THE
TEXAS
FOOD
BIBLE

THE
TEXAS

FROM LEGENDARY DISHES

FOOD

TO NEW CLASSICS

BIBLE

★

DEAN FEARING

with JUDITH CHOATE and ERIC DREYER

Photographs by Dave Carlin

GRAND CENTRAL
Life & Style
NEW YORK • BOSTON

Grand Central Life & Style
Hachette Book Group
237 Park Avenue
New York, NY 10017

www.GrandCentralLifeandStyle.com

Printed in the United States of America

Q-MA

First Edition: April 2014
10 9 8 7 6 5 4 3 2 1

Grand Central Life & Style is an imprint of Grand Central Publishing.
The Grand Central Life & Style name and logo are trademarks of Hachette Book Group, Inc.

The Hachette Speakers Bureau provides a wide range of authors for speaking events. To find out more, go to www.HachetteSpeakersBureau.com or call (866) 376-6591.

The publisher is not responsible for websites (or their content) that are not owned by the publisher.

Library of Congress Cataloging-in-Publication Data

Fearing, Dean.
  The Texas food bible : from legendary dishes to new classics / Dean Fearing ; photographs by Dave Carlin. — First edition.
     pages cm
  Includes index.
  ISBN 978-1-4555-7430-8 (hardcover) — ISBN 978-1-4555-7431-5 (ebook) 1. Cooking, American—Southwestern style. 2. Cooking—Texas.
I. Title.
  TX715.2.S69F44 2013
  641.59764—dc23
                              2013034361

Design by Jason Snyder

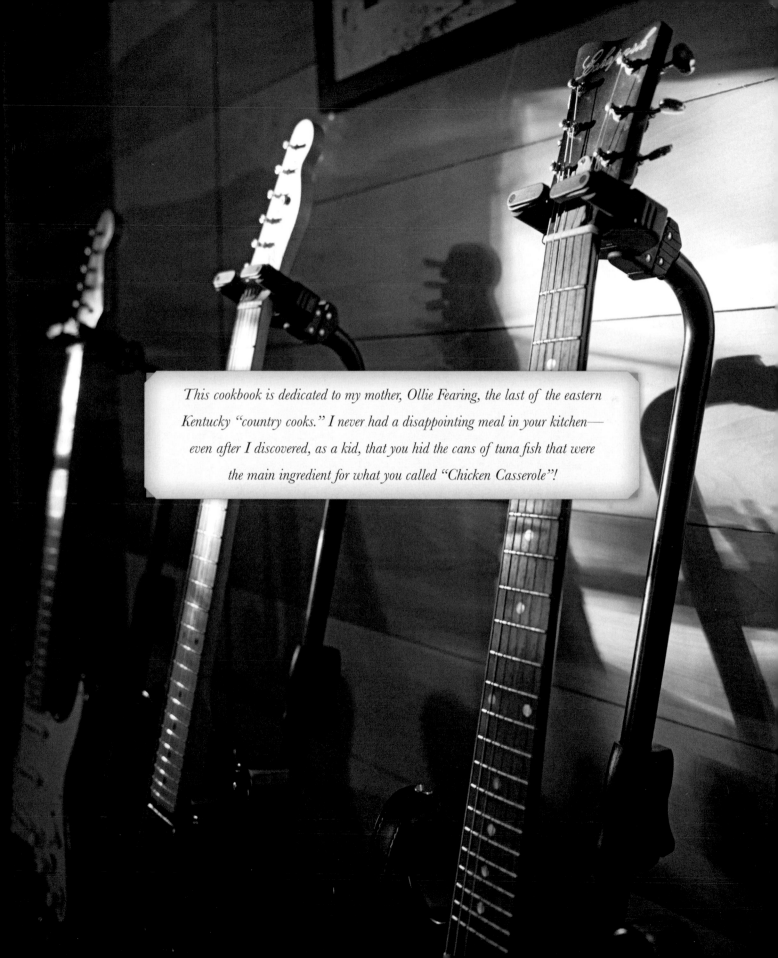

This cookbook is dedicated to my mother, Ollie Fearing, the last of the eastern Kentucky "country cooks." I never had a disappointing meal in your kitchen— even after I discovered, as a kid, that you hid the cans of tuna fish that were the main ingredient for what you called "Chicken Casserole"!

CONTENTS

★ ★ ★ ★ ★ ★ ★ ★ ★ ★ ★

INTRODUCTION

★ ★ ★ ★ ★ ★ ★ ★ ★ ★

I bet that you didn't know that the word *Texas* comes from the Native American word *tejas*, which means "those who are friends." And no matter what you might hear, Texans are the friendliest people in the world. I learned that very quickly when I moved to Dallas and found myself being asked to "come on over," "sit right here," "pull up a chair," and "have another," as I was introduced to both the hospitality and the meals of folks all across the state. Home cooked, around the campfire, in backyards, or in the restaurants of my friends, I got to experience the most amazing foods—good old-fashioned meals like my mom made, ethnic dishes that I had never tasted, grilled meats on an open fire, and innovative dishes in a restaurant setting. It didn't take long for me to become an aficionado of Texas cuisine.

When I began my career in the kitchen, I had no idea that I would end up wearing cowboy boots in front of the stove. I was a Kentucky boy trained in the classic French culinary tradition when I arrived in Texas almost thirty-five years ago to be the fish cook (*poissonnier* in French) at the Pyramid Room in the Fairmont Hotel, the finest French restaurant in Dallas. From there I was invited to be the opening chef at Agnew's, Dallas' first fine-dining restaurant featuring "modern American cuisine" rather than Continental or French.

The cooks that I worked with were mostly from Mexico, and I found I loved the foods that they prepared for their own meals. And they loved nothing more than introducing me to the ingredients and recipes taught to them, usually by their mothers. Off times in the kitchen I was able to learn the basic salsas, enchiladas, tamales, moles, and snack foods of their homeland. Since each cook came from a different region, I got to taste many different regional cooking styles. They had grilling, marinating, and braising techniques that were completely new to me, and the ingredients were unheard of—a variety of chiles, herbs like cilantro and epazote, citrus, mango, tomatillos, cactus paddles, chayote, dried corn, and so many other extraordinary products. I vividly remember calling my produce supplier in 1979 and asking for cilantro

with his response "What's that?" Sometimes the cooks would bring me the produce they grew, and sometimes they would take a trip "home" and come back with sacks of new things to try. Agnew's became the first fine-dining restaurant in Dallas to use these "ethnic" ingredients, and it was where I began to see the direction I wanted to take my cooking. It was, for me, a major stepping-stone to the evolution of modern Texas cuisine.

"Oh, Lordy," as much as I loved my immersion in the foods of Mexico, it didn't take long for me to fall head over cowboy boots in love with Texas—the larger-than-life people, the climate, agriculture, music, and wide-open spaces, and, most of all, the beautiful blend of cultures that had settled the state, and the foods that reflected that mix in an extraordinary way. It all couldn't have been further from the discipline and rigorous adherence to the past that I was trained to observe. Texas was—and is—an amazing place to live, learn, and cook!

I began to really stretch my culinary wings at the Mansion on Turtle Creek, where I, along with a number of other young chefs throughout the state, inaugurated the "new Southwestern cuisine," introducing everyday "ethnic" ingredients into four-star dining. When Bob Zimmer, president of the Mansion, asked me to join the team, I told him that I would do so only if we could promote

"Southwest" cuisine, using local purveyors and local ingredients in the restaurant. He agreed and the Mansion became the first internationally known boutique hotel and restaurant to feature an authentic Texas dining experience.

I like to think that this was also the beginning of the "locavore" movement, as we cooked with those Mexican, Native American, and other regional ingredients that were grown on farms, in small plots, and in gardens all through Texas. We looked at the past in a different way as we incorporated the ancient foods of Native Americans, the simple cooking styles of frontier settlers, indigenous game, ingredients used in the meals of early immigrants from Germany and Eastern Europe, the rich cultural and agricultural spirit of the American South, the diverse seafood found in the Gulf, and, most of all, those bold, flavorful tastes of the Mexican population. We were taking what ordinary Texans had been doing in the kitchen for generations and fusing that cooking with classic culinary techniques and a sense of adventure. In the end, what we created was nothing less than a four-star experience using local ingredients, and along the way "new Southwestern cuisine" was born.

★   ★   ★

In 2007 I opened Fearing's at the Ritz-Carlton Hotel, my dream restaurant. Not only is the restaurant a reflection of my own vision of Texas design and comfort, but it is also where I embraced the richness of the state's agriculture, folkways, artisanal foods, and lifestyle. The restaurant itself is filled with the colors and light that so identify the openness of the land, and our staff's welcome is relaxed and neighborly, the same greeting I received when I first arrived. There is no dress code—jeans and cowboy boots are as fancy as we get. I often travel the state exploring the wonderful products and cooking styles that have made Texas such a leader in new American cooking. Throughout my restaurant career I have kept a diary of the regional recipes and foods that have caught my attention. I have a large collection of old cookbooks that grows through the generosity of home cooks who frequently send me their own handwritten recipes and hand-me-down recipe books. Over the years so many people have asked me about Texas ingredients, "Tex-Mex" cooking, and how I incorporate all of the various "ethnic" styles to make recipes my own that I began to create my own Texas food bible as a resource for my cooks. It is something we constantly use.

I easily recognize that the "new" Texas cuisine that I serve daily has come about through years of evolving "new" ingredients, "new" farming methods, "new" cooking methods, "new" immigrants, and even "new" appliances. And I also know that, to quote that old song, "Everything Old Is New Again." This is particularly true in cooking, where through the past twenty years we have seen "heirloom" produce, "artisanal" craftsmen, and "farm to table" reintroduced. And, since we know that in Texas everything is bigger, all of this has had an even bigger impact on my *Texas Food Bible*.

Before we get to the nitty-gritty, I'll give you a brief rundown on the main influences in how Texans cook. In the beginning, we had the Native American tribes of the Southwest who raised sheep (but, for the most part, didn't eat them) and cultivated the holy trinity of "beans, squash, and corn" while they treasured the gifts of the land. The exploring Spaniards of the seventeenth century introduced a meat-protein diet, adding poultry and pork along with rice, onions, and tomatoes. And, since they had arrived through Mexico, the explorers also introduced chocolate, tropical fruits, vanilla, avocados, chiles, and nuts that were indigenous to the pre-Columbian world.

As the United States spread westward, new foods came with the travelers, some of whom settled on homesteads throughout the state. Foods that had typically been prepared only in the Southern states (primarily by domestic servants) very quickly became everyday meals on the range. New settlers from Europe, particularly those from Germany and Eastern Europe, brought recipes that are now part of Texas culinary lore. Our famous chicken-fried steak is nothing more than an adaptation of the classic German Wiener schnitzel, and it is said that the familiar barbecue evolved through the skill of German butchers smoking and curing pork. Texans will travel quite a piece to get to West, Texas (the town, not the area), to buy kolaches (sweet or savory) from the Czech Stop. Of course, we can't forget the cowboys who spent weeks and sometimes months moving cattle and cooking on an open fire. Although the experts say that barbecue came from the Germans, in my opinion it more likely came from range cooking and the ranch cookhouse.

Chili, Texas' best-known dish, seems to be lost in its heritage. Some say it came from trail cooks, some from Mexican home cooks, some from a Texas ranger, some from a Spanish nun teaching Native Americans a new dish. I'd say that it is a legendary dish made from legend. The only thing that you need to know for certain is that Texas chili does *not* contain beans or tomatoes and you will learn how to make an authentic version in *The Texas Food Bible*.

In recent memory, we have the enormous influx of Mexican peoples, whose foods are now a part of every American's diet—burritos, tacos, enchiladas, and on it goes. Did you know that salsas now outsell ketchup, an amazing statistic to a lover of that signature American condiment? And, finally, there is the bounty of the state: the Gulf provides superb seafood; longtime cultivation along the Colorado River makes Texas the fourth-largest producer of rice; cattle ranches offer some of the best beef in the world; game farms provide a wide array of meats; citrus groves flourish; and orchards abound. Bigger in Texas and better in Texas, I'd say.

Now, all this leads us to *The Texas Food Bible*.

In the following pages we will first take a look at the ingredients that make Texas cuisine explode with bold, rich flavors. Then we will give a heads-up to those sauces and salsas and other good things that help the cook take an ordinary recipe to new heights. Recipes will range from traditional to modern interpretations of the classics through my personal favorites, old and new. We will wander from Navajo fry bread to sweet potato spoonbread from the South, from tacos to shrimp diablo "tamales," from Granny Fearing's "paper bag–shook" fried chicken to chicken-fried Texas quail on bourbon-jalapeño creamed corn, and from Texas-style chili to bacon-jalapeño biscuits. Simple taco and salsa recipes will have a starred place right beside the culinary treasures that make new Texas cuisine internationally famous. I'll show you step-by-step methods and techniques for grilling and smoking. In addition, you will get to meet some of the many other chefs and artisans whom I've met and worked with along the way. While it's educational, I hope that *The Texas Food Bible* will also serve as a daily reference in every cook's kitchen.

Pull on your boots, push back your Stetson, and come join me for some of the world's greatest food deep in the heart of Texas.

—*Dean Fearing*

FEARING'S TEXAS PANTRY

★ ★ ★ ★ ★ ★ ★ ★ ★ ★

STAPLES

A WORD ABOUT STOCKS

Stocks are probably the most important kitchen staple, both in a restaurant and at home, so almost every cookbook has recipes for them. Rather than give you another one, let me tell you why a good homemade stock will make all the difference in the world to any recipe calling for one. First and foremost, when you make your own stocks you have complete control of the quality of the ingredients and the seasoning. It is a good idea to make a big batch of stock and freeze it in small quantities so you will always have it on hand. Starting with a ratio of about 1 part bones/meat to 6 parts water, here's what you do:

If you want a richer stock, first roast the bones (poultry or game bird carcasses or veal or beef bones) and, if using, pieces of fresh meat. This is true for all types, including chicken. Bones that are not browned will yield a light stock, in both color and flavor.

Cover the bones with cold water. This ensures that the collagen (the gelatin-forming agent) is extracted as the stock cooks. Adding the bones to hot water would seal them, keeping the collagen inside, and since much of the flavor comes from the collagen and cartilage in the bones, you don't want to lose any of the deliciousness.

Do not add salt to the water. Salt can be added when you use the stock in a recipe.

Bring the bones to a boil. Add the vegetables (hunks of carrots, onion or leek, and celery, known as mirepoix) and herbs. I use a little sachet of fresh thyme, parsley, bay leaf, and peppercorns, but this really is the cook's choice. For a hint of Texas, I often add a few ancho chiles to the pot. For a very rich beef or veal stock, I use chicken stock as the cooking liquid and, before it is added, I cover the bones with about 2 cups of red wine and reduce the liquid by half. Once the red wine has reduced, I add the chicken stock. This yields a very rich stock that can be further reduced for sauces. Be sure to skim off the scum that rises to the top.

Once the stock comes to a boil, lower the heat and cook at a bare simmer, skimming frequently. Simmer for at least 4 hours to extract the maximum flavor.

Strain through a very-fine-mesh sieve (you can even line it with cheesecloth for greater clarity, but for home use this really isn't necessary).

Chill the strained stock in an ice bath. As it chills, the fat will rise to the top or form little balls, which can then be skimmed off.

Store the stock in 1-cup measures. Be sure to label and date them. The shelf life of the stock, refrigerated, is 1 week; frozen, 3 months.

Now, if you don't have stock on hand, or you do not have time to make it, buy the best-quality canned, non-fat, low-sodium chicken broth you can find. Besides, it is always a good idea to keep a supply of canned stock or broth in the pantry for emergencies.

BEANS

I have no idea how many types of beans can be found throughout the world, but in Texas we primarily use only four: black, pinto, and red as well as black-eyed peas. Each one is inexpensive, packed with nutrition, agriculturally enriching, easy to store, and delicious. The edible seeds of pod-bearing plants, and one of nature's most balanced foods, beans are low in fat, and what fat they do contain is unsaturated. They are cholesterol-free, yet help manage

Dried pinto, red, and black beans

blood cholesterol and glucose, and are high in vegetable protein, fiber, vitamins, and minerals. Wearing any number of disguises, either combined with animal protein or working their magic with rice, beans can come to the table in everyday meals or in four-star recipes.

Buying and storing dried beans and peas: Always purchase dried beans from stores with a high turnover, such as health food stores, or directly from the farmer. This ensures that you have the freshest product. Dried beans should be stored in a cool spot in see-through, airtight containers. Dried beans seem to keep indefinitely, but the older they are, the longer they will take to cook.

Cooking dried beans and peas: Presoak in 10 times as much cold water as beans for at least 8 hours in a cool spot. Some cooks no longer do the presoak, but I think that soaking results in a creamier bean. Discard the soaking liquid and cover with enough fresh liquid (water, broth, or stock) so that there are 2 inches of liquid above the beans. Place over high heat and bring to a boil; then lower the heat and simmer for about 1 hour, or until tender.

If you don't have time for a good, long presoak, place the dried beans in a large pot and cover with at least 3 inches of cold water. Place over high heat and bring to a boil. Boil for 5 minutes; then remove from the heat, cover, and let stand for no less than 1 hour and no more than 2 hours. Drain and rinse well before proceeding with your recipe.

Black Beans: Small, with a shiny exterior and a richly flavored interior, black beans are native to South America. They are also known as turtle beans or *frijoles negros*. They are used in soups, sauces, dips, side dishes, and entrées.

Pinto Beans: A variety of haricot, or common bean, pinto beans are the most frequently used dried bean in the United States. Medium in size, pale brownish-pink in color with a slightly mottled exterior, and mellow in flavor, pinto beans are most often used for refried beans, for fillings for burritos and other stuffed Mexican dishes, and in chilies that have beans as a component.

Red Beans: Similar to pinto beans, except deeply red in color and somewhat denser in texture, red beans are a very meaty bean, often used in combination with rice to create a filling, nutritious meal.

Black-Eyed Peas: Available fresh, frozen, and dried, black-eyed peas are often associated with dishes from the American South. Medium in size, pale yellow with a black heel (or dot), thin-skinned, and relatively quick cooking, they are also known as cowpeas or field peas. Black-eyed peas were brought to Texas by cooks from the Southern states as they moved west around the time of the Civil War.

I don't know where I'd be without the rich, zesty flavor that chiles, either fresh or dried, add to dishes. When I started cooking, chiles were not in my culinary vocabulary, but they certainly are now. I am amazed at the variety that we have available, even from the local supermarket. I would guess that there are thousands of types of chiles grown around the world, but in Texas, and particularly at Fearing's, we generally use just a few. The spicy heat carried in a chile is measured in Scoville units, which range from zero to the millions. Bell peppers are down in the zero spectrum, while habaneros can be in the millions. These heat units indicate the amount of capsaicin in an individual chile, noting that within a type the heat amount can vary greatly from chile to chile. If you remove the seeds and the interior white membrane from most chiles, you can decrease the amount of heat somewhat.

Fresh Chiles: Fresh chiles should be firm to the touch with smooth, shiny skin. There should be no evidence of spotting or softening around the base of the stem end. If not used immediately, chiles should be wrapped in paper towels and stored, refrigerated, in a resealable plastic bag.

When working with fresh chiles, it is a good idea to wear disposable rubber gloves. If using the chile raw, cut or pull off the stem end, slice the chile in half lengthwise, and carefully remove and discard the seeds and membrane. When you are finished working with chiles, whether you wear gloves or not, always wash your hands in hot, soapy water to remove any oils, and never rub your face or eyes until your hands are very, very clean and dry.

If roasting small chiles, place the whole chile on an ungreased frying pan or griddle and, using tongs, frequently turn until all sides are blistered. Then remove from the pan and stem and seed as for raw. If you're roasting large chiles and if you want to peel them before use, you can fire-roast them by using tongs to hold the chile directly over an open flame. Roast, turning frequently, for about 1 minute, or until all sides are lightly blistered. You don't want to blacken or burn the chile. You can also roast them, as you would small chiles, on the stovetop, char under a broiler, roast in a 400°F oven, or fry in hot oil to blister the skin. Transfer the hot chile to a resealable plastic bag, seal, and let steam for no more than 5 minutes to loosen the skin. You can also wrap the hot chile in a towel for a couple of minutes and then use the towel to push off the blackened skin.

ANAHEIM: Mild but flavorful, this long, slender green chile is usually slightly sweet in flavor. Anaheims are also known as long green, California, or Magdalena chiles. A hotter version of this same chile is grown in New Mexico (see New Mexico chile below). The heat level of Anaheim chiles can vary from very mild to quite pungent. They are often stuffed to make chiles rellenos, as well as used for chile con queso, a favorite snack of cheese and chiles that originated in Texas. When dried, they are red and known as *seco del norte*.

HABANERO: Ooo-eee! These are hot little guys; Scoville units begin in the mid-hundred thousands. The lantern-shaped habaneros are a soft green as they ripen, and then turn a beautiful orange or deep red when fully mature, although they can also be found in other colors. Because they have such a defined citrusy sweetness with the heat, habaneros are one of the most popular chiles used in Mexican and Mexican-style dishes. In recent years, Texas growers have bred a new habanero that retains the distinct flavor with less heat.

JALAPEÑO: These are probably the best-known chile in the United States. Shiny-skinned with a great vibrant, dark green color, a rather stumpy look, and a full fat top tapering to a rather rounded point, jalapeños range in size from 1 inch to 3 inches long. They have a wide variation in heat, running from extremely mild to blisteringly hot. When fully ripe, the green turns to bright red. Jalapeños are also frequently sold pickled and canned.

NEW MEXICO: See Anaheim (above), although the long green chiles grown in New Mexico frequently contain more heat than those grown in Texas and California.

POBLANO: Triangular in shape, thick-skinned, and fleshy, this chile begins to ripen at a purplish-green color and then progresses to a deep red color when fully mature. Quite large, about 5 inches long, with a fat, ridged top, these chiles have a very complex flavor that is best experienced when cooked. Because of its thick skin, the poblano is almost always charred and peeled before use. The Scoville unit measurement is usually from 2,500 to 6,000. Poblanos are often used for chiles rellenos.

SERRANO: Small, shiny-skinned chiles with a thin layer of crisp flesh, serranos are piquant and herbal in flavor when in the early green-colored stage of maturation, and richer in flavor when extremely ripe and red. They are frequently used in salsas and cooked sauces. The heat range is from hot to tongue-blistering.

Dried Chiles: Chiles are dried, for the most part, simply for preservation. They are most often used in cooked sauces but are occasionally fried for use as a garnish. Generally a specific recipe will designate how to prepare the dried chile that is called for. Since chiles are often sun-dried on the ground, they are usually dusty and dirty. The first step to prepare dried chiles is to gently wipe the dust with a damp paper towel. Next, remove the stem and seeds. Sometimes the chile is toasted, sometimes soaked, sometimes roasted for a short period of time. It is important to follow the instructions given, as the preparation method impacts on the final flavor. Toast chiles, turning frequently, over an open flame for about 1 minute or until all sides are lightly blistered. You don't want to blacken or burn the chile. Chiles can be soaked by covering with hot water for 20 minutes. You can also roast dried chiles in a 400°F oven for about 3 minutes.

ANCHO: A deep red fully ripe poblano that has been dried, a desirable ancho is about 3 inches wide and 4 to 5 inches long, flexible, reddish-brown (not black) in color, with wrinkly skin. Anchos are used for moles, soups, or cooked sauces, or are ground to a powder.

CHILE DE ÁRBOL: An extremely hot, bright red, long, thin dried chile, the chile de árbol is generally used in cooked table sauces or in stews, although it is popular ground to a powder to be sprinkled on fresh fruit, nuts, or crisp vegetables. It is usually toasted before use.

CHIPOTLE: A fully ripened jalapeño that has been smoke-dried, which gives it a defined tobacco-like flavor, the dried chile has a very tough, wrinkled outer skin and is usually about 1 inch wide and a couple of inches long. Chipotles are also available canned, either pickled or in adobo (red chile) sauce.

GUAJILLO: One of the least expensive and most popular dried chiles, the guajillo chile is long, thin, smooth-skinned, and dark red, and ranges from extremely hot to tangy in flavor. The thinner the chile, the hotter the taste. Guajillos are generally ground for use in combination with other chiles for seasoning mixes.

PASILLA: Wrinkled, shiny-skinned, almost black in color, this very long, thin chile is a dried *chilaca*. It is almost always toasted and soaked before use in cooked sauces. It can also be rehydrated and used whole, and stuffed with meat or cheese and fried.

FRESH HERBS

Although there is a wide variety of culinary herbs, I have listed only those that I use frequently, or those that are found in regional dishes.

Chives: This long, slender, hollow-stemmed herb is related to the onion family. It is used primarily as a garnish on dishes that require just a slight oniony accent.

Cilantro: Now commonplace, cilantro was almost totally unknown thirty years ago. Its widespread availability indicates just how popular Mexican cooking is throughout the United States. Cilantro is a slightly pungent but fragrant, light green leafy herb with a flavor that some call "soapy." Quite fragile, with a tendency to wilt and brown quickly, it is best bought and stored with its roots intact. It is used to flavor both raw and cooked sauces, as a garnish for tacos, in moles, and with seafood, among a host of other dishes. Both the leaves and the stems can be used.

Epazote: Known as pigweed to American gardeners, epazote is usually pulled and discarded. Only in Mexico do cooks prize its sharp, distinct flavor, which some liken to turpentine or detergent. It is a tall, rangy herb with pointed, serrated leaves that is a required ingredient for

Mexican black beans and zesty soups. It is available in Mexican markets and at some farmers' markets or, maybe, in your backyard.

Flat-Leaf Parsley: This common bright green herb, sometimes called Italian parsley, is used either chopped or as whole leaves to flavor many cooked dishes or as a garnish for finished dishes. Both leaves and stems can be used to add a slightly peppery accent.

Marjoram: This tall, light green herb with rounded, slightly fuzzy leaves has a delicate citrusy, almost mint-like, sweet flavor. Also known as sweet marjoram, it is used to flavor sauces and stews.

Oregano: There are two types of oregano used in our kitchen, Mediterranean and Mexican. The former is much less pungent than the Mexican, but the flavor of both mimics marjoram, although stronger. Both the soft green leaves, slightly rounded to a point, and the purple flowers are used. Because of its pungency, oregano is generally added with caution, as a little goes a long way.

Sage: A lovely soft gray-green herb with oval-shaped fuzzy leaves, sage has a flat but intense, almost medicinal, flavor. An ancient herb, it is used in flavoring a wide variety of dishes as well as in sausage making.

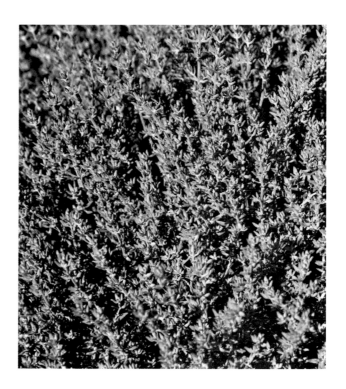

Thyme: A woody, low-growing herb with tiny greenish-gray leaves. thyme has a strong citrusy, woodsy flavor. It is used to make a classic French bouquet garni along with parsley and bay leaf. There are now a variety of fresh thymes, such as lemon, caraway, orange, and variegated, which are frequently available at farmers' markets.

DRIED SPICES AND HERBS AND SEEDS

A spice pantry should be stocked with only small amounts of those dried spices and herbs that are used frequently, as they very quickly lose their intensity of flavor and aroma. Dried spices can be heated just a bit to pull out the flavor, but ground spices and herbs cannot be revived once the flavor has dissipated. Texas cooking does not use a wide variety of dried spices or herbs; in fact, we primarily use only the three "c's" cinnamon, cumin, and coriander— and also oregano. At home and in the restaurant, I keep black peppercorns, which I grind as needed to ensure fresh, pungent flavor.

The one commercially packaged dried spice that most cooks don't realize is a blend of a few herbs and spices is chile powder, unless it is labeled as pure chile powder.

The commercial blend is usually a mixture of dried chiles, cumin, garlic, oregano, coriander, and cloves. Pure chile powder will usually be labeled with the type of chile, such as ancho chile powder, or as pure chili/chile powder.

The one seed or nut used consistently in Tex-Mex cooking is the pumpkin seed, also called pepita. These seeds are used in a wide variety of sauces and stews and as a garnish for finished dishes. In cooking, pepitas are the dark green interior kernel of a pumpkin seed, but the whole seed can also be referred to as a pepita. They are used both raw and roasted to add a delicate, slightly nutty flavor to a dish.

In my kitchens, both at home and in the restaurant, I use a finely ground sea salt, such as *La Baleine*, for general seasoning. It dissolves quickly and gives a pleasant salty flavor to a dish.

Cornmeal: A meal made from grinding dried corn kernels, it can be fine, medium, or coarse ground by either a water or a steel grinding method. Water grinding (also known as stone-ground) is the old-fashioned method, in which the grinding stones are powered by water. It produces the most desirable type of cornmeal, which carries the richest flavor and the most nutritional value since it includes some of the hull and germ of the corn. It does, however, have a short shelf life. Steel-ground cornmeal is substantially more shelf stable but has much lighter flavor and less nutritional value. Cornmeal may be yellow, white, or blue. We use the extraordinary cornmeal produced by the Homestead Gristmill (see Sources, page 242).

Masa: The literal translation of the Spanish word *masa* is "dough," but it now is generally taken to mean masa harina, a powdery flour that is used to make tortillas. Real masa is a fresh dough made from treated, soaked, and ground corn mixed with water that is traditionally used to make both tortillas and tamales. Smooth fresh masa is used for tortillas, while coarse ground is specifically for tamales. Masa harina is fresh masa that has been dried and then ground to a smooth, flour-like consistency. Although easy to use, it lacks the deep corn flavor of fresh masa. Both the Quaker Oats and the Maseca brands are available in many supermarkets and most Hispanic markets.

OILS

Lard: Rendered, clarified pork fat, lard is used for frying or baking. The best quality is leaf lard, which comes from the visceral fat around the pig's kidneys. Most lard available today has been processed to soften the flavor and increase shelf life. Some artisanal lards are now available at farmers' markets and specialty butchers, and like many products, the quality of the lard is dependent upon the quality of the animal and the processing method.

Texas Olive Oil: Texas Olive Ranch 100% Pure Texas Extra Virgin Olive Oil is pressed from arbequina variety olives grown at Texas Olive Ranch between Carrizo Springs and Asherton. The arbequina was developed in Spain and is especially suitable for growing in the sandy loam soil of the Middle Rio Grande Valley, where the climate is very similar to that of southern Spain. The growing season in Texas is extremely hot, and the olives are usually harvested the first week of September. (See Source, page 242).

CHEESES

Queso Asadero (Queso Oaxaca): *Queso* simply means "cheese" in Spanish. Asadero is a mild, chewy cheese traditionally used to fill chiles rellenos and chile con queso. If asadero is unavailable, teleme or Muenster cheese is a good substitute.

Cotija: In Mexico, Cotija is a dry, salty aged cheese, similar to Parmesan, primarily used for grating over tacos or beans, or as a crumble to add flavor to soups or stews. However, it is also available in the United States as a softer fresh cheese similar to feta.

SAUCES AND GRAVIES

★ ★ ★

TEXAS-STYLE BARBECUE SAUCE

MAKES ABOUT 2 CUPS

Uses: **Brush on or dip for all types of grilled or smoked items.**

- 1 tablespoon bacon fat
- 1 large yellow onion, cut into ¼-inch dice
- 1 cup ketchup
- ¼ cup Worcestershire sauce
- 2 tablespoons molasses
- 1 tablespoon malt vinegar
- 2 teaspoons Creole mustard
- 1 teaspoon Tabasco sauce
- Fresh lemon juice
- Salt

Preheat the oven to 375°F.

Heat the bacon fat in a small ovenproof frying pan over medium heat. Add the onion and fry for about 5 minutes, or until softened. Remove from the heat and set aside.

Combine the ketchup, Worcestershire, molasses, vinegar, mustard, and Tabasco in a small bowl and stir to blend. Add lemon juice and salt to taste.

Pour the ketchup mixture over the diced onions and stir to blend. Cover, place in the preheated oven, and bake for 30 minutes.

Remove from the oven, transfer to a blender, and puree until smooth. Strain the sauce through a coarse-mesh strainer.

Use as directed in a specific recipe, or store, tightly covered and refrigerated, for up to 1 week.

APRICOT BARBECUE SAUCE

MAKES ABOUT 3 CUPS

Uses: **Brush on or dip; grilled or smoked pork, game, poultry.**

- 1 cup chopped dried apricots
- 1 cup chopped cold-smoked onion (see page 177)
- ½ cup packed light brown sugar
- 1 tablespoon minced garlic
- 1 teaspoon seeded and minced jalapeño chile
- 2 cups fresh orange juice
- 2 tablespoons malt vinegar
- 1 tablespoon Worcestershire sauce
- 1 teaspoon fresh lime juice
- ½ teaspoon Tabasco sauce
- Salt

Combine the dried apricots, onion, brown sugar, garlic, and chile in a heavy-bottomed saucepan. Stir in the orange juice, vinegar, Worcestershire sauce, lime juice, and Tabasco. Bring to a boil over medium-high heat. Season with salt to taste, lower the heat, and cook at a gentle simmer for 20 minutes.

Remove the sauce from the heat and scrape into a blender. Process to a smooth puree. Taste and adjust the seasoning if necessary.

Use as directed in a specific recipe, or store, covered and refrigerated, for up to 1 week. Reheat before using.

SMOKY BACON BARBECUE SAUCE

MAKES ABOUT 3 CUPS

Uses: **Even though this is not used in a main-dish recipe, it is such a terrific Texas-style barbecue sauce that I had to include it. It can be used for everything grilled or smoked.**

> 1 tablespoon bacon fat
>
> 1 cup ¼-inch-dice onion
>
> 2 cups ketchup
>
> ¼ cup Worcestershire sauce
>
> 2 tablespoons molasses
>
> 1 tablespoon malt vinegar
>
> 2 teaspoons Creole mustard
>
> 2 teaspoons fresh lemon juice
>
> 1 teaspoon Tabasco sauce
>
> Salt
>
> ¼ cup chopped cooked smoky bacon

Preheat the oven to 375°F.

Heat the bacon fat in a small ovenproof frying pan over medium heat. Add the onion and cook, stirring occasionally, for about 4 minutes, or until the onion has softened. Remove from the heat.

Combine the ketchup, Worcestershire sauce, molasses, vinegar, mustard, lemon juice, and Tabasco in a small bowl and whisk to combine. If necessary, season with salt.

Pour the ketchup mixture over the onion, cover, and transfer the pan to the preheated oven. Bake for 30 minutes.

Remove from the oven and stir in the cooked bacon.

Serve warm or as directed in a specific recipe, or store, tightly covered and refrigerated, for up to 1 week. Reheat before serving.

FEARING'S MOP SAUCE

MAKES 1 QUART

Uses: **Brushed on all steaks at the end of the cooking process—I can't eat a steak without this sauce!**

> 1 tablespoon olive oil
>
> 1 cup chopped onion
>
> 2 tablespoons chopped shallots
>
> 1 tablespoon chopped garlic
>
> 1 tablespoon freshly cracked pepper
>
> 1 bottle Shiner Bock beer (see sidebar, page 77)
>
> 2 cups molasses
>
> 1 cup Worcestershire sauce
>
> ½ cup balsamic vinegar
>
> 2 teaspoons Dijon mustard
>
> 1 teaspoon ground chile de árbol
>
> ¼ cup cornstarch dissolved in ¼ cup cold water
>
> Fresh lime juice
>
> Salt

Heat the oil in a large saucepan over medium-high heat. Add the onion and sauté for about 3 minutes, or until lightly browned. Stir in the shallots, garlic, and pepper and continue to sauté for 2 minutes more.

Add the beer and, using a heatproof spatula, scrape the browned bits from the bottom of the pan. Cook, stirring occasionally, for about 5 minutes, or until the liquid has reduced by half.

Add the molasses, Worcestershire, vinegar, mustard, and chile and bring to a boil. Immediately lower the heat and cook at a gentle simmer for 5 minutes.

Whisking constantly, add the cornstarch mixture in a slow, steady stream. Continue to cook for a few minutes more, or until the sauce is thick and the cornstarch taste has cooked out. Season to taste with lime juice and salt.

Serve as directed in a specific recipe, or store, tightly covered and refrigerated, for up to 1 week.

"D1" Sauce

MAKES 1 QUART

Uses: **My version of the famous A1 Steak Sauce. Use as a glaze for any roasted, grilled, or smoked items.**

1 tablespoon olive oil

1 cup roughly chopped yellow onions

¼ cup roughly chopped carrots

1 tablespoon chopped garlic

1 tablespoon freshly cracked pepper

1 cup balsamic vinegar

½ cup **Worcestershire sauce**

2 cups rich beef stock or nonfat,
    low-sodium beef broth

½ cup ketchup

2 tablespoons brown sugar

¼ cup cornstarch dissolved in ¼ cup cold water

Salt

Heat the oil in a large saucepan over medium-high heat. Add the onions and cook, stirring, for 3 minutes, or until just beginning to color. Stir in the carrots, garlic, and cracked pepper and cook, stirring, for 2 minutes, or until the carrots have taken on some color.

Stir in the vinegar and Worcestershire and, using a heatproof spatula, scrape the browned bits from the bottom of the pan. Cook, stirring occasionally, for about 5 minutes, or until the liquid has reduced by half.

Add the stock, ketchup, and brown sugar and bring to a boil. Immediately lower the heat and simmer for 5 minutes.

Whisking constantly, add the cornstarch mixture in a slow, steady stream. Cook, stirring constantly, for 5 minutes, or until quite thick.

Remove the sauce from the heat and pour into a blender. Holding the lid down with a folded kitchen towel to prevent a steam explosion, process to a smooth puree. Season with salt to taste.

Use as directed in a specific recipe, or store, tightly covered and refrigerated, for up to 1 week. Reheat before using.

Tabasco Butter Sauce

MAKES 2 CUPS

Uses: **This is a great all-around sauce for everything—I really love it with fish.**

2 tablespoons vegetable oil

¼ cup chopped shallots

¼ cup chopped leek

¼ cup chopped celery

¼ cup chopped red bell pepper

1 tablespoon chopped garlic

3 chiles de árbol

2 fresh thyme sprigs

¼ cup chopped fresh parsley stems

1 teaspoon freshly cracked black pepper

¼ cup dry white wine

¼ cup **Tabasco sauce**

½ cup heavy cream

1 pound (4 sticks) unsalted butter,
    at room temperature

Fresh lemon juice

Salt

Heat the oil in a heavy-bottomed saucepan over medium heat. Add the shallots, leek, celery, bell pepper, and garlic. Cook, stirring frequently, for about 4 minutes, or until the vegetables have softened.

Stir in the chiles, thyme, parsley stems, and black pepper. Add the wine and cook, scraping up the browned bits from the bottom of the pan. Bring to a simmer and cook until the liquid has almost totally evaporated.

Stir in the Tabasco and cream and bring to a boil. Cook for about 2 minutes, or until the cream has thickened slightly.

Whisk in the butter, a bit at a time, and continue to whisk until all the butter has been incorporated into the sauce.

Remove the sauce from the heat and strain through a fine-mesh sieve into a clean saucepan. Season to taste with lemon juice and salt. Keep warm until ready to use.

CILANTRO HOLLANDAISE SAUCE

MAKES ABOUT 2 CUPS

Uses: Great at breakfast time with eggs, or anytime over roasted or grilled vegetables.

- 3 large egg yolks, at room temperature
- 2 tablespoons cold water
- 1 cup (2 sticks) warm clarified unsalted butter or ghee
- 2 tablespoons chopped fresh cilantro
- 1½ tablespoons fresh lime juice
- Tabasco sauce
- Salt

Fill a medium saucepan about halfway with water. Place over medium heat and bring to a simmer.

Combine the egg yolks with the cold water in a heat-resistant bowl that will fit into the top of the water-filled pan. Set the bowl on top of the simmering water, taking care that the bottom of the bowl does not touch the water. Cook, stirring, for 10 minutes.

Slowly begin adding the clarified butter (melted butter with the floating solids skimmed off, warm but not hot) in a thin stream, whisking constantly until all of the butter has been added and the sauce has a mayonnaise-like consistency. Whisk in the cilantro and lime juice. Add Tabasco and salt to taste. Keep warm until ready to use.

BACON BÉCHAMEL SAUCE

MAKES ABOUT 3 CUPS

Uses: This is what I would call an "add-to" sauce, as I use it as a cream element for spinach or other sautéed greens.

- ½ cup bacon fat
- ¼ cup small-dice onion
- ¼ cup small-dice celery
- 1 teaspoon chopped fresh thyme
- ½ cup all-purpose flour
- 2 cups rich chicken stock or nonfat, low-sodium chicken broth
- 1 cup whole milk
- Fresh lemon juice
- Salt
- Freshly ground pepper

Heat the bacon fat in a medium saucepan over medium heat. Add the onion and celery and cook, stirring, for about 4 minutes, or until translucent. Add the thyme and then, stirring constantly, sprinkle in the flour. Cook, stirring constantly, for about 8 minutes, or until a golden-brown roux has formed.

Stirring constantly, slowly add the stock and milk. Reduce the heat and cook at a bare simmer for about 10 minutes, or until the sauce is thick.

Remove from the heat and season to taste with lemon juice and salt and pepper.

Use as directed in a specific recipe, or store, covered and refrigerated, for up to 2 days. Reheat before using.

ANCHO SAUCE

Uses: **A very versatile sauce, particularly good with eggs, but can add some Texas flair to almost anything you cook.**

- **10 dried ancho chiles**
- **2 tablespoons olive oil**
- **1 cup chopped onion**
- **½ cup chopped carrot**
- **2 corn tortillas, cut into strips**
- **1 jalapeño chile, stemmed, seeded, and chopped**
- **1 teaspoon chopped garlic**
- **2 medium tomatoes, cored and chopped**
- **½ cup chopped fresh cilantro**
- **2 cups chicken stock or nonfat, low-sodium chicken broth**
- **2 teaspoons fresh lime juice**
- **2 teaspoons pure maple syrup**
- **Salt**

Remove the stems and seeds from the ancho chiles. Place the chiles in a heatproof bowl with hot water to cover by about 2 inches. Set aside to soak and soften for about 20 minutes.

Drain the chiles well and transfer to a blender or food processor fitted with the metal blade and process to a smooth puree. Scrape into a measuring cup; you should have 1 cup of puree. Set aside.

Heat the oil in a medium saucepan over medium heat. Add the onion and cook, stirring frequently, for about 5 minutes, or until golden brown. Add the carrot and continue to cook for an additional 4 minutes. Stir in the tortillas, jalapeño, and garlic and cook, stirring, for 2 minutes.

Add the tomatoes and cilantro along with the ancho puree and stir to blend. Add the stock and bring to a boil. Lower the heat and simmer for 20 minutes.

Remove from the heat and pour into a blender. Puree until very smooth. Add the lime juice, maple syrup, and salt to taste and process to blend. Taste the sauce and, if necessary, adjust the seasoning.

Use as directed in a specific recipe, or store, covered and refrigerated, for up to 1 week.

RANCHERO SAUCE

Uses: **As a sauce for egg dishes like huevos rancheros, or for enchiladas or tacos.**

- **2 teaspoons olive oil**
- **1 cup finely diced onion**
- **½ cup finely diced celery**
- **½ cup finely diced carrot**
- **½ cup finely diced red bell pepper**
- **2 tablespoons seeded and minced jalapeño chiles**
- **2 teaspoons minced garlic**
- **1 cup Ancho Chile Paste (page 40)**
- **2 cups vegetable stock or nonfat, low-sodium vegetable broth**
- **1 tablespoon chopped fresh cilantro**
- **Fresh lime juice**
- **Salt**

Heat the oil in a medium saucepan over medium-high heat. Add the onion, celery, carrot, and bell pepper. Cook, stirring occasionally, for about 5 minutes, or until the vegetables are light brown.

Stir in the chiles and garlic and sauté for 1 minute.

Add the chile paste and cook for about 3 minutes to "fry" the paste.

Add the stock and bring to a boil. Lower the heat and cook at a gentle simmer for about 30 minutes, or until the sauce is thick enough to coat the back of a spoon.

Remove from the heat and stir in the cilantro and lime juice to taste. Season with salt.

Use as directed in a specific recipe, or store, tightly covered and refrigerated, for up to 1 week. Reheat before using.

Charred Tomato Sauce

MAKES ABOUT 3 CUPS

Uses: As a sauce for almost any Mexican, Mexican-style, or Southwest recipe. It adds a rich, smoky finishing touch.

- 6 large ripe tomatoes
- 1 tablespoon vegetable oil
- 2 cups large-dice onions
- 1 bay leaf
- ½ cup smashed **Roasted Garlic** (see page 41)
- ½ cup veal demi-glace (see **Note**)
- 2 tablespoons seeded and chopped jalapeño chiles
- 2 teaspoons ground cumin
- 2 tablespoons chopped fresh cilantro
- Fresh lime juice
- Salt

Place the tomatoes in a stovetop grill pan over high heat. Grill, turning frequently, for about 12 minutes, or until nicely charred on all sides and softened. Remove from the heat and set aside until cool enough to handle.

When cool enough to handle, core and chop the tomatoes, and set aside.

Heat the oil in a large frying pan over medium heat. Add the onions and cook, stirring occasionally, for about 15 minutes, or until the onions are golden and well caramelized. Add the reserved tomatoes along with the bay leaf, garlic, demi-glace, chiles, and cumin and stir to combine. Bring to a boil. Immediately lower the heat, and cook, stirring occasionally, for about 20 minutes, or until the sauce is well flavored and thickened.

Remove from the heat and remove and discard the bay leaf. Stir in the cilantro. Taste and season with lime juice and salt.

Use as directed in a specific recipe, or store, tightly covered and refrigerated, for up to 1 week. Reheat before using.

NOTE: If you don't make your own demi-glace, it is available from fine butcher shops, at specialty food stores, and online.

Roasted Green Chile Sauce

MAKES 1 QUART

Uses: A great alternative for any dish that would use a Mexican red chile sauce.

- 2 cups chopped tomatillos
- 5 garlic cloves, peeled
- 1 jalapeño chile, stemmed, seeded, and chopped
- 2 cups chopped poblano chiles
- 1 cup chopped onion
- 1 tablespoon olive oil
- Salt
- Freshly ground pepper
- 3 cups chicken stock or nonfat, low-sodium chicken broth
- ½ cup chopped fresh spinach leaves
- 1 tablespoon chopped fresh cilantro
- Fresh lime juice

Preheat the oven to 350°F.

Combine the tomatillos with the garlic, jalapeño, poblanos, and onion in a bowl. Add the olive oil, season with salt and pepper to taste, and toss to coat well.

Transfer the seasoned vegetables to a baking pan and spread them out in a single layer. Place in the preheated oven and roast for 20 minutes, or until lightly browned.

Remove the vegetables from the oven and scrape into a medium saucepan. Add the chicken stock and bring to a boil over medium-high heat. Lower the heat and simmer for 15 minutes. Remove from the heat and set aside to cool slightly.

When cool, transfer to a blender. Add the spinach and process to a smooth puree. Pour into a clean container. Stir in the cilantro along with lime juice to taste. Taste and, if necessary, adjust the seasoning with additional salt and pepper.

Serve warm as directed in a specific recipe, or store, tightly covered and refrigerated, for up to 1 week. Reheat before serving.

DIABLO SAUCE

MAKES ABOUT 2 CUPS

Uses: **I like this sauce with shrimp, but it adds a great all-around kick to any dish.**

- **1 tablespoon olive oil**
- **1 cup chopped smoked red bell pepper (see page 176)**
- **¼ cup seeded and minced jalapeño chile**
- **2 tablespoons minced shallot**
- **1 tablespoon minced garlic**
- **1 teaspoon whole cumin seed**
- **1½ cups chicken stock or nonfat, low-sodium chicken broth**
- **½ cup diced mango**
- **1 teaspoon peeled and grated fresh ginger**
- **Fresh lime juice**
- **Salt**

Heat the oil in a medium saucepan over medium-high heat. Add the bell pepper, chile, shallot, garlic, and cumin and cook, stirring, for 3 minutes.

Add the stock, mango, and ginger and bring to a boil. Immediately lower the heat and cook at a gentle simmer for 10 minutes.

Scrape the mixture into a blender and process until very smooth. Season the sauce with lime juice and salt.

Use as directed in a specific recipe, or store, tightly covered and refrigerated, for up to 1 week.

GREEN CHILE MOJO

MAKES ABOUT 1 CUP

Uses: **A light, flavorful sauce that works well in the heat of summer on grilled fish and meat.**

- **½ cup vegetable oil**
- **2 roasted poblano chiles, stemmed, peeled, and seeded**
- **2 garlic cloves, roughly chopped**
- **½ bunch scallions, green part only, roughly chopped**
- **½ bunch fresh cilantro, roughly chopped**
- **¼ cup mango, roughly chopped**
- **¼ cup fresh lime juice**
- **Salt**

Heat the oil in a medium saucepan over medium-high heat. Add the chiles, garlic, scallions, and cilantro and bring to a simmer. Lower the heat and cook at a gentle simmer for 10 minutes, or until the chiles and garlic are very tender.

Remove from the heat and pour through a fine-mesh sieve; reserve the chile mixture solids and the hot oil separately.

When the chile mixture has cooled a bit, transfer to a blender. Add the mango and process to a smooth puree, then add the reserved hot oil, a bit at a time, to make a smooth consistency. Add the lime juice, season with salt to taste, and process to blend.

Serve the sauce immediately, or store, covered and refrigerated, for up to 1 week.

QUESO ASADERO

Uses: The only thing I can say about the use of this is … "Where are the chips?"

1 cup chicken stock or nonfat,
   low-sodium chicken broth

1 cup heavy cream

2 tablespoons cornstarch dissolved
   in 2 tablespoons cold water

2 cups shredded asadero cheese

½ cup of your favorite tomato salsa

Fresh lime juice

Salt

Combine the chicken stock and cream in a medium saucepan over medium heat. Watching carefully to prevent spillover, bring to a boil. Immediately lower the heat to a gentle simmer. Stirring constantly, add the cornstarch mixture in a thin, steady stream. Cook, stirring, for about 10 minutes, or until the gravy is very thick.

Remove from the heat, add the cheese, and stir until completely melted. Stir in the salsa and season to taste with lime juice and salt.

Use immediately or keep warm in the top half of a double boiler over a saucepan of simmering water until ready to serve.

TEX-MEX GRAVY

Uses: A great smother over eggs or enchiladas.

2 tablespoons bacon fat

1 pound ground beef

2 garlic cloves, minced

1 medium onion, finely chopped

3 tablespoons pure chile powder

2 teaspoons ground cumin

2 teaspoons chopped fresh oregano

4 cups chicken stock or nonfat,
   low-sodium chicken broth

Salt

Freshly ground pepper

1 tablespoon masa harina (see page 18)

Heat the bacon fat in a large cast-iron skillet over medium-high heat. Add the ground beef and fry, stirring frequently, for about 5 minutes, or until the meat has begun to brown. Stir in the garlic and onion and continue to fry, stirring, for 2 minutes. Add the chile powder, cumin, and oregano and stir to blend. Add the chicken stock and season to taste with salt and pepper. Bring to a boil; then lower the heat and simmer for about 30 minutes, or until the meat is thoroughly cooked and the liquid has reduced slightly.

Remove about ¼ cup of the cooking liquid and place it in a small bowl. Stir in the masa and when blended, stir the mixture into the meat until well incorporated. Bring to a simmer and cook, stirring occasionally, for an additional 10 minutes, or until the gravy has thickened. Remove from the heat.

Use as directed in a specific recipe, or store, covered and refrigerated, for up to 3 days. Reheat before using.

POBLANO CREAM GRAVY

MAKES ABOUT 3 CUPS

Uses: **This is a terrific alternative to the traditional cream gravy for the Texas breakfast favorite biscuits and gravy.**

3 tablespoons unsalted butter (or bacon fat)

½ cup small-dice onion

1 tablespoon minced garlic

1 tablespoon seeded and minced jalapeño chile

3 tablespoons all-purpose flour

2½ cups whole milk

½ cup heavy cream

4 roasted poblano chiles, stemmed, seeded, and chopped

Tabasco sauce

Fresh lime juice

Salt

Freshly ground pepper

Heat the butter (or bacon fat) in a medium saucepan over medium heat. Add the onion, garlic, and jalapeño and cook, stirring, for about 4 minutes, or until the onion is translucent. Sprinkle the flour over the top and stir to incorporate.

Add the milk and then the cream in a slow, steady stream and stir to blend. Cook, stirring constantly, for about 3 minutes, or until thickened.

Stir in the poblanos and bring to a boil. Lower the heat and simmer, stirring occasionally, for 20 minutes.

Remove the gravy from the heat and transfer to a blender. Process to a smooth puree. Taste and season with Tabasco, lime juice, salt, and pepper as needed.

Serve hot as directed in a specific recipe, or the gravy may be made in advance and stored, covered and refrigerated, for a few hours. Reheat before serving.

SMOKED TOMATO GRAVY

MAKES ABOUT 4 CUPS

Uses: **Great for anything fried, even fried green tomatoes!**

3 tablespoons bacon fat (or unsalted butter)

½ cup small-dice onion

1 tablespoon minced garlic

1 tablespoon seeded and minced jalapeño chile

¼ cup all-purpose flour

2½ cups whole milk

½ cup heavy cream

2 cups cold-smoked tomatoes (see page 177)

Fresh lime juice

Salt

Freshly ground pepper

Heat the bacon fat in a medium saucepan over medium heat. Add the onion, garlic, and chile and sauté for 3 minutes, or until the onion is translucent.

Sprinkle the flour over the onion mixture and cook, stirring, for 3 minutes, or until light brown.

Combine the milk and cream in a small bowl and begin adding to the onion mixture in a slow, steady stream, whisking constantly. Cook, stirring constantly, for about 5 minutes, or until thick.

Add the tomatoes and bring to a boil. Immediately lower the heat and cook at a simmer, stirring occasionally, for 20 minutes.

Remove from the heat and pour into a blender. Process to a smooth puree. Season to taste with lime juice, salt, and pepper.

Use as directed in a specific recipe, or store, tightly covered and refrigerated, for up to 1 day.

POBLANO-PEPITA PESTO

MAKES ABOUT 2 CUPS

Uses: **A great summertime sauce. I enjoy this with tomatoes or anything grilled. It also offers a really different Mexican flavor to pasta dishes.**

2 roasted poblano chiles, stemmed,
    peeled, and seeded

Juice of 1 lemon

½ pound fresh basil leaves, washed and dried

½ pound fresh spinach leaves, washed and dried

1 garlic clove, chopped

¼ cup roasted pepitas

2 tablespoons grated **Cotija** or
    Mexican farmer's cheese

2 tablespoons cold water

½ cup olive oil

Salt

Freshly ground pepper

Combine the poblanos with the lemon juice and basil and spinach leaves in a blender. Process to chop. Add the garlic, pepitas, and cheese along with the cold water and continue to process until very smooth. With the motor running, add the oil in a slow, steady stream and process until a very smooth paste forms. If too thick, add additional water, a bit at a time. Taste and season with salt and pepper.

CILANTRO-LIME SOUR CREAM

MAKES ABOUT 1 CUP

Uses: **No limits!**

1 cup sour cream

1 tablespoon finely chopped fresh cilantro

1 pinch ground cumin

Juice of 1 lime

Salt

Combine the sour cream, cilantro, and cumin in a small bowl. Whisk in the lime juice and season to taste with salt.

Use as directed in a specific recipe, or store, tightly covered and refrigerated, for up to 1 day.

HORSERADISH CREAM SAUCE

MAKES ABOUT 2½ CUPS

Uses: **I am such a lover of horseradish that I could eat this all by itself. Use it on everything!**

One 8- to 10-inch piece fresh horseradish,
    peeled and grated (see **Note**)

2 cups sour cream

1 teaspoon **Worcestershire** sauce

1 teaspoon **Tabasco** sauce

1 teaspoon fresh lemon juice

1 tablespoon chopped fresh chives

Salt

Freshly cracked pepper

Combine the horseradish with the sour cream, Worcestershire, Tabasco, and lemon juice in the bowl of a food processor fitted with the metal blade. Process just enough to blend well.

Scrape the sauce from the processor bowl into a clean container. Stir in the chives and season to taste with salt and cracked pepper.

Serve as directed in a specific recipe, or store, tightly covered and refrigerated, for up to 3 days. Bring to room temperature before serving.

NOTE: Horseradish is very tough. It can be peeled with a strong vegetable peeler and can be grated by hand on the small holes of a box grater or on the grating blade of a food processor, but beware, it is very, very pungent so you may shed a few tears in the process. Do not try to process chunks of the root when mixing with the sour cream. It must be grated first or it won't be fine enough in the final sauce.

SMOKED-BACON GASTRIQUE

MAKES ABOUT ½ CUP

Uses: **On all fish dishes.**

½ cup small-dice smoked bacon

2 garlic cloves, minced

½ cup small-dice onion

1 cup turkey stock or nonfat,
   low-sodium turkey broth

¼ cup Tabasco sauce

2 tablespoons dry white wine

1 tablespoon molasses

2 teaspoons minced fresh thyme

In a small saucepan over medium-high heat, cook the bacon, stirring occasionally, for about 5 minutes, or until all of the fat has rendered out.

Stir in the garlic and onion and cook, stirring, for 2 minutes. Add the stock, Tabasco, wine, molasses, and thyme and bring to a boil. Lower the heat and cook at a gentle simmer for about 15 minutes, or until reduced by half and thick enough to coat the back of a spoon.

Use as directed in a specific recipe, or store, tightly covered and refrigerated, for up to 3 days. Reheat before using.

THICKENED CHICKEN STOCK

MAKES 2¾ CUPS

Uses: **To thicken any other sauces you like.**

2½ cups chicken stock or nonfat,
   low-sodium chicken broth

2 tablespoons cornstarch dissolved
   in 2 tablespoons cold water

In a small saucepan over medium-high heat, bring the chicken stock to a boil. Whisking constantly, begin adding the cornstarch mixture in a slow, steady stream. When all of the cornstarch has been incorporated, lower the heat to a simmer. Cook at a gentle simmer, whisking constantly, for about 5 minutes, or until smooth and thick and the starchiness has cooked out.

Use as directed in a specific recipe, or store, tightly covered and refrigerated, for up to 3 days. Reheat before using.

WATERMELON-JALAPEÑO GLAZE

MAKES ABOUT 4 CUPS

Uses: **A wonderful summer glaze that can be used on all grilled items.**

4 cups fresh watermelon juice

1 cup chicken stock or nonfat,
   low-sodium chicken broth

4 jalapeño chiles, stemmed and
   chopped, seeds included

3 shallots, chopped

1 bunch fresh cilantro stems

2 tablespoons cornstarch dissolved
   in 2 tablespoons cold water

Fresh lime juice

Salt

Combine the watermelon juice with the stock, chiles, shallots, and cilantro stems in a medium, heavy-bottomed saucepan over high heat. Bring to a boil and immediately whisk in the cornstarch mixture. Return to a boil, lower the heat, and cook at a gentle simmer for 20 minutes.

Remove the glaze from the heat and strain through a fine-mesh sieve into a clean container. Season to taste with lime juice and salt.

Use as directed in a specific recipe, or store, tightly covered and refrigerated, for up to 1 week.

SALSAS

★ ★ ★

GUACAMOLE

MAKES ABOUT 2 CUPS

Uses: **Chips, chips, chips!!**

3 large ripe avocados, pitted and peeled (see sidebar below)

1 jalapeño chile, stemmed, seeded, and minced

¼ cup finely diced onion

1 tablespoon chopped fresh cilantro

Salt

Fresh lime juice

Place the avocados in a shallow bowl and, using a kitchen fork, mash until smooth. Add the chile, onion, and cilantro and stir to blend. Season generously with salt and lime juice.

Serve the guacamole immediately if possible. If not serving immediately, reserve a pit and place it in the guacamole. Then cover the container with plastic wrap, pushing it directly onto the surface of the guacamole to prevent air from getting in; this will keep it from discoloring.

PICO DE GALLO

MAKES 2 CUPS

Uses: **Anything you like.**

1 cup ¼-inch-dice ripe tomatoes

2 tablespoons ¼-inch-dice red onion

1 tablespoon seeded and minced jalapeño chile

1 tablespoon finely chopped fresh cilantro

Fresh lime juice

Salt

Combine the tomatoes, onion, chile, and cilantro in a medium bowl. Season to taste with lime juice and salt and toss to combine. Let stand for 10 minutes before serving.

Pico de gallo is best when made within a couple of hours of use. Although the flavors blend over time, as it sits the tomatoes and onion soften and the fresh texture is lost.

Removing the Flesh from an Avocado

To extract the flesh from an avocado, first cut the avocado in half, from stem end around. Using your knife blade and a gentle, single motion, tap into the pit and pull up. The pit should pull away from the flesh. Remove the pit. Using a large serving spoon, push the spoon between the skin and the flesh and, following the curve of the avocado, move the spoon against the skin to lift out the flesh. The goal is to extract all of the flesh from the skin, leaving a perfectly clean shell of skin.

Yellow Tomato Pico de Gallo

MAKES ABOUT 1 CUP

Uses: **Anything you like.**

- **1 large yellow tomato, peeled, cored, seeded, and cut into small dice**
- **1 medium jalapeño chile, stemmed, seeded, and finely diced**
- **1 small shallot, finely diced**
- **Juice of 1 lime**
- **Salt**
- **Freshly ground pepper**

Combine the tomato with the chile and shallot in a small bowl. Add the lime juice and season to taste with salt and pepper.

Use as directed in a specific recipe, or store, tightly covered and refrigerated, for no more than a couple of hours. Longer storage will cause the tomatoes to become mushy.

Mango Pico de Gallo

MAKES ABOUT 4 CUPS

Uses: **A naturally sweet version of the traditional pico that is great with fish, shellfish, and pork.**

- **2 ripe mangoes, peeled and cut into ¼-inch dice**
- **1 medium ripe tomato, peeled, cored, seeded, and cut into ¼-inch dice**
- **1 jalapeño chile, stemmed, seeded, and minced**
- **½ small red onion, cut into ¼-inch dice**
- **¼ cup fresh lime juice**
- **1 tablespoon finely chopped fresh cilantro**
- **Salt**

Combine the mango with the tomato, chile, onion, lime juice, and cilantro in a bowl and toss to blend. Taste and season with salt.

Let rest for 10 minutes before serving. The pico may be made in advance and stored, covered and refrigerated, for up to 1 day. Bring to room temperature before serving.

Watermelon Pico de Gallo

MAKES ABOUT 3 CUPS

Uses: **My summertime version of a traditional pico.**

- **1½ cups ¼-inch-dice seedless watermelon**
- **½ cup ¼-inch-dice jicama**
- **¼ cup ¼-inch-dice honeydew melon**
- **¼ cup ¼-inch-dice cantaloupe**
- **¼ cup ¼-inch-dice red onion**
- **1 jalapeño chile, stemmed, seeded, and chopped**
- **½ cup chopped fresh cilantro leaves**
- **2 tablespoons fresh lime juice**
- **Pure maple syrup**
- **Salt**

Combine the watermelon, jicama, honeydew, cantaloupe, and onion in a medium bowl. Gently stir in the chile, cilantro, and lime juice, being careful not to mash the fruit. Taste and season with maple syrup and salt as needed.

Use as directed in a specific recipe, or store, tightly covered and refrigerated, for no more than an hour or so. Longer storage will cause the melon to become mushy.

Yellow Tomato Salsa

MAKES ABOUT 3 CUPS

Uses: **A bright, colorful, and exciting salsa for dipping, chipping, or garnishing grilled pork, chicken, fish, or shellfish.**

- 2 pints yellow cherry tomatoes, or 1 pound yellow tomatoes, peeled and cored
- 2 small white onions, minced (½ cup)
- 2 garlic cloves, minced
- 1 jalapeño chile, stemmed, seeded, and minced
- 1 tablespoon minced fresh cilantro
- Fresh lime juice
- Salt
- 1 tablespoon pure maple syrup (optional)

Place the tomatoes in a food processor fitted with the metal blade and process until well chopped; do not puree.

Transfer the tomatoes along with their juices to a bowl. Add the onions, garlic, jalapeño, cilantro, and lime juice, and mix well to combine. Season to taste with salt. Add maple syrup, if needed, to balance the flavor and sweeten slightly.

Do not make the salsa ahead; the mixture must be very fresh.

Charred Tomato Salsa

MAKES ABOUT 2 CUPS

Uses: **This is my all-around great ole sauce to use on just about everything.**

- 6 large ripe tomatoes, cored
- 3 tablespoons olive oil
- 6 garlic cloves, peeled
- 2 jalapeño chiles, stemmed
- 1 medium onion, thinly sliced
- 1 tablespoon chopped fresh cilantro
- Salt
- Fresh lime juice

Preheat the broiler.

Place the tomatoes in a baking pan that will fit under the broiler. Using 1 tablespoon of the olive oil and a pastry brush, lightly coat the top of each tomato.

Place under the broiler and broil for about 8 minutes, or until the skin is well charred and quite black. Remove from the broiler and set aside.

Turn off the broiler and set the oven temperature to 375°F.

Combine the garlic, chiles, and onion with the remaining 2 tablespoons olive oil and toss to coat well. Place in a baking pan and transfer to the preheated oven. Bake, stirring occasionally, for about 15 minutes, or until golden brown and cooked through. Remove from the oven and set aside.

Combine the tomatoes with the garlic, chiles, onion, and cilantro in a food processor fitted with the metal blade. Process, using quick on-and-off turns, until blended but still slightly chunky; do not puree.

Generously season the salsa with salt and lime juice to taste and serve, or store, tightly covered and refrigerated, for up to 1 week. Bring to room temperature before using.

NOTE: If you have a meat grinder, use it to make this salsa, as it results in a more authentic texture.

DRESSINGS AND VINAIGRETTES

★ ★ ★

ANCHO CHILE MAYONNAISE

MAKES ABOUT 1½ CUPS

Uses: **A terrific sandwich spread.**

4 dried ancho chiles, stemmed and seeded

1 large egg yolk, at room temperature

2 tablespoons balsamic vinegar

1 tablespoon Dijon mustard

1 cup olive oil

Juice of 1 lime

Salt

Place the chiles in a heatproof bowl with hot water to cover by at least 1 inch. Set aside to soak for 20 minutes.

Drain the chiles well and transfer to a food processor fitted with the metal blade. Process to a smooth puree. Add the egg yolk, vinegar, and mustard and process to blend completely.

With the motor running, add the oil in a slow, steady stream, processing until completely emulsified. When emulsified, blend in the lime juice and, if necessary, season with salt to taste.

Use as directed in a specific recipe, or transfer to a plastic squeeze bottle and cover the opening with plastic wrap and then with the cap. Refrigerate until ready to use, or for up to 2 days.

ROASTED GARLIC MAYONNAISE

MAKES ABOUT ½ CUP

Uses: **I like to use this as a dip for French fries, or as a glue for smoked pecans (see page 139) on top of grilled or baked fish.**

8 large Roasted Garlic cloves (page 41), peeled

½ cup mayonnaise

Combine the garlic with the mayonnaise in a food processor fitted with the metal blade and process to a smooth puree.

Use as directed in a specific recipe, or scrape into a clean container and store, tightly covered and refrigerated, for up to 1 week.

POINT REYES BLUE CHEESE DRESSING

Uses: **It's the cheese that makes this my favorite blue cheese dressing for salads.**

- **1 cup crumbled Point Reyes Blue Cheese or other fine-quality blue cheese**
- **1 cup buttermilk**
- **½ cup sour cream**
- **Juice of ½ lemon**
- **2 teaspoons Worcestershire sauce**
- **1 teaspoon freshly ground pepper**
- **Splash Tabasco sauce**
- **Salt**

Combine the blue cheese with the buttermilk in a medium bowl. Add the sour cream along with the lemon juice, Worcestershire sauce, pepper, and Tabasco, vigorously whisking to blend completely. The mixture should be almost smooth with just a few lumps of cheese remaining. Taste and season with salt if necessary.

Use as directed in a specific recipe, or store, tightly covered and refrigerated, for up to 1 week.

BARBECUED THOUSAND ISLAND DRESSING

MAKES ABOUT 2 CUPS

Uses: **This is a modern take on the traditional Thousand Island dressing—it just can't be beat to give a hint of Texas to sandwiches and salads.**

- **1 cup mayonnaise**
- **¼ cup Texas-Style Barbecue Sauce (page 19) or other smoky barbecue sauce**
- **2 tablespoons ketchup**
- **1 tablespoon distilled white vinegar**
- **1 tablespoon fresh lemon juice**
- **1 hard-boiled egg, peeled and finely chopped**
- **2 teaspoons sweet pickle relish**
- **1 teaspoon finely minced white onion**
- **1 teaspoon dry mustard powder**
- **1 tablespoon minced capers, well drained**
- **1 teaspoon minced garlic**
- **1 teaspoon Worcestershire sauce**
- **1 teaspoon chopped fresh flat-leaf parsley**
- **1 teaspoon snipped fresh chives**
- **Salt**
- **Freshly ground pepper**

Put the mayonnaise in a small bowl. Stir in the barbecue sauce, ketchup, vinegar, and lemon juice. When blended, add the chopped egg, relish, onion, mustard powder, capers, garlic, Worcestershire sauce, parsley, and chives and stir to mix thoroughly. Taste and season with salt and pepper.

Use as directed in a specific recipe, or store, tightly covered and refrigerated, for up to 3 days.

Jalapeño Ranch Dressing

MAKES ABOUT 2 CUPS

Uses: **My take on ranch dressings—use this for salads and sandwiches and as a glaze on grilled fish or pork.**

- **1 cup buttermilk**
- **½ cup mayonnaise**
- **⅓ cup seeded and chopped jalapeño chile**
- **One 1-ounce package ranch dressing mix**
- **Tabasco sauce**
- **Fresh lime juice**

Put the buttermilk in a blender along with the mayonnaise and chile. Add the dressing mix and process to a smooth puree. Add the Tabasco and lime juice to taste and process to blend.

Use as directed in a specific recipe, or store, tightly covered and refrigerated, for up to 1 week.

Smoked Chile Aioli

MAKES 2 CUPS

Uses: **Versatile; use on a salad or to accompany a steak.**

- **2 anchovy fillets**
- **1 red bell pepper, stemmed, seeded, and cold smoked (see page 177)**
- **1 roasted red jalapeño chile, stemmed, seeded, and chopped**
- **1 cup mayonnaise**
- **2 tablespoons Dijon mustard**
- **2 teaspoons sherry vinegar**
- **1 tablespoon minced garlic**
- **1 tablespoon Worcestershire sauce**
- **1 teaspoon Tabasco sauce**
- **1 teaspoon smoked paprika**
- **½ cup olive oil**
- **Fresh lime juice**
- **Salt**

Combine the anchovies, bell pepper, chile, mayonnaise, mustard, vinegar, garlic, Worcestershire, Tabasco, and smoked paprika in a blender. Process until very smooth.

With the motor running, add the oil in a slow, steady stream. When well emulsified, add the lime juice and salt to taste.

Use as directed in a specific recipe, or store, tightly covered and refrigerated, for up to 1 week.

FIRECRACKER DRESSING

MAKES ABOUT 1½ CUPS

Uses: **Where's the Fourth-of-July picnic? Bring this to your table for salads and sandwiches all year long.**

- **1 cup mayonnaise**
- **1 tablespoon ketchup**
- **1 tablespoon Texas-Style Barbecue Sauce (page 19) or your favorite smoky sauce**
- **1 tablespoon Sriracha sauce**
- **½ tablespoon cask-aged sherry vinegar**
- **1 teaspoon minced garlic**
- **1 teaspoon anchovy paste**
- **1 teaspoon dry mustard powder**
- **1 teaspoon Worcestershire sauce**
- **1 teaspoon chopped fresh cilantro**
- **1 teaspoon snipped fresh chives**
- **Fresh lime juice**
- **Salt**
- **Freshly ground pepper**

Put the mayonnaise in a medium bowl. Stir in the ketchup, barbecue sauce, Sriracha, and vinegar. When blended, stir in the garlic, anchovy paste, mustard powder, Worcestershire, cilantro, and chives. Taste and season with lime juice, salt, and pepper as needed.

Use as directed in a specific recipe, or store, tightly covered and refrigerated, for up to 3 days.

CREAMY BASIL DRESSING

MAKES ABOUT 1½ CUPS

Uses: **My favorite dressing to drizzle over juicy, ripe summertime tomatoes, but it is also delicious on grilled vegetables or in potato salad.**

- **2 packed cups fresh basil leaves**
- **¼ cup olive oil**
- **1 cup mayonnaise**
- **1 tablespoon Dijon mustard**
- **1 tablespoon sherry vinegar**
- **1 teaspoon minced shallot**
- **Salt**
- **Freshly ground pepper**

Combine the basil and oil in a blender and process to a smooth puree.

Put the mayonnaise in a medium bowl. Whisk the basil puree into the mayonnaise in a slow, steady stream. Add the mustard, vinegar, and shallot and stir to blend well. Taste and season with salt and pepper.

Use as directed in a specific recipe, or store, tightly covered and refrigerated, for up to 3 days.

CARROT-CUMIN VINAIGRETTE

MAKES 1½ CUPS

Uses: **An unusual vinaigrette, this is terrific for salads, grilled veggies, and meats.**

- 1½ cups peeled, roughly chopped, cold-smoked carrots (see page 177)
- 3 tablespoons olive oil
- 1 teaspoon cumin seeds
- Salt
- 2 teaspoons pure maple syrup
- 1 tablespoon sherry vinegar
- Fresh lime juice

Preheat the oven to 300°F.

Combine the carrots with 1 tablespoon of the oil and the cumin seeds in a small baking pan and season with salt. Transfer to the preheated oven and bake for 10 minutes, or until the carrots are tender.

Scrape the carrots into a blender and, with the motor running, add the remaining 2 tablespoons oil along with the maple syrup and vinegar. Season to taste with lime juice and, if necessary, add water to adjust the consistency. Season with additional salt if needed.

Use as directed in a specific recipe, or store, tightly covered and refrigerated, for up to 3 days.

MUSTARD-SAGE VINAIGRETTE

MAKES ABOUT 1¾ CUPS

Uses: **Great with raw, steamed, or grilled root vegetables.**

- 1 cup mayonnaise
- ¼ cup Dijon mustard
- 2 tablespoons malt vinegar
- 1 teaspoon fresh lime juice
- ¼ cup olive oil
- 1 tablespoon finely chopped fresh sage
- 1 teaspoon salt
- 1 teaspoon freshly ground pepper

Combine the mayonnaise with the mustard, vinegar, and lime juice in a small bowl. Whisking constantly, add the oil in a slow, steady stream. When emulsified, whisk in the sage and season with the salt and pepper.

Use as directed in a specific recipe, or store, tightly covered and refrigerated, for up to 2 days. Bring to room temperature and whisk before using.

HONEY-MUSTARD DRESSING

MAKES ABOUT ¾ CUP

Uses: **This is an all-time favorite of mine, and my kids love it, too. Serve it with fried chicken or, in fact, any deep-fried fish, shellfish, or meat tenders.**

- ½ cup mayonnaise
- 2 tablespoons honey
- 2 tablespoons Dijon mustard
- 1 teaspoon fresh lemon juice
- 1 tablespoon snipped chives
- Salt
- Freshly ground pepper

Combine the mayonnaise with the honey, mustard, lemon juice, and chives in a small bowl and stir to blend completely. Taste and, if necessary, season with salt and pepper.

Use as directed in a specific recipe, or store, tightly covered and refrigerated, for up to 3 days.

Smoky Cumin-Lime Vinaigrette

MAKES ABOUT 2 CUPS

Uses: You will love the mysterious smoke flavor that comes from this vinaigrette, as it adds zest to almost any grilled meat, fish, or vegetable.

- 1 cup fresh orange juice
- ½ cup diced cold-smoked onion (see page 177)
- 3 tablespoons pure maple syrup
- 2 tablespoons malt vinegar
- ½ tablespoon toasted cumin seeds
- ½ cup olive oil
- ½ cup vegetable oil
- ¼ cup fresh lime juice
- Salt

Combine the orange juice with the smoked onion, maple syrup, vinegar, and cumin in a small nonreactive saucepan over high heat and bring to a boil. Lower the heat and simmer for about 10 minutes, or until the liquid has almost completely evaporated.

Transfer the onion mixture to a blender and process to a smooth puree. With the motor running, add both the olive and vegetable oils in a slow, steady stream, processing until completely emulsified. Add the lime juice and salt to taste.

Use as directed in a specific recipe, or store, tightly covered, for up to 1 week. Bring to room temperature before using.

Sherry Vinaigrette

MAKES ABOUT 1½ CUPS

Uses: Great for all salads, tossed, green, or otherwise.

- ½ cup cask-aged sherry vinegar
- ½ cup apple juice
- 2 tablespoons Dijon mustard
- 1 tablespoon honey
- 1 small shallot, minced
- ½ cup olive oil
- 1 cup vegetable oil
- Salt
- Freshly ground pepper

Combine the vinegar, apple juice, mustard, and honey in a small bowl. Stir in the shallot. Whisking vigorously, add the olive oil and vegetable oil in a slow, steady stream. Season to taste with salt and pepper.

Use as directed in a specific recipe, or store, tightly covered and refrigerated, for up to 3 days. Bring to room temperature before using.

Lime Vinaigrette

MAKES 1 CUP

Uses: This vinaigrette is especially good with raw vegetable salads.

- ½ cup olive oil
- ½ cup fresh lime juice
- 1 teaspoon honey
- Pinch cayenne pepper
- Salt

Combine the oil and lime juice in a small bowl. Add the honey and cayenne and whisk vigorously until completely blended. Add salt to taste.

Serve as directed in a specific recipe, or store, tightly covered and refrigerated, for up to 1 week. Bring to room temperature before using.

SPICE MIXES, POWDERS, PASTES, AND GARNISHES

★ ★ ★

FEARING'S BARBECUE SPICE BLEND

MAKES ABOUT ¾ CUP

Uses: **On anything roasted, grilled, smoked, or fried.**

- ¼ cup **Pendery's chile powder blend** (see Sources, page 242)
- 1 tablespoon ground chipotle chile
- 1 tablespoon ground dried ancho chile
- 1 tablespoon hickory-smoked salt
- 1 tablespoon sugar
- 1 tablespoon cayenne pepper
- 1 tablespoon paprika
- 1 tablespoon smoked paprika
- ½ tablespoon ground cumin
- ½ tablespoon granulated garlic
- ½ tablespoon Aleppo pepper
- ¼ tablespoon freshly ground pepper

Place the Pendery's chile powder in a small bowl. Add the remaining ingredients and stir to combine. Store, tightly covered, in a cool, dark spot until ready to use. Keeps for 3 months.

FEARING'S BARBECUE SPICE FLOUR MIXTURE

MAKES ABOUT 2¼ CUPS

Uses: **This is the best chicken-fried flour blend known to man!**

- 2 cups all-purpose flour
- ½ cup Fearing's Barbecue Spice Blend (at left)

Place the flour in a small bowl. Add the spice blend and stir to combine.

Store, tightly covered, in a cool, dark spot until ready to use. Keeps for about 6 weeks.

BARBECUE SPICED PEPITAS

MAKES 2 CUPS

Uses: **A garnish for almost anything you want to give a Texas hit to!**

- 2 cups green Mexican pumpkin seeds
- 2 tablespoons Fearing's Barbecue Spice Blend (at left)
- Salt

Preheat the oven to 350°F.

Place the pumpkin seeds in a single layer on a baking sheet with sides. Transfer to the preheated oven and roast for about 8 minutes, or until fragrant and lightly colored.

Pour the hot seeds into a medium bowl. Add the spice blend and toss to coat. Add salt to taste.

Use as directed in a specific recipe, or store, tightly covered, in a cool spot, for up to 1 month.

PUMPKIN SEED POWDER

MAKES ¼ CUP

Uses: **A fine garnish for the world of Texas cuisine.**

¼ cup toasted unsalted pumpkin seeds (pepitas)

Pour the pumpkin seeds into the bowl of a food processor fitted with the metal blade. Process to a fine powder.

Store, tightly covered, at room temperature, for up to 1 week.

GUAJILLO CHILE PASTE

MAKES ABOUT 2 CUPS

Uses: **The best enhancement I know for burgers, ground meats, and sausage making.**

10 guajillo chiles

1 small carrot, peeled, trimmed, and roughly diced

1 cup fresh orange juice

½ onion, roughly diced

½ jalapeño chile, stemmed, seeded, and chopped

5 fresh cilantro sprigs

Place the guajillos in a cast-iron frying pan over medium heat. Toast, turning, for about 4 minutes, or just until the chiles have taken on some color but are not burned. Remove from the pan and set aside to cool.

When cool, using a sharp knife, split the guajillos in half lengthwise. Remove and discard the seeds.

Combine the seeded guajillos with the carrot, orange juice, onion, jalapeño, and cilantro in a medium saucepan. Add just enough water to cover the chiles completely, and bring to a boil over high heat. Lower the heat and simmer for 20 minutes.

Remove from the heat and pour into a blender. Process to a smooth puree.

Use as directed in a specific recipe, or store, tightly covered and refrigerated, for up to 1 month.

ANCHO CHILE PASTE

MAKES ABOUT 1 CUP

Uses: **For all-around great Texas chili making.**

1 tablespoon olive oil

1 small onion, chopped

1 tablespoon minced jalapeño chile

1 teaspoon minced garlic

1 teaspoon cumin seed

4 dried ancho chiles, stemmed and seeded

2 cups vegetable stock or nonfat, low-sodium vegetable broth

1 cup diced, peeled, and seeded tomato

1 teaspoon minced fresh cilantro

Fresh lime juice

Salt

Heat the oil in a medium saucepan over medium-high heat. Add the onion, jalapeño, garlic, and cumin and cook, stirring, for 2 minutes.

Add the ancho chiles along with the stock, tomato, and cilantro and bring to a boil. Lower the heat and simmer for 20 minutes.

Remove from the heat and pour into a blender. Process to a smooth puree.

Pour into a clean container and season with lime juice and salt.

Use as directed in a specific recipe, or store, tightly covered and refrigerated, for up to 3 days.

FEARING'S GARLIC POWDER/SALT

MAKES ¼ CUP

Uses: **This is my staple for anything roasted or grilled.**

24 garlic cloves, peeled

Preheat the oven to 200°F.

Fill a medium saucepan about two-thirds full with cold water. Add the garlic and bring to a boil over medium-high heat. Lower the heat and simmer for 15 minutes, or until the garlic is very soft but not falling apart.

Remove from the heat and drain well. Transfer to a blender or food processer fitted with the metal blade and process to a smooth puree.

Coat a 13 by 7-inch pan with nonstick vegetable spray. Scrape the garlic puree onto the pan and, using a spatula, spread it out in an even layer. It should be about ¼ inch thick.

Transfer to the preheated oven and bake for about 4 hours, or until the garlic has dried out completely and hardened. Remove from the oven and set aside to cool completely.

When cool, transfer to a blender and process until the garlic is powder. Remove from the blender and pour through a fine-mesh sieve to remove any remaining large pieces.

Store, tightly covered, in a cool, dark spot for up to 3 months.

NOTE: To make garlic salt, add ½ cup coarse sea salt when blending, and continue with the process.

ROASTED GARLIC

MAKES AS MUCH AS YOU LIKE

Uses: **A great addition to mashed potatoes, dressings, and sauces.**

Heads or cloves of unpeeled garlic, as much as you like or need

Olive oil, for coating

Preheat the oven to 350°F.

If roasting whole heads, lay the heads on their sides and, using a sharp knife, cut about ⅛ inch off the stem ends.

Lightly coat the entire garlic heads or cloves with olive oil. Wrap them tightly in aluminum foil, place them on a baking pan, and roast in the preheated oven until soft and aromatic; whole heads should take about 25 minutes and individual cloves about 12 minutes.

Remove from the oven, unwrap, and let cool slightly.

Using your fingertips, push the pulp from the skin. The clove may or may not pop out whole, but either way it doesn't matter, as roasted garlic usually gets mashed or pureed before use.

Store, covered and refrigerated, for up to 1 week.

PICKLES, RELISHES, AND CHUTNEYS

★ ★ ★

BLUE RIBBON CHOWCHOW

MAKES 4 PINTS

Uses: **A great accompaniment to grilled meats, poultry, or fish or as a side dish on the table, picnic or otherwise.**

5 cups coarsely chopped green tomatoes

5 cups (about 1½ pounds) coarsely chopped cabbage

1½ cups finely chopped yellow or sweet onion

2 cups coarsely chopped red bell pepper

⅓ cup kosher salt or pickling salt

2½ cups apple cider vinegar

2 garlic cloves, finely minced

1 cup packed light brown sugar

1 tablespoon yellow mustard seeds

1 teaspoon celery seeds

½ teaspoon crushed red pepper flakes, or as needed (optional)

Combine the tomatoes, cabbage, onion, and bell pepper in a large nonreactive bowl or saucepan. Add the salt and toss to blend thoroughly. Cover and let stand for 4 hours, or refrigerate overnight.

Drain the mixture well in a colander and rinse under cold running water. Squeeze out excess liquid. Set aside.

Combine the vinegar with the garlic, sugar, mustard seeds, celery seeds, and red pepper flakes in a large nonreactive saucepan over high heat and bring to a boil. Immediately lower the heat to a simmer. Simmer for 5 minutes.

Add the well-drained vegetables, raise the heat, and bring to a boil. Lower the heat and simmer for 10 minutes.

Pack into hot, sterilized canning jars, leaving about ¼ inch headspace. Wipe the edges of the jars clean, immediately cover with sterilized lids, and seal with the band. Make sure that the lids are evenly set and that the bands are on correctly, but not too tight. They will continue to seal in the canning process.

Place the filled jars on a rack in a large deep saucepan. Add enough water to cover by at least 1 inch and place the pan over high heat. Bring to a boil, cover, and boil for 10 minutes.

Using tongs, remove the jars from the boiling water. Transfer to wire racks to cool.

Check the seals (the middle of the caps should have made a popping sound while cooling). The lids should stay depressed.

Store in a cool, dark spot for up to 1 year.

PICKLED RED ONIONS

MAKES ABOUT I CUP

Uses: **These can accompany almost any dish to add a little Texas two-step!**

1 red onion

½ cup white wine vinegar

½ cup sugar

Pinch salt

Peel the onion and cut in half lengthwise. Cut each half lengthwise into very thin half-moon strips. Place in a small nonreactive bowl and set aside.

Combine the vinegar and sugar in a small nonreactive saucepan over medium heat. Cook, stirring constantly, for a couple of minutes, or just until the sugar has dissolved. Immediately remove from the heat and stir in a pinch of salt.

Pour the hot vinegar mixture over the onions, gently stirring to blend. Cover and refrigerate for no less than 8 hours, but no more than 12.

Drain well and keep chilled until ready to use, or for up to 2 weeks in the fridge.

BREAD-AND-BUTTER JALAPEÑO CHILES

MAKES ABOUT I QUART

Uses: **A sweet, spicy, addictive addition to sandwiches, salads, and the picnic table.**

3 cups distilled white vinegar

10 garlic cloves

5 bay leaves

1 bunch fresh marjoram

2 cups sugar

2 tablespoons salt

2 tablespoons mustard seeds

2 teaspoons ground turmeric

2 teaspoons celery seeds

1 teaspoon peeled and minced fresh ginger

4 pounds jalapeño chiles, stemmed and cut crosswise into thin slices

2 pounds onions, cut crosswise into thin slices

Combine the vinegar with the garlic, bay leaves, marjoram, sugar, salt, mustard seeds, turmeric, celery seeds, and ginger in a large nonreactive saucepan over high heat. Bring to a boil.

Add the chiles and onions, cover, and return to a boil.

Immediately remove from the heat and let stand, covered, for 12 hours or overnight.

Transfer to a sterilized container, cover, and refrigerate for as long as you like. These will keep almost indefinitely but are mighty good, so they might only last a week or so.

It's Not a Big "Dill" Horseradish Pickles

MAKES 5 QUARTS

Uses: **These are my all-time favorite pickles, but watch out, they are addictive and will disappear quicker than you can make them.**

- 40 small pickling cucumbers
- 1¾ cups distilled white vinegar
- 1¼ cups sugar
- 1 teaspoon pickling spices
- 7 cups cold water
- 15 fresh dill sprigs
- 10 garlic cloves, peeled
- 10 large strips fresh horseradish root
- 5 tablespoons pickling salt

Soak the cucumbers in ice-cold water to cover for 2 to 3 hours.

Combine the vinegar, sugar, and pickling spices in a large nonreactive saucepan. Add the 7 cups of cold water and place over high heat. Bring to a boil and cook, stirring, for about 3 minutes, or until the sugar has dissolved. Lower the heat and cook at a gentle simmer while you complete the recipe.

Drain the cucumbers and, using a small, sharp knife, trim the ends and make a slit in the skin of each one so that the brine can soak in.

Place 3 sprigs of the dill, 2 cloves of the garlic, 2 strips of the horseradish, and 1 tablespoon of pickling salt in each of 5 sterilized 1-quart canning jars.

Pack 8 cucumbers (or to fit) into each jar.

Pour the hot brine into each jar, taking care that the cucumbers are completely covered. Wipe the edges of the jars clean, immediately cover with sterilized lids, and seal with the band. Make sure that the lids are evenly set and the bands are on correctly, but not too tight. They will continue to seal in the canning process.

Place the filled jars on a rack in a large deep saucepan. Add enough water to cover by at least 1 inch and place over high heat. Bring to a boil, cover, and boil for 10 minutes.

Using tongs, remove the jars from the boiling water. Transfer to wire racks to cool.

Check the seals (the middle of the caps should have made a popping sound while cooling). The lids should stay depressed.

Store in a cool, dark spot for up to 1 year.

Mexican Relish

MAKES ABOUT 3 CUPS

Uses: **Can be used as a stand-alone salad or as an accompaniment to grilled meats, poultry, or fish to add a little heat and spice.**

- 1 cup corn kernels, cut from 2 ears of grilled corn (see page 189)
- ½ cup cooked black beans
- ½ cup small-dice mango
- ½ cup small-dice peeled and seeded tomato
- ¼ cup small-dice red bell pepper
- ¼ cup small-dice red onion
- 1 tablespoon seeded and minced jalapeño chile
- 2 tablespoons olive oil
- 1 tablespoon fresh lime juice
- Pinch smoked paprika
- Salt
- Freshly ground pepper

Combine the corn with the beans, mango, tomato, bell pepper, onion, and chile in a medium bowl. Stir in the olive oil and lime juice. Season with paprika and salt and pepper to taste.

Serve as directed in a specific recipe, or store, tightly covered and refrigerated, for up to 3 days.

JALAPEÑO-PEACH CHUTNEY

MAKES ABOUT 2 CUPS

Uses: **A summertime favorite garnish for almost anything off the grill.**

- **5 ripe peaches, peeled and pitted**
- **1 jalapeño chile, stemmed, seeded, and minced**
- **1 tablespoon peeled and minced fresh ginger**
- **1 tablespoon sugar**
- **2 teaspoons fresh lemon juice, plus more if needed**
- **1 teaspoon ground cinnamon**

Cut 3 of the peaches into ½-inch dice and transfer to a medium bowl. Plan on using these immediately, as peaches discolor as they sit. Or add a touch of fresh lemon juice, which will keep them from doing so.

Put the remaining 2 peaches in a food processor fitted with the metal blade and process to a smooth puree. Scrape the puree into a small nonreactive saucepan and place over medium heat. Stir in the chile, ginger, sugar, 2 teaspoons lemon juice, and cinnamon and bring to a boil. Lower the heat and cook, stirring occasionally, for about 6 minutes, or until thickened.

Stir in the diced peaches and cook for an additional 3 minutes, or until heated through. Remove from the heat and set aside to cool.

When cool, use as directed in a specific recipe, or store, tightly covered and refrigerated, for up to 3 days.

PEAR CHUTNEY

MAKES ABOUT 3 CUPS

Uses: **A great fall/winter chutney to accompany grills and roasts.**

- **Juice of 1 lemon**
- **5 ripe Bosc pears, peeled and cored**
- **1 tablespoon peeled and finely diced fresh ginger**
- **1 tablespoon sugar**
- **2 teaspoons lemon juice**
- **1 teaspoon ground cinnamon**

Acidulate a bowl of cold water with the juice of 1 lemon. Cut 3 of the pears into medium dice. Place in the bowl and set aside.

Chop the remaining 2 pears, transfer to a blender, and process to a smooth puree.

Transfer the pear puree to a medium saucepan. Stir in the ginger, sugar, the 2 teaspoons lemon juice, and cinnamon and place over medium heat. Cook the puree, stirring occasionally, for about 6 minutes, or until quite thick.

Drain the diced pears and add them to the pureed mixture. Return to a simmer and cook, stirring occasionally, for about 3 minutes, or until very hot.

Remove from the heat and serve as directed in a specific recipe, or store, tightly covered and refrigerated, for up to 1 week.

BREAKFAST

and

BRUNCH

EGGS RANCHERO   SERVES 4

There are a few components to this dish, but it all comes together pretty quickly. If you have four small pans, it goes even faster, as you can cover the stovetop and crank out the eggs, which is what I do when a crowd gathers for a weekend brunch. Eggs Ranchero (or huevos rancheros) is one of the most popular breakfast/brunch dishes throughout Texas, made simply with the availability of so many prepared sauces and beans.

8 corn tortillas

4 cups Mashed Black Beans (page 194)

4 tablespoons (½ stick) unsalted butter

8 large eggs, at room temperature

Salt

Ancho Sauce (page 23)

Guacamole (page 30)

About ¼ cup grated Cotija cheese

4 fresh cilantro sprigs (optional)

Preheat the oven to its lowest setting.

Heat a griddle over medium heat. Working with one at a time, heat 4 of the tortillas until just slightly darkened. As they are heated, place 1 tortilla in the center of each of four luncheon plates. Cover each tortilla with about 1 cup of the mashed beans, spreading them out to completely cover. Heat the remaining 4 tortillas and place 1 on top of each bean-covered tortilla. Transfer to the warm oven while you make the eggs.

Melt 1 tablespoon of the butter in a small nonstick frying pan over low heat. When melted, slide 2 eggs into the pan and season with salt. Cover and cook for about 5 minutes, or until the egg white solidifies and the yolk thickens slightly. Continue frying eggs, adding a tablespoon of butter to the pan for each 2 eggs.

Remove the tortilla stacks from the oven and place 2 eggs over the top of each one. Generously spoon the sauce over the eggs, allowing some to spill off onto the plate. Place a good helping of guacamole on the side, sprinkle with an equal portion of the cheese, and garnish with a cilantro sprig.

Texas Barbecue Sirloin Steak *and* Eggs *with* Jalapeño Grits   SERVES 4

Nothing in the world beats steak and eggs for breakfast when the steak is glazed with a Texas-style barbecue sauce. We use a local brand of heritage grits; the grits are deeply aromatic and I fix 'em up so that they are filled with savory flavors, unlike my mom, who put them on a breakfast plate with just a pat of butter to mix in. I loved my childhood breakfast, but I sure like my grown-up Texas one a lot more.

You might get a helper or two to begin frying the eggs and making the grits as you cook the steak. That way everything will come together in a few minutes and you can all sit down together.

Four 8-ounce center-cut beef sirloin steaks, trimmed of all fat and silverskin

Salt

Freshly ground pepper

2 tablespoons olive oil

1 cup Texas-Style Barbecue Sauce (page 19) or your favorite barbecue sauce

4 tablespoons (½ stick) unsalted butter

8 large eggs, at room temperature

Jalapeño Grits (page 200)

Pickled Red Onions (page 43)

Generously season the steaks on both sides with salt and pepper.

Preheat the gril, or heat the oil in a large cast-iron skillet over medium-high heat. When very hot but not smoking, lay the steaks in the pan or on the grill. Sear for 4 minutes. Then turn and sear the opposite sides for 3 to 5 minutes more, or until the desired degree of doneness is reached. You can test with an instant-read thermometer; remember, the steaks will continue cooking from carryover heat as they sit, so take them off of the heat while they are a bit underdone. While still in the pan, using a pastry brush, generously coat both sides of the steaks with the barbecue sauce. Remove from the heat and set aside.

With your extra set of hands, while the steak is cooking begin frying the eggs.

Place a small nonstick frying pan over low heat. Add 1 tablespoon of the butter and allow it to slowly melt. Then crack 2 eggs into the pan and cover. Continue cooking approximately 5 minutes, or until the egg white solidifies and the yolk thickens slightly. Do not flip the eggs, but leave them sunny-side up. Remove the eggs from the pan and repeat the process using the remaining butter and eggs.

Spoon an equal portion of the grits on one side of each of four warm plates. Place a steak on top of each one. Place 2 eggs on the other side of the plate, garnish with a small pile of the pickled onions, and serve immediately.

Homestead Grits

The grits that I use come from the Homestead Gristmill, located in the Ploughshare Institute for Sustainable Culture in Waco, Texas. It has evolved from a mill that was begun in 1814 in New Jersey and operated there through the early part of the last century. After years of neglect, the property was dismantled and rebuilt in Central Texas in 2001. In addition to three types of wheat and corn, the Gristmill also grinds oats, rye, spelt, rice, buckwheat, and soybeans using the single-step process of grinding with natural granite stones. (See Sources, page 242.)

CHILAQUILES SERVES 4

Chilaquiles are so much a part of the Texas breakfast routine that you'd be hard-pressed to find a native who hasn't begun their day with this deliciously spicy start. The dish always begins with crisp tortilla pieces, but from there almost anything goes. The salsa can be red or green or mole; the protein, just the cheese and eggs or any type of meat the cook has on hand. This is a true clean-out-the-fridge dish.

Some prefer the tortilla pieces to soften nicely to thicken up the salsa, while others opt for the crisp, fried texture.

2 tablespoons olive oil

3 corn tortillas, cut into strips

½ cup finely diced onion

1 tablespoon seeded and minced jalapeño chile

1 teaspoon minced garlic

½ cup cooked, crumbled Mexican chorizo, well drained

4 large eggs, beaten

¼ cup grated jalapeño Jack cheese

1 tablespoon chopped fresh cilantro

Juice of ½ lime

Salt

Freshly ground pepper

¼ cup **Pico de Gallo** (page 30)

2 tablespoons grated **Cotija** cheese

Heat the olive oil in a frying pan over medium heat. Add the tortilla strips and fry, tossing and turning, for about 4 minutes, or until very crisp and nicely colored. Add the onion, jalapeño, and garlic and fry, stirring, for 3 minutes. Mix in the cooked chorizo and stir in the eggs. Cook, stirring, for about 2 minutes, or just until lightly scrambled. Fold in the Jack cheese and cilantro followed by the lime juice. Season to taste with salt and pepper.

Remove from the heat and spoon equal portions of the egg mixture into the center of each of four luncheon plates. Generously sprinkle the pico de gallo over the eggs and around the plate, distributing it evenly among the plates. Garnish with a bit of the Cotija cheese. Serve immediately.

Breakfast Burritos with Charred Tomato Salsa and Smoky Black Beans SERVES 4

If you have the salsa and beans ready to go, this dish comes together in a Texas minute. Although we put it on the table in the morning, it is substantial enough to make a satisfying lunch or dinner. It's the type of Tex-Mex dish that is also the perfect ending to an evening of music and dancing, especially under the starlight.

3 tablespoons olive oil

3 corn tortillas, cut into strips

2 cups diced Idaho potatoes

1 small onion, finely diced

3 strips applewood- or hickory-smoked
   bacon, cooked and crumbled

2 garlic cloves, minced

1 jalapeño chile, seeded and minced

½ cup cooked, crumbled Mexican chorizo sausage

6 large eggs, beaten

1½ cups grated jalapeño Jack cheese

¼ cup shredded fresh cilantro

Salt

Fresh lime juice

Four 6-inch fresh flour tortillas, warmed

Charred Tomato Salsa (page 32)

Mashed Black Beans (page 194)

Preheat the oven to 300°F.

Heat 2 tablespoons of the oil in a large frying pan over medium-high heat. Add the corn tortilla strips and fry, tossing and turning, for about 4 minutes, or until very crisp. Using a slotted spoon, transfer to a double layer of paper towels to drain. Set aside.

Heat the remaining 1 tablespoon oil in a medium frying pan over medium-high heat. Add the potatoes and fry for about 7 minutes, or until beginning to soften. Stir in the onion, lower the heat slightly, and continue to fry for about 2 minutes, or just until the onion is translucent.

Add the bacon, garlic, chile, and chorizo and cook, stirring, for another 4 minutes. Add the eggs and continue to cook, stirring, for about 2 minutes, or just until the eggs are softly scrambled. Immediately remove the pan from the heat, add the cheese, and stir until it has completely melted into the eggs and the mixture is creamy.

Stir in the reserved corn tortilla strips and cilantro. Season with salt and lime juice.

Spoon an equal portion of the egg mixture into the center of each of 4 flour tortillas. Then roll each tortilla up, cigar-fashion, and place, seam side down, in the center of each of four warm plates. Spoon the salsa around the edge of the tortilla and garnish each side with a small mound of the beans. Serve immediately.

Evolution of the Burrito

Although introduced into the American vocabulary only in the 1930s, burritos, or wrapped foods resembling what we now call a burrito, have been eaten throughout northern Mexico and the American Southwest since ancient times. Traditionally, a corn or other grain tortilla was wrapped around a simple meat or bean filling so it could be easily consumed out of hand. It is only in recent times that burritos have been overstuffed with a variety of meat, cheese, and vegetable mixtures.

Carmella's Truck-Stop Enchiladas
with Griddled Jalapeño Potatoes   SERVES 4

My Oklahoma-born assistant, Carmella, is a fountain of home-cooking recipes. She introduced my kitchen to this dish, which we all loved so much we put it on our brunch menu. Guess what? Texans love it as much as Sooners do. And I love it 'cause it is truck-stop-full of flavor. These enchiladas really hit it big when topped with a couple of fried eggs!

8 corn tortillas

2 tablespoons vegetable oil

1 pound lean ground beef

½ medium onion, minced

½ cup fresh corn kernels (or thawed frozen)

½ cup roasted, stemmed, peeled, seeded, and chopped poblano chiles (see page 15)

2 cups Tex-Mex Gravy (page 26)

1 cup grated jalapeño Jack cheese

Salt

Freshly ground pepper

Griddled Jalapeño Potatoes (recipe follows)

About Enchiladas

As early as the 1880s, American travelers to Mexico remarked on the "greasy sandwich" called an enchilada. Originally, they were probably just about that, as an enchilada was simply a tortilla dipped in chile sauce and fried. Even today, in Mexico, while now quite substantial and filling, enchiladas can still be quite a greasy but delicious mess. Throughout Texas, enchiladas follow the Mexican rule— substantial, a bit spicy, and a little messy to eat, but, oh, so delicioso!

Preheat the oven to 375°F.

Heat a griddle over medium-high heat. One at a time, lightly color each tortilla on the griddle. Wrap the tortillas in a kitchen towel and keep warm.

Heat the oil in a cast-iron skillet (or other heavy-bottomed frying pan) over medium heat. Add the ground beef and fry, stirring frequently, for about 5 minutes, or until lightly browned. Add the onion, corn, and poblanos and continue to fry, stirring, for another 3 minutes.

Stir in the gravy and bring to a simmer. Simmer for about 5 minutes, or until quite thick. Fold in ½ cup of the cheese and season to taste with salt and pepper. Remove from the heat.

Unwrap the tortillas and lay them out on a clean work surface. Spoon an equal portion of the ground beef mixture into the center of each tortilla and then roll each up, cigar-fashion, and place, seam side down, in a nonstick baking pan. Spoon the remaining gravy over all, generously covering each enchilada. Sprinkle the remaining ½ cup cheese evenly over the top.

Bake in the preheated oven for about 5 minutes, or until the cheese has melted and the enchiladas are very hot.

Remove from the oven and, using a spatula, carefully transfer 2 enchiladas to each of four warm plates. Spoon an equal portion of the griddled potatoes beside each portion and serve.

GRIDDLED JALAPEÑO POTATOES

2 cups small-dice peeled Idaho potatoes

½ cup small-dice onion

¼ cup small-dice red bell pepper

2 tablespoons seeded and minced jalapeño chiles

½ cup vegetable oil

Salt

Freshly ground black pepper

Preheat the oven to 375°F.

Combine the potatoes with the onion, bell pepper, and chiles in a large bowl. Add the oil and season with salt and black pepper.

Spread the potato mixture in a single layer in a large baking pan and transfer to the oven. Roast, turning occasionally, for about 20 minutes, or until golden brown and fork-tender.

Remove from the oven and serve immediately.

Gulf Coast Crab Benedict
with Cilantro Hollandaise   SERVES 4

Rather than the usual ham and eggs, this Texas take on the classic brunch dish uses the extraordinary Gulf Coast crab in combo with farm-fresh eggs. Of course, if you don't have access to the Gulf, use the best lump crabmeat you can find. If you get yourself organized, this is an easy recipe to put together and yet one that will still impress your guests with your cooking style. It can be done in stages, leaving the poaching of the eggs until just before you are ready to serve.

1 pound fresh **Gulf Coast (or other) lump crabmeat**, picked clean of all shell and cartilage

1 tablespoon snipped fresh chives

1 tablespoon olive oil

½ teaspoon salt, plus more as needed

Freshly ground pepper

8 Bacon-Jalapeño Biscuits (page 212)

Cilantro Hollandaise Sauce (page 22)

8 large farm-fresh eggs, at room temperature

2 quarts cold water

1 tablespoon champagne or apple cider vinegar

4 fresh cilantro sprigs, for garnish

About Blue Crab

Blue crab, the most common edible crab along the Texas coast, is a prized catch, both economically and at the table. It's one of the most widely harvested crabs in the world, and the Gulf waters of Texas lead in the yearly catch. The "blue" in the name comes from the bright jewel-like tint on the claws. Blue crabmeat is extremely sweet and flavorful and can be enjoyed simply, as in an informal beachside crab boil, or as the main ingredient in many four-star dishes.

Preheat the oven to its lowest setting.

Place the crabmeat in a small bowl. Add the chives and olive oil and toss to combine. Season to taste with salt and pepper, cover, and refrigerate until ready to serve.

Prepare the biscuits and the hollandaise.

Cut each biscuit in half crosswise, wrap in aluminum foil, and place in the preheated oven to keep warm.

Break each egg into a separate small container—small bowls or cups work nicely. Set aside.

Pour the water into a large shallow saucepan. Add the vinegar along with the ½ teaspoon salt. Bring to a rolling boil over high heat. When the water is boiling, slowly slide in the eggs, one at a time, and cook for about 4 minutes for soft yolks, 5 minutes for medium, and about 10 minutes for well-done.

While the eggs are poaching, place 2 biscuits on each of four warm plates. Lift off the top of each one, positioning it next to the bottom.

Remove the crabmeat mixture from the refrigerator and spoon an equal portion on top of each biscuit bottom.

Using a slotted spoon in one hand, with a double layer of paper towels held under it with the opposite hand, and working with one at a time, carefully lift the cooked eggs from the poaching liquid and touch the spoon to the paper towels in your opposite hand to absorb the excess water. Transfer one egg to the top of the crabmeat on each biscuit. Cover with the biscuit top and then spoon a generous portion of the hollandaise sauce over the top. Garnish with a sprig of cilantro and serve immediately.

TORTILLA STACK *with* POBLANO CREAM GRAVY

SERVES 4

I believe that this dish traveled from Oklahoma to Texas as settlers moved to new ground. Since there is nothing Texans like better than getting a group together to party, this dish is a perfect easy-to-put-together "let's party" dish. You can throw it all together like a scramble in a casserole and let everyone serve themselves.

Eighteen 6-inch griddled corn tortillas

1 tablespoon vegetable oil

1 cup diced bacon

½ cup small-dice red bell pepper

¼ cup small-dice red onion

1 tablespoon minced garlic

1 tablespoon seeded and minced jalapeño chile

2 medium ripe tomatoes, peeled, cored, seeded, and chopped

1 cup cooked Mexican chorizo

Salt

Freshly ground pepper

12 large eggs, beaten

2 cups grated jalapeño Jack cheese

½ cup heavy cream

¼ cup loosely packed chopped fresh cilantro

Poblano Cream Gravy (page 27)

Preheat the oven to 350°F.

Spray a 9 by 11-inch baking dish with nonstick vegetable spray. Lay 6 tortillas over the bottom of the dish, slightly overlapping. Set aside.

Heat the oil in a large frying pan over medium-high heat. Add the bacon and fry, stirring occasionally, for 4 minutes, or just until the fat has rendered out. Add the bell pepper, onion, garlic, and jalapeño and continue to cook, stirring occasionally, for about 4 minutes, or until the onion is translucent. Add the tomatoes and chorizo and cook for 2 minutes more. Season with salt and pepper. Remove from the heat and set aside to cool.

When cool, stir in the eggs, cheese, cream, and cilantro. Adjust the seasoning with salt and pepper.

Ladle half of the egg mixture into the tortilla-lined baking dish. Top with 6 of the remaining tortillas and then ladle the remaining egg mixture over the tortillas. Top with the remaining 6 tortillas and cover tightly with aluminum foil.

Bake in the preheated oven for 30 to 40 minutes, or until the eggs are thoroughly cooked and set.

Remove from the oven and serve with the hot poblano cream gravy.

Jaxson *and* Campbell-Style Pancakes

Year-round all over Texas—in big towns and small—you will find charity pancake breakfasts. For a couple of dollars, your plate will be piled high with buttermilk cakes, eggs, bacon or ham, and sometimes biscuits, too. My sons, Jaxson and Campbell, have accompanied me on cooking jaunts all over the state and have had the opportunity to begin their day with some of the best eats in the world. However, they still feel that the pancakes we make at home are the absolute tops!

3 cups sifted (1 pound) all-purpose flour

1 teaspoon baking powder

1 teaspoon salt

½ teaspoon baking soda

2 cups buttermilk

3 large eggs, at room temperature

1 tablespoon vegetable oil

1 tablespoon honey

Vegetable oil or unsalted butter, for frying

Unsalted butter, for serving

Pure maple syrup, for serving

Combine the flour, baking powder, salt, and baking soda in a medium bowl. Set the dry ingredients aside.

Place the buttermilk in a separate medium bowl. Add the eggs, oil, and honey and whisk to blend. When blended, whisk in the dry ingredients and mix until just barely blended.

Place a griddle (nonstick is great) over medium heat and brush lightly with oil or melted unsalted butter. When hot, ladle about ¼ cup of batter into the pan for each pancake. Don't crowd the griddle—leave plenty of room for the cakes to puff and brown around the edges. Most griddles will fit three pancakes.

Cook for about 2 minutes, or until bubbles form and pop on top of each cake and the bottom is golden brown. Using a spatula, turn and cook on the opposite sides for another 2 minutes, or until golden brown and cooked through.

Serve immediately, or stack the cakes on a warm platter and tent lightly with aluminum foil to keep warm while you continue to make the remaining pancakes.

Serve hot with butter and pure maple syrup.

STARTERS
and
SOUPS

Mango, Poblano, *and* Caramelized Onion Quesadillas *with* Cilantro-Lime Sour Cream

MAKES 2 QUESADILLAS

When I was a kid, nobody had heard of a quesadilla; two pieces of bread and some American cheese in a frying pan was what we had. Nowadays, even school lunch programs feature cheese quesadillas, and restaurants can always throw one together for picky children. But a Tex-Mex quesadilla is a thing of beauty, for sure. This is one I often star on my brunch menu, but you can truly put anything between two tortillas, corn or flour, as long as there is a little cheese to hold it all together. This is a particularly great combo—a little sweet, a little hot, and a little gooey.

1 ripe mango, peeled, pitted, and cut into thin strips

1 poblano chile, roasted, stemmed, peeled, seeded, and cut into thin strips (see page 15)

½ packed cup caramelized sliced onions (see **Note**)

1 tablespoon seeded and minced jalapeño chile

2 tablespoons chopped fresh cilantro

Fresh lime juice

3 cups grated jalapeño Jack cheese

4 large flour tortillas

2 tablespoons clarified butter or vegetable oil (see **Note**)

Charred Tomato Salsa (page 32)

Cilantro-Lime Sour Cream (page 28)

Combine the mango with the poblano, onions, jalapeño, and cilantro in a medium bowl. Stir in the lime juice to taste. When blended, add the cheese and toss to mix.

Lay 2 of the tortillas out on a clean, flat work surface. Place an equal portion of the mango mixture in the center of each one. Cover the top of each one with a remaining tortilla.

Heat 1 tablespoon of the clarified butter in a frying pan over medium heat. Slide one of the tortilla "sandwiches" into the pan and cook for about 4 minutes, or until golden brown. Using a large spatula, carefully turn and cook for an additional 3 minutes, or until the cheese has melted and the quesadilla is golden brown on both sides. Remove from the pan and keep warm while you cook the second quesadilla in the remaining 1 tablespoon clarified butter.

When both quesadillas are cooked, using a sharp knife, cut each into 6 wedges and serve with the salsa and the cilantro-lime sour cream for dipping.

NOTE: Caramelized onions are nothing more than sliced onions sautéed in oil (the type is your choice) until golden brown and slightly sweet.

For real Mexican flavor, quesadillas are cooked in a pan with a nice slick of clarified butter, but if you don't mind missing out on the rich, buttery kick, use a nonstick pan. It will save calories and fat but sacrifice a bit of the richness many love in Tex-Mex cooking.

About Quesadillas

The original quesadilla was a simple cooked corn tortilla folded over some type of "stringy" cheese, such as Oaxaca braided cheese. Often the tortilla was freshly made with the cheese placed in the center of the raw dough, the dough then folded over, and the half-moon shape griddled on all sides (even on the fold) so that all of the dough was evenly cooked, speckled with brown, and toasty. Throughout centuries, quesadillas have been one of the most popular of all traditional Mexican street foods—fried, baked, or griddled.

Quesadillas as Texas cooks make them are almost always made with a filling sandwiched between two large flour tortillas. The filling may still be as simple as some type of "runny" cheese, but it may also be an elaborate mix of meat, vegetables, and herbs, always with some added heat.

Charred Corn *and* Chorizo Street Tacos *with* Avocado Fries   SERVES 4

Everything about this basic taco says "street food" except for the inclusion of homemade chorizo—at Fearing's we make these with pheasant. Although it sounds elegant, it really serves as an economical way for me to use all parts of the pheasant in the restaurant. If you want to make your own, you could easily use any other gamey meat or even chicken thighs or, of course, you can also pick up ready-made Mexican chorizo. Any flavor will work. Charred corn on the cob and Cotija cheese are favorite go-togethers both south and north of the border, and here they partner to make a terrific taco combo.

2 ears fresh yellow corn, shucked and all tassels removed

1 small red onion, cut crosswise into ½-inch-thick slices

4 tablespoons olive oil

Salt

Freshly cracked pepper

2 cups Mexican chorizo

2 cups grated jalapeño Jack cheese

Fresh lime juice

Eight 4-inch round corn tortillas, warmed

About ¼ cup Green Chile Mojo (page 25)

Avocado Fries (page 203) (optional)

⅓ cup crumbled Cotija cheese

⅓ cup coarsely ground toasted pepitas

4 fresh cilantro sprigs, for garnish

2 cups Queso Asadero (page 26)

Preheat a grill to medium heat.

Using a pastry brush, generously coat the ears of corn and onion slices with 1 tablespoon of the olive oil. Season to taste with salt and pepper and place on the hot grill. Grill, turning occasionally, for about 6 minutes, or until cooked and lightly charred. Remove the vegetables from the grill and set aside to cool to room temperature.

When cool enough to handle, using a sharp knife and holding the cob vertically, slice the kernels from each cob.

Cut the cooled, cooked onion slices into a small dice, about ¼ inch. Combine with the corn kernels and set aside.

Heat 1 tablespoon of the remaining olive oil in a large frying pan over medium heat. Add the chorizo and cook, stirring frequently, for about 6 minutes, or until nicely browned. Remove from the heat and scrape into a fine-mesh sieve set over a bowl. Press lightly on the meat to extract any excess fat and let the meat drain while you proceed with the recipe.

Heat the remaining 2 tablespoons olive oil in a clean frying pan over medium heat. Add the reserved corn-onion mixture and cook, stirring occasionally, for about 2 minutes, or until heated through. Add the drained chorizo and cook for an additional 2 minutes.

Remove the pan from the heat, add the Jack cheese, and stir until completely melted into the chorizo mixture. Season to taste with lime juice and salt.

Place 2 tortillas in the middle of each of four warm plates. Working with one at a time, spoon an equal portion of the chorizo mixture into the center of each tortilla and then roll each up, cigar-fashion. Place 2 filled tortillas, seam side down, in the center of each plate. Ladle about a tablespoonful of the mojo into the front of each "taco" and stack the fries like Lincoln Logs in the back. Sprinkle Cotija cheese and pepitas over the top and garnish with a sprig of cilantro. Serve immediately with a small dish of the cheese sauce for each serving for dipping the fries.

MODERN BUFFALO TACOS *with* BLUE CHEESE DRESSING *and* SMOKED CHILE AIOLI   SERVES 4

Here we redefine the classic taco with a wild combination of flavors, each one building upon the others. This dish began early in the days of Fearing's when we used the buffalo scraps to make the "family meal." One of the cooks decided to use the meat in tacos, which we all loved. Shortly after, we added it to the bar menu, where it has become one of our most requested dishes. At home, it would make a great party dish, as many of the components can be made in advance. To many cooks, Sriracha sauce has become the new "ketchup." It is pretty fiery, so eliminate it if you are a heat-resistant Yankee or you don't like to get overheated.

1 cup pure maple syrup

1 tablespoon minced garlic

1 tablespoon minced shallot

1 tablespoon freshly cracked black pepper

1 teaspoon finely chopped fresh sage

1 teaspoon finely chopped fresh thyme

Crushed red pepper flakes

1 pound buffalo tenderloin, trimmed of all fat and silverskin

2 tablespoons vegetable oil

Salt

Freshly ground pepper

8 white corn tortillas, griddled

¼ cup Point Reyes Blue Cheese Dressing (page 34)

¼ cup Smoked Chile Aioli (page 35)

Sriracha sauce (see Note)

Yellow Tomato Pico de Gallo (page 31)

½ cup grated Cotija cheese

Combine the maple syrup with the garlic, shallot, cracked pepper, sage, thyme, and red pepper flakes in a resealable plastic bag. Add the tenderloin, seal, and toss to coat completely. Place in the refrigerator and allow to marinate, turning occasionally so that all sides are covered, for 2 hours, or up to overnight.

Remove the tenderloin from the marinade. Using a sharp knife, cut the meat into thin strips.

Heat the oil in a large frying pan over medium-high heat. When very hot, but not smoking, add the buffalo, season with salt and black pepper, and sear for 2 minutes. Turn and sear for an additional 2 minutes, or until the desired degree of doneness is reached. Remove from the heat.

Place 2 warm tortillas on each of four warm plates. Spoon an equal portion of the buffalo into the center of each one. Top with a tablespoon of the blue cheese dressing and then a tablespoon of the aioli. Drizzle a bit of Sriracha over all. Finish the plate with a mound of the pico de gallo and then sprinkle cheese over each plate. Serve immediately.

NOTE: Sriracha is a Thai chile sauce that carries quite a bit of heat. It is available from Asian markets, specialty food stores, and well-stocked supermarkets. The most common brand in the United States, Huy Fong, is also known as "rooster" sauce because of the rooster logo on the jar. I love its flavor and often use it with abandon.

Buffalo Meat

Buffalo herds could be found in northern Texas in the early settlement days, but those days are long gone. However, today managed herds are found on game ranches, particularly in Texas Hill Country, where guided hunts yield not only the "trophy" but also a goodly supply of meat that is lower in fat, cholesterol, and calories than beef. Buffalo steaks and chops have become increasingly popular over the past few years, with diners appreciating the healthy alternative.

Evolution of the Taco

The Mexican cooks who gave me my first introduction to their favorite snack would find the current American take on tacos to be *muy loco*. To them, a taco was nothing more than poor people's street food—a warm, thick, fresh-from-the-griddle corn tortilla wrapped around a tiny bit of protein—meat or cheese—sprinkled with some type of tangy sauce, a smattering of chopped onion, and a touch of cilantro. Filling, but not overstuffed or well garnished, and certainly not fancy dining. If you want to follow the basics, make fresh tortillas or buy Mexican-made ones and improvise the filling, using whatever you have on hand, as many Texas cooks still do. When you want to move away from that stand-on-the-street food, try one of my versions of this traditional Mexican dish that is now recognized as a Tex-Mex classic.

The traditional method of heating a tortilla is to brush one side with oil and then heat it, oiled-side down, on a griddle. This softens the tortilla and also gives it the authentic taste.

BARBECUE SHRIMP TACOS *with* MANGO-PICKLED RED ONION SALAD SERVES 4

For years one of my signature dishes was a lobster taco. After making it for so long, I wanted a change. Rather than the now-popular fried fish taco, I have created a lighter, zestier shellfish version. I use the extraordinary wild-caught Texas Gulf shrimp when available. Are they bigger and better? You bet; they have deep flavor and terrific taste and make the best shrimp taco you can imagine.

1 tablespoon vegetable oil

1 cup (about 6 ounces) diced, peeled, and
    deveined Gulf or other high-quality shrimp

Salt

Freshly cracked pepper

1 cup Texas-Style Barbecue Sauce (page 19)

½ cup grated jalapeño Jack cheese

Four 6-inch round flour tortillas, warmed

2 cups Mango–Pickled Red Onion Salad (page 100)

⅓ cup grated Cotija or Mexican farmer's cheese

⅓ cup toasted and coarsely chopped pepitas

4 fresh serrano chiles, for garnish

4 fresh cilantro sprigs, for garnish

Heat the oil in a large sauté pan over medium heat. Add the shrimp, season with salt and pepper, and cook, stirring, for about 1 minute, or until the shrimp turns color. Stir in the barbecue sauce and bring to a boil. Immediately remove the pan from the heat and add the Jack cheese and stir until completely melted.

Place a tortilla in the middle of each of four warm plates. Working with one at a time, spoon an equal portion of the shrimp mixture into the center of each tortilla and then roll up, cigar-fashion. Place the filled tortilla, seam side down, in the center of the plate. Spoon an equal portion of the salad on top of each taco followed by a sprinkle of Cotija cheese and the pepitas. Garnish with a fresh serrano chile—to be eaten like a pickle for the adventurous—and a sprig of cilantro, and serve.

Texas Shrimp Hotline

Gulf shrimp are wild-caught out in the deep waters off the Texas coast. Since Texas is one of the nation's top providers of this superb shellfish, the Texas Department of Agriculture supports the fishing industry through a strong marketing program. They even provide a hotline for consumers, Texas Shrimp Hotline (877-TX-CATCH) that tells you not only where to buy wild-caught Texas shrimp, but how to cook and serve them as well. We try to do our part, too.

Tamales *with* Barbecued Corn *and* Fiesta Salad MAKES 12 TAMALES

Tamales are one Tex-Mex food that is totally Mexican in heritage. When researching them early in my cooking career, I found that although evolved from the ancient Mayan culture, tamales can be found throughout Central and South America as well as the Caribbean. And, in some Deep South areas of the United States, street vendors have sold tamales since the beginning of the last century. It took Texas to introduce them to me, and I quickly embraced them—filling, flavorful, interesting to make, and easy to serve—a chef's dream! Tamales can be filled with almost anything—either sweet or savory. Once you master making masa (see Note, page 70), the tamale fillings can be made to fit your menu. Tamales can also be served plated or on a buffet platter.

> 12 large dried corn husks
>
> 5 cups Maseca corn flour (see Note, page 70, and page 18)
>
> 1 tablespoon baking powder
>
> 1 teaspoon salt
>
> ½ cup hot water
>
> ½ cup cold water
>
> 1 cup lard, cut into small pieces (see Note, page 70, and page 18)
>
> ½ cup Texas-Style Barbecue Sauce (page 19) or your favorite barbecue sauce
>
> Barbecued Corn Filling (recipe follows)
>
> Fiesta Salad (page 100)
>
> ¼ cup crumbled Cotija cheese
>
> Fresh cilantro sprigs, for garnish (optional)

Place the corn husks in a container large enough to allow them to lie flat. Cover with warm water. Place a weight on top to keep the husks submerged. Soak for at least 3 hours, or overnight.

Meanwhile, make the masa filling: Combine the corn flour, baking powder, and salt in the bowl of a heavy-duty stand mixer fitted with the paddle attachment. Begin mixing on low speed as you slowly add the hot water. Continue to beat until well combined and then slowly begin adding the cold water, beating until a soft dough forms. Increase the speed to medium-high and begin adding the lard, one piece at a time, beating until all of the lard is completely incorporated into the dough. Lower the mixer speed and begin adding the barbecue sauce in a slow, steady stream. Increase the speed to high and beat for about 5 minutes, or until light and airy.

Drain the corn husks and pat very dry. Pull a long "string" from one edge of each husk to make a tie for the finished tamale. Set aside.

Working with one husk at a time, using wet hands and a small spatula, spread about 2 tablespoons of the masa filling over the bottom two-thirds, leaving about ¼ inch uncovered on either side. Add about 1 tablespoon of the barbecued corn filling to the center of the masa, leaving about 3 inches uncovered at the pointed end and 1½ inches at the wider end.

Turn the right side of the husk over to the center of the filling and fold the left side over the filling, allowing the uncovered husk to wrap around the filling. Fold the top end down over the bottom end. Tightly secure the two ends by tying closed with a corn husk string. The tamales can be made up to this point and stored, tightly wrapped and refrigerated, for up to 1 week.

Bring about 2 inches of water to a gentle boil in a 4-quart saucepan, or steamer, over high heat. Place a steamer rack over the boiling water and place the tamales, folded sides down, on the rack. Cover and steam for 30 minutes, or until cooked through and very hot. If you want to test for doneness, remove a tamale from the center of the steamer rack, carefully untie and open; the properly cooked tamale should be firm and should easily pull away from the husk.

Remove from the steamer and unwrap. Using a paring knife, cut an opening down the center of each tamale and place on a serving platter. Garnish each tamale with a small mound of the salad on top of the opening. Sprinkle with the cheese and, if using, cilantro sprigs.

BARBECUED CORN FILLING

MAKES ENOUGH FILLING
FOR 12 TAMALES

2 tablespoons olive oil

2 ears yellow corn, shucked and cleaned

1 small red onion, cut crosswise
   into ½-inch-thick slices

Salt

Freshly ground pepper

1 cup Texas-Style Barbecue Sauce (page 19)
   or your favorite barbecue sauce

Preheat the grill to medium.

Using 1 tablespoon of the oil and a pastry brush, lightly coat the ears of corn and the onion. Season with salt and pepper.

Place the corn on the hot grill and grill, turning constantly, for about 4 minutes, or until the kernels begin to char.

Add the onion slices to the grill and grill, turning once, for 10 minutes, or until lightly charred. Remove the corn and the red onion from the grill and set aside to cool to room temperature.

When cool enough to handle, using a sharp knife and holding the cob vertically, slice the kernels from each cob. Discard the cobs and set the kernels aside.

Cut the onion into ¼-inch pieces and set aside.

Heat the remaining 1 tablespoon oil in a medium frying pan over medium heat. Add the reserved corn and onions and cook, stirring frequently, for about 3 minutes, or until softened. Add the barbecue sauce and cook, stirring occasionally, for about 10 minutes, or until reduced by half and quite thick. Season to taste with salt and pepper and remove from the heat.

NOTE: The masa that I make is somewhat lighter than the dark, dense mix favored by authentic Mexican cooks, although I use the same Maseca brand corn flour that they do. It is 100 percent natural, and I have found it to be the best flour to use for tortillas and tamales. It is available from Hispanic markets and some supermarkets, particularly those located in neighborhoods with a large Hispanic population.

I use Manteca lard, which we have found is the most readily available across the United States. It is usually found in the refrigerated section of the supermarket, even though it is shelf stable.

Making Tamales

Tamales are nothing more than a terrific eat-out-of-hand food made from a masa dough wrapped around almost any type of well-seasoned filling, from beans to shrimp to fruit, and then wrapped in corn husks or palm or banana leaves and steamed. One of the ancient foods of Central America, tamales are, in fact, one of the foods that early Spanish explorers carried back to the Old World to signify a thriving culture in the new. Unbelievably, they have also been a staple in parts of the United States since the late 1800s. As early as the mid-1700s, tamales were making their way into the cuisine of the Mississippi Delta via early Spanish settlers in Louisiana, and by the 1800s roaming tamale sellers could be found throughout the eastern part of the United States. "They're Red Hot," a red-hot blues song by the famous American blues artist Robert Johnson, sings the praises of the tamale sellers and their wares. But not all tamales evolved from the ancient peoples of other countries. Native Americans, particularly Cherokee tribes, were making a type of tamale using flour (or masa) from ground hominy that had been soaked in wood ash (rather than the lime used for Central American masa), filled with beans and other vegetables, and cooked, wrapped in the green leaves of a cornstalk. Nowadays there are numerous tamale festivals around the country; two of the most notable ones are in Indio, California, and Zwolle, Louisiana.

SMOKED CHICKEN NACHOS   SERVES 6

Unlike the standard messy piled-high nachos, these are handmade with the garnishes placed on individual chips. Although we smoke our own chicken breasts, you could certainly use any fine-quality commercially smoked chicken for these bar-style nachos. Or almost any other type of smoked meat would work as well. Just leave the meat off half of the batch and you can satisfy the vegetarians in the crowd.

2 cups Mashed Black Beans (page 194)

16 large crisply fried tortilla chips (see page 161)

2 cups Guacamole (page 30)

1 pound smoked chicken breast
   (see page 176), diced

2 cups grated jalapeño Jack cheese

1 jalapeño chile, stemmed, seeded,
   and cut crosswise into very thin
   slices, for garnish (optional)

Charred Tomato Salsa (page 32)

Preheat the oven to 375°F.

Spread a light portion of the mashed beans on each tortilla chip. Top with a thin spread of guacamole. Top with an equal portion of chicken and then generously pile cheese on top.

Place the nachos on a rimmed baking sheet and bake in the preheated oven for about 3 minutes, or until the cheese is melting and bubbly.

Remove from the oven, garnish with a slice of fresh jalapeño, if desired, and serve immediately with the salsa for dipping.

A Word About Nachos

Nachos are probably more Tex than Mex, as they are now far removed from the simple Mexican dish of pieces of tortillas baked with a bit of cheese. Even though they were born in Mexico, Texas was where they began their move to international stardom. Beginning in the 1950s, Texas home cooks were making nachos with commercially made tortilla chips topped with what was probably Cheez Whiz, which made its debut in 1953. Then, with the introduction of so many commercially made Tex-Mex-style salsas and sauces, the cheese got topped with a variety of additions and meats. Now there are even commercial seasoned cheese products called "Nacho Cheese." I have eaten nachos all over the world with some very strange toppings—pineapple in Hawaii, barbecued pork and slaw in North Carolina, and sauerkraut in Germany.

BARBECUED BACON-WRAPPED QUAIL
with JALAPEÑO RANCH DRESSING SERVES 4

At Fearing's we purchase our quail from a great rancher, Texas Quail Farms (www.texquail .com), out in Lockhart, Texas. I have eaten quail and other little game birds all over the world, and I can tell you these are the most flavorful quail I have ever tasted. This may be the reason that this is a dish that is never off my menu; diners would hang me up by my boots if it was. It is a simple but delicious typical Texas recipe.

Four 4-ounce semiboneless quail

Salt

Freshly ground pepper

8 thin strips seeded jalapeño chile

8 strips smoked bacon

1 cup warm Texas-Style Barbecue Sauce (page 19) or use your favorite sauce

1 cup Jalapeño Ranch Dressing (page 35)

Texas Game Birds

Hunters from all over the world converge on Texas to hunt quail, chukar, pheasant, and dove, both on game farms and during wild bird and waterfowl migration. These small birds all provide superb eating. If you don't hunt, almost all of them are available through online companies, such as Texas Quail Farm.

Preheat the oven to 375°F.

Place the quail on a clean cutting board. Working with one at a time and using a small, sharp knife, cut the wing tips and legs from each bird. Cut down the center of the backbone of each quail, opening up the body. Lay flat, skin side down.

Generously season all sides of each quail with salt and pepper. Lay 2 strips of chile down the center of each one and, working from one cut side, roll the birds into a tight cylinder.

Working with one bird at a time, place 2 strips of bacon, side by side, on a clean surface. Place a rolled quail on one end, and again roll into a tight cylinder, completely enclosing the quail. Repeat the process to cover all the birds.

Place the rolled quail, seam side down, in a baking pan, leaving about 2 inches between birds. Transfer to the preheated oven and roast for about 12 minutes, or until the bacon is thoroughly cooked and nicely browned.

Remove from the oven and let rest for 5 minutes.

Using a serrated knife, cut each quail roll crosswise into ½-inch-thick rounds. Place a small skewer through each round, going straight through the center, entering and exiting through the bacon wrap. Dip the quail rolls into the barbecue sauce to glaze slightly.

Place on a platter and serve warm with the ranch dressing for dipping.

CRISPY BARBECUED GULF OYSTERS
"ROCKEFEARING" SERVES 4

This is my take on the classic New Orleans dish Oysters Rockefeller, but I turn it into a Texas classic using Gulf oysters and crab and locally smoked bacon. The fried oysters alone would make a terrific cocktail treat or a po'boy.

The braised leeks fancy this recipe up, but you really don't have to make them. However, you may find that they will become a go-to garnish for all types of grilled meats and fish. I particularly like the way they look wrapped around the oyster shells.

Fearing's Barbecue Spice Flour Mixture (page 39)

12 large Gulf oysters, shucked with liquor and shells reserved (see Note)

2 cups safflower oil

Spinach-Crab Mix (recipe follows)

12 Braised Baby Leeks or Scallions (recipe follows) (optional)

1 cup Texas-Style Barbecue Sauce (page 19) or your favorite barbecue sauce

Place the spice flour in a resealable plastic bag. Add the oysters and shake to coat. Remove the oysters from the bag and shake off excess flour. Set aside.

Heat the oil in a medium frying pan over medium heat. When very hot, but not smoking, add the oysters, 6 at a time. Fry for 1 minute, or until golden brown. Using a slotted spoon, transfer the fried oysters to a double layer of paper towels to drain. Keep warm while you fry the remaining 6 oysters.

Place 3 warm oyster shells on each of four luncheon plates. Spoon an equal portion of the spinach-crab mixture onto each shell. Top with a fried oyster. If using, wrap a braised leek or scallion around each shell, and pool barbecue sauce around the plate. Serve immediately.

NOTE: When you want to use oyster shells for serving, be sure to boil them for about 5 minutes to make sure that they are very clean and sanitized. They should be warmed in hot water and dried before adding any hot filling to them. In the restaurant, we put a little dab of mashed potatoes on the plate to stabilize the shell on the plate as served.

Shiner Bock

Shiner Bock is a dark lager beer that has been produced in Texas since the early part of the last century by the Spoetzl Brewery located in Shiner, Texas. Although originally operated as the Shiner Brewing Company, it was purchased by a Bavarian brewer named Spoetzl in 1914, which led to the production of a variety of much-loved German-style beers. It was operated as a small, independent, and very local business until the late 1980s, when it was purchased by a San Antonio businessman, Carlos Alvarez. The new management broadened the distribution of the esteemed local brew, making Spoetzl Brewery the fourth-largest craft brewer in the United States. Although nationally distributed, Shiner Bock remains a statewide favorite and is our beer of choice in many recipes.

SPINACH-CRAB MIX

2 cups chopped, cooked spinach

6 ounces Gulf (or other lump) crabmeat, picked clean of all shell and cartilage

¼ cup cooked, crumbled smoky bacon

1 cup Bacon Béchamel Sauce (page 22)

Salt

Freshly ground pepper

Combine the spinach with the crabmeat, bacon, and about three-fourths of the béchamel in a small saucepan over medium-low heat. Cook, gently stirring so that you don't mash the crabmeat, for about 2 minutes, or just until heated through; it should be the consistency of creamed spinach. If it isn't, add the remaining béchamel. Season to taste with salt and pepper and remove from the heat. Use immediately.

BRAISED BABY LEEKS OR SCALLIONS

12 baby leeks or scallions, root ends trimmed

1 cup chicken stock or nonfat, low-sodium chicken broth

¼ cup Shiner Bock beer (see sidebar at left)

1 fresh thyme sprig

1 bay leaf

1 teaspoon crushed red pepper flakes

Salt

Freshly ground black pepper

Place the leeks (or scallions) in a shallow saucepan large enough to hold them in a single layer. Add the stock, beer, thyme, bay leaf, and red pepper flakes. Season with salt and black pepper and place over medium heat. Bring to a simmer; then cover, lower the heat, and cook at a gentle simmer for about 30 minutes, or until very soft. Remove and discard the bay leaf.

Remove from the heat and keep warm until ready to use. Alternatively, store in the cooking liquid, covered and refrigerated, for up to 2 days. Reheat before serving.

CORPUS CHRISTI SEAFOOD CEVICHE SERVES 4

Corpus Christi sits on the Gulf of Mexico with great deep-sea fishing. Sportsmen come from all over the world to fish the waters for pompano, black drum, sheepshead, flounder, and redfish, among others. Although I use tuna and shrimp, you can use almost any fish you like. When available, the flavor of sheepshead is particularly great for ceviche, as the fish dines on all types of crustaceans, including the great Gulf shrimp, which give its flesh extraordinary flavor. Although you won't find coconuts growing on the Gulf, I love the sweet balance of coconut milk in this slightly spicy dish.

½ pound tuna, cut into ½-inch cubes

½ pound lightly poached Gulf shrimp, peeled and deveined, cut in half lengthwise

½ cup unsweetened coconut milk

¼ cup fresh lime juice

¼ cup fresh orange juice

½ cup small-dice peeled and seeded cucumber

¼ cup seeded and minced jalapeño chile

1 tablespoon peeled and minced fresh ginger

1 tablespoon Damiana Liqueur (see Note)

¼ cup pitted and diced avocado

2 tablespoons finely julienned fresh cilantro leaves

2 tablespoons finely julienned scallions

Salt

¼ cup Pickled Red Onions (page 43)

4 fresh cilantro sprigs

Combine the tuna and shrimp in a nonreactive container with a lid. Add the coconut milk, lime and orange juices, cucumber, chile, ginger, and liqueur and gently stir to combine. Cover and refrigerate for 1 hour.

Remove from the refrigerator and fold in the avocado along with the julienned cilantro and scallions. Season with salt to taste.

Serve immediately, garnished with pickled red onions and a cilantro sprig.

NOTE: Damiana Liqueur is flavored with damiana, an herb that grows in Baja California, Mexico. It has a light herbal scent that adds an undefinable note to the ceviche. Its packaging is unique, as the bottle is shaped in the form of an Incan goddess—a great conversation piece to say the least. It is thought that the first margaritas were made with Damiana rather than triple sec or Cointreau.

Pan-Fried Texas Crab Cakes
with Mango Pico de Gallo SERVES 4

Who doesn't love a crab cake? For as long as I've been cooking, crab cakes have been a customer favorite. Although crab cakes seem to be identified with Maryland, Texans have made them their own, using the rich, luscious meat from Gulf crabs. Crabbing in Gulf waters is one great family fun day that often ends with a Gulf Coast favorite, a crab barbecue. These very popular Fearing crab cakes get the best of both worlds—a little Southern style and lots of Texas spice.

3 tablespoons finely diced toasted
   white bread, crusts removed

¼ cup mayonnaise

2 tablespoons heavy cream

1 tablespoon fresh lemon juice

1 teaspoon Old Bay Seasoning

1 teaspoon paprika

1 teaspoon Worcestershire sauce

1 teaspoon dry mustard powder

3 to 4 drops Tabasco sauce

1 pound lump Gulf crabmeat, picked
   clean of all shell and cartilage

Salt

Freshly ground pepper

About 2 cups vegetable oil

1 recipe Mango Pico de Gallo (page 31)

Combine the bread with the mayonnaise, heavy cream, lemon juice, Old Bay Seasoning, paprika, Worcestershire, mustard powder, and Tabasco in a medium bowl. Using your hands, mix until the bread has absorbed the liquid.

Gently fold the crabmeat into the bread mixture until just barely combined. You do not want to mash the crab. Taste and, if necessary, adjust the seasonings. The mixture should be firm enough to hold its shape when formed into cakes.

Line a platter with waxed paper. Set aside.

Using your hands, form the crab mixture into eight 2-ounce cakes. Transfer to the waxed paper–lined platter as they are formed.

When all of the crab cakes have been formed, transfer to the refrigerator for about 20 minutes, or until the exterior is slightly dry.

In a frying pan large enough to accommodate the crab cakes without crowding, add oil to the depth of about ½ inch. Heat the oil over high heat until it registers 350°F on a candy thermometer.

Add the crab cakes and fry, turning once, for about 3 minutes, or until golden brown on both sides.

Using a slotted spatula, transfer the cooked cakes to a double layer of paper towels to drain.

Place 2 crab cakes in the center of each of four luncheon plates. Spoon an equal portion of the pico de gallo over each plate and serve.

SMOKED SALMON TARTARE *with* ROASTED JALAPEÑO CREAM

SERVES 4 AS A STARTER OR 8 AS AN HORS D'OEUVRE

Although I know that you wouldn't find smoked salmon on a traditional Texas menu, it is so popular as a starter that, since my first days cooking in Dallas, I have had a smoked salmon dish on the menu. This one is easy to make, particularly if you keep both roasted garlic and roasted chiles on hand, as I always do. You can easily double the recipe to feed a crowd.

3 Roasted Garlic cloves (page 41)

2 anchovy fillets

1 tablespoon olive oil, plus more for drizzling

1 teaspoon ground cumin

½ cup sour cream

2 tablespoons heavy cream

2 teaspoons fresh lime juice

1 cup very-small-dice smoked salmon

¼ cup very-small-dice mango

¼ cup very-small-dice red onion

1 tablespoon well-drained capers

2 tablespoons roasted, seeded, and chopped jalapeño chile (see page 15)

1 tablespoon chopped fresh cilantro

Salt

Freshly cracked pepper

16 crisp tortilla chips

16 small fresh cilantro sprigs

Combine the garlic, anchovy, 1 tablespoon of olive oil, and the cumin in a small bowl. Using a kitchen fork, mash the mixture into a rough paste. Stir in the sour cream, heavy cream, and lime juice and mix until completely blended.

Add the salmon, mango, red onion, capers, chile, and chopped cilantro and stir to just lightly blend. Season with salt and pepper to taste. The mixture should be quite thick, but not dry.

When ready to serve, spoon a tablespoon of the salmon mixture onto each of 16 tortilla chips. Drizzle with a bit of the remaining olive oil, garnish with a sprig of cilantro, and serve.

GRANNY FEARING'S BLUE CHEESE BALLS

MAKES 2 BALLS; EACH SERVES 10 TO 12

When I was growing up in eastern Kentucky, holiday time meant cheese balls with Triscuits and Ritz crackers. I still remember running through the living room of my granny's house after coming in from playing outside with my siblings and cousins with the smell of bourbon and blue cheese filling the air. We'd pinch off a piece of the cheese ball, grab a couple of Triscuits, and head right back outside. The grown-ups just lay back, sipped their bourbon on the rocks, and waited for one of Granny's great meals to appear. To this day, cheese balls and Triscuits mean "Granny" to me.

Once I moved to Texas I discovered that cheese balls were not invented by my granny, but were part and parcel of Texas culinary history, too. Every home cook seems to have a favorite blend. They can be made from blue cheese, cheddar cheese, cream cheese—whatever cheese your family likes. Since they keep so well, tightly wrapped and refrigerated, cheese balls are a terrific have-on-hand treat when unexpected (or expected) company arrives.

You don't need a fancy aged cheddar cheese for this recipe; a cheese aged less than 6 months will be just fine.

One 8-ounce package cream cheese, cut into pieces, at room temperature

1 pound fine-quality blue cheese, such as Maytag, cut into pieces, at room temperature

½ cup grated Parmesan or pecorino Romano cheese

1 pound sharp white cheddar cheese, cut into pieces, at room temperature

2 tablespoons snipped fresh chives

1 tablespoon Worcestershire sauce

1 teaspoon Tabasco sauce

Salt

Freshly ground pepper

2 cups chopped pecans

Combine the cream cheese with the blue cheese, Parmesan, and cheddar in the bowl of a stand mixer fitted with the paddle attachment. Begin mixing on low speed, then increase the speed to medium and beat, scraping down the sides of the bowl and the paddle from time to time, for about 8 minutes, or until completely blended and smooth.

Add the chives, Worcestershire, and Tabasco and beat for about 1 minute, or until blended. Season to taste with salt and pepper.

Remove the bowl from the mixer and scrape down the sides and the paddle. Cover with plastic wrap and refrigerate for about 1 hour, or until firm.

When firm, remove from the refrigerator and divide the cheese mixture into 2 equal portions. Using your hands, form each portion into a smooth ball.

Spread the pecans out on a rimmed baking sheet. Gently roll each cheese ball in the pecans, taking care that the cheese is completely covered.

Wrap each ball in plastic wrap, twisting the wrap closed to form a tight seal. Place in the refrigerator, twisted side down, pressing down lightly to make a smooth resting place; this is so the cheese ball will sit on the level when ready to serve. Refrigerate for at least 1 hour, or up to a month or so.

One hour before you are ready to serve, unwrap the cheese ball and place on a serving plate. Let stand at room temperature to soften. Surround the cheese ball with crackers or toasts and serve.

FOURTH-OF-JULY DEVILED EGGS

MAKES 2 DOZEN DEVILED EGGS

You tell me—who doesn't love a deviled egg? And these are really deviled, with a nice hit of spice that takes them far and away from the usual. I always feature them on the Fourth of July—even in the restaurant—because it wouldn't be an old-fashioned celebration without them. You can, of course, make less than two dozen, but why? The two dozen will be gone before all your guests arrive for the annual down-home picnic!

1 dozen hard-boiled eggs, peeled

¼ cup mayonnaise

¼ cup minced smoked ham

1 tablespoon Dijon mustard

1 tablespoon dill pickle relish

1 tablespoon chopped Pickled
    Red Onions (page 43)

1 tablespoon Tabasco Chipotle
    sauce, or as needed

Salt

Freshly ground pepper

Fearing's Barbecue Spice Blend
    (page 39), for garnish

Using a sharp knife, cut the eggs in half lengthwise. Carefully remove the yolk half, being careful not to break the white.

Place the yolks in the bowl of a food processor fitted with the metal blade. Add the mayonnaise, ham, mustard, relish, red onion, and Tabasco Chipotle and process until smooth. Add salt and pepper to taste and process to blend.

Using a teaspoon or a plastic bag fitted with a plain tip, fill the cavity of each egg white half with the seasoned yolk mixture.

Sprinkle the top of each egg with the barbecue spice and serve.

Texas Caviar on Navajo Fry Bread SERVES 4

When I first heard the words "Texas caviar" I couldn't imagine what it might be, but I can tell you that I had no idea that in Texas caviar was black-eyed peas. I guess you have figured out that it isn't the mucho-expensive black pearls, but simply humble black-eyed peas all dressed up.

This dish was invented by Helen Corbitt, who for many years ran the restaurant at the Neiman Marcus flagship store in Dallas. It is said that when she discovered that Texans didn't care for the real deal of caviar and blinis (which, by the way, I've found that they do), she devised this dip to be served with tortilla chips at cocktail parties. I like to serve it with Navajo Fry Bread for a Native American twist.

2 cups dried black-eyed peas, soaked

1 cup fine-dice tomato

¾ cup fine-dice red onion

2 tablespoons seeded and minced jalapeño chile

2 tablespoons crumbled cooked smoked bacon

1 tablespoon finely diced green olives

1 teaspoon minced garlic

1 teaspoon ground cumin

¾ cup extra-virgin olive oil

1 tablespoon red wine vinegar

1 tablespoon fresh lime juice

Salt

Freshly ground pepper

Navajo Fry Bread (page 220), for serving

Cook the black-eyed peas according to the directions on page 14. Drain well through a fine-mesh sieve and transfer to a bowl.

While the beans are still warm, add the tomato, red onion, chile, bacon, olives, garlic, and cumin and stir to combine. Stir in the oil, vinegar, and lime juice and season to taste with salt and pepper.

Cover and let marinate for at least 1 hour before serving with warm fry bread or a basket of tortilla chips for dipping.

Black Bean Soup *with* Smoked Tomatoes *and* Cilantro Sour Cream SERVES 6 TO 8

Without black beans, we wouldn't have an authentic Tex-Mex soup. But when you add some smoky tomatoes and cilantro-flavored sour cream to the mix, you have Tex-Mex heaven. This is a great make-ahead recipe because the flavors just get better 'n' better as they blend over a couple of days. You can certainly serve it without the tomatoes and sour cream, but you will be missing that extra oomph!

2 cups dry black beans, soaked according to directions on page 14

2 tablespoons olive oil

1 cup chopped onion

½ cup chopped leek, white part only

½ cup chopped celery

2 tablespoons chopped garlic

2 tablespoons seeded and chopped jalapeño chile

2 teaspoons ground cumin

1 large smoked ham hock

6 cups rich chicken stock or nonfat, low-sodium chicken broth

1 tablespoon chopped fresh epazote or cilantro

Salt

Freshly ground pepper

Fresh lime juice

½ cup Cilantro-Lime Sour Cream (page 28)

1 cup chopped cold-smoked tomatoes (see page 177)

¼ cup grated Cotija cheese

Drain the soaked beans and set aside.

Heat the oil in a large soup pot over medium-high heat. Add the onion, leek, celery, garlic, and chile and sauté for 4 minutes, or until the onions are translucent. Add the cumin and cook, stirring, for 1 minute. Add the reserved beans along with the ham hock, stock, and epazote. Season to taste with salt and pepper and bring to a boil. Lower the heat and cook at a gentle simmer for about 1 hour, or until the beans are very soft.

Remove the beans from the heat. Remove and discard the ham hock.

Pour the beans into a blender and process to a smooth puree; this may have to be done in batches. The puree should be thick, but of a soup-like consistency. If too thick, thin with chicken stock until the correct consistency is achieved.

Add lime juice and taste. If necessary, season with additional salt and pepper. The soup may be made up to this point and stored, covered and refrigerated, for up to 5 days or frozen for up to 3 months. Reheat the soup before serving.

Ladle equal portions of soup into each of six warm large shallow soup bowls. Place a tablespoon of the sour cream in the center and sprinkle cold-smoked tomatoes and cheese over the top. Serve immediately.

Dean's Tortilla Soup *with* South-of-the-Border Flavors   SERVES 4

I don't know how many bowls of tortilla soup I've prepared, or how many different preparations I have eaten, but I can tell you the figure is in the thousands. Throughout the years, as it became one of my signature dishes, I have had ample opportunity to refine it, so what you are getting is the absolute best tortilla soup you will ever eat. My version is based on the traditional Mexican soup that I experienced in Mexico many, many years ago, which was nothing more than a highly seasoned chicken broth thickened with tortillas and topped with some crumbled cheese. This is a bit more elaborate. It can easily be made an exciting vegetarian dish by replacing the chicken stock with a good homemade vegetable stock.

8 tablespoons olive oil

8 corn tortillas, cut into long strips and divided in half

8 garlic cloves, peeled

2 cups fresh onion puree (see Note)

6 cups chicken stock or nonfat, low-sodium chicken broth

4 cups fresh tomato puree (see Note)

5 roasted ancho chiles, stemmed, and seeded (see page 15)

2 jalapeño chiles, stemmed, seeded, and chopped

1 tablespoon chopped fresh epazote or 2 tablespoons chopped fresh cilantro

1 tablespoon ground cumin

1 teaspoon ground coriander

1 large bay leaf

Salt

Fresh lemon juice

Cayenne pepper

1 cup small-dice boneless, skinless, smoked chicken breast (see page 176)

1 cup cubed avocado

½ cup shredded sharp cheddar cheese, preferably Veldhuizen (see facing page)

¼ cup finely diced cabbage

¼ cup finely julienned red radish

1 tablespoon seeded and minced jalapeño chile

Evolution of My Tortilla Soup

When I was chef at the Mansion on Turtle Creek, the owner, Mrs. Caroline Rose Hunt, brought us the recipe for the Argyle tortilla soup. The Argyle is a private club in San Antonio owned by the Southwest Foundation for Biomedical Research. It has a long, long history of fine dining, which was established by the superb cooking skills of one of its early owners, Miss Alice O'Grady. Tortilla soup is just one of many now-classic Texas recipes that came from the club. Although Mexican in origin, the soup had been somewhat Anglicized, and over the years I pretty much kept to my take on the original recipe. It became so identified with me (and with the new Southwest cooking that sprang up in the 1980s) that I knew I would never be able to take it off of any menu. So when I opened Fearing's, I decided to take it back to its heritage and give it a bit more basic Mexican flavor. The broth remains the classic, but with a little more heat and spice. It remains my million-dollar baby!

Heat about 5 tablespoons of the olive oil in a large frying pan over medium-high heat. Add one-half of the tortilla strips and fry, turning occasionally, for about 5 minutes, or until very crisp. Carefully transfer to a double layer of paper towels to drain. Reserve.

Heat the remaining 3 tablespoons oil in a large saucepan over medium heat. Add the garlic along with the remaining half of the tortilla strips and fry, stirring frequently, for about 5 minutes, or until the tortillas are crisp. Add the onion puree and bring to a simmer. Simmer, stirring occasionally, for 10 minutes.

Stir in the chicken stock and tomato puree along with the roasted anchos, jalapeños, epazote, cumin, coriander, and bay leaf. Season with salt to taste, raise the heat, and bring to a boil. Lower the heat and cook at a gentle simmer for 40 minutes, skimming off any fat that rises to the surface. Remove from the heat, transfer to a blender, and process to a smooth puree. If too thick, add chicken stock, a bit at a time, to reach a smooth soup consistency. The soup may be made up to this point and stored, covered and refrigerated, for up to 3 days or frozen for up to 3 months.

When ready to serve, place the soup in a large saucepan over low heat. Remove and discard the bay leaf. Season with lemon juice and cayenne and, if necessary, additional salt.

Place an equal portion of smoked chicken, avocado, cheese, cabbage, radish, minced jalapeño, and reserved tortilla crisps in the center of each of four warm shallow soup bowls. Ladle 8 ounces of soup over the garnish and serve immediately.

NOTE: Fresh onion and tomato puree can be made by processing the fresh vegetables in a food processor fitted with a metal blade. You will need about 3 medium peeled onions to yield 2 cups of puree and about 2½ pounds of peeled, cored, and seeded tomatoes to yield 4 cups of puree.

Veldhuizen Cheeses

The Veldhuizen cheeses come from a small family farm in Dublin, Texas, where they are handcrafted using their own raw milk. Three generations of the family work together producing a small line of artisanal farmstead raw milk cheeses and milk products. We particularly love their Redneck Cheddar and Texas Gold cheeses. (See Sources, page 242.)

Yellow Tomato Gazpacho
with Smoked Red Tomato Cream SERVES 4

Who doesn't love a chilled tomato soup on a hot Texas day? I reverse the roles here and use yellow tomatoes for the soup and red tomatoes in the garnish. You can make the gazpacho early in the day, but don't refrigerate it much longer than a few hours, as the vegetables will soften and not be as appetizing as they are with a bit of crunch.

1½ pounds yellow tomatoes, coarsely chopped

1 cup chopped peeled-and-seeded cucumber

½ cup chopped yellow bell pepper

1 tablespoon minced serrano chile

1 tablespoon minced shallot

1 teaspoon minced garlic

1 tablespoon white wine vinegar, or as needed

1 tablespoon minced fresh cilantro

1 tablespoon minced fresh basil

Fresh lime juice

Salt

Few drops of pure maple syrup, if needed

Smoked Red Tomato Cream (recipe follows)

Place the tomatoes in a food processor fitted with the metal blade and process, using quick on-and-off turns, to just chop coarsely. They should not be pureed. Scrape the tomatoes into a large bowl.

Place the cucumber, bell pepper, chile, shallot, and garlic in the food processor still fitted with the metal blade and process, using quick on-and-off turns, to just chop coarsely; remember not to puree. All of the vegetables should be of an even size.

Scrape the mixture into the tomatoes. Stir in the vinegar along with the cilantro and basil. Season to taste with lime juice and salt.

Taste and, if the soup is too acidic, add a few drops of maple syrup.

Cover with plastic wrap and refrigerate for at least 1 hour, or until very cold.

Pour an equal portion into each of four chilled shallow soup bowls. Spoon the smoked red tomato cream over the soup.

SMOKED RED
TOMATO CREAM

½ pound ripe red tomatoes, cored and halved

1 tablespoon olive oil

1 tablespoon minced shallot

1 tablespoon minced serrano chile

1 teaspoon minced garlic

½ cup very cold heavy cream

Fresh lime juice

Salt

Cold-smoke the tomatoes for 20 minutes according to the directions on page 177.

Heat the oil in a small saucepan over medium heat. Add the shallot, chile, and garlic and sauté for 1 minute. Add the smoked tomatoes and bring to a slow boil, using a wooden spoon to break up the tomatoes and release their juices. Cook, stirring constantly, for 12 minutes, or until very thick.

Transfer the tomato mixture to a blender and puree until smooth and thick. Transfer to a clean container and refrigerate for 1 hour, or until very cold.

Pour the cream into a chilled bowl and, using a hand-held mixer, whip to form soft peaks. Fold in the chilled tomato mixture. When blended, season with lime juice and salt.

Cover and refrigerate until ready to serve.

CORN *and* POBLANO CHOWDER
with SHRIMP HUSH PUPPIES   SERVES 4

Although the word *chowder* seems to conjure up visions of a New England chilly winter day, to me corn chowder does just the opposite. I think late summer, sweetness, and light. To "Texas-ify" this classic American soup, I add some heat and savor with both fresh and roasted chiles. It is one of the most popular soups at Fearing's, where diners often remark that it is one of the best chowders they have ever tasted.

6 ears corn, husked and all tassels removed

3 thick-cut bacon slices, finely diced

1 cup finely diced onion

½ cup finely diced celery

½ cup finely diced leek, white part only

1 tablespoon minced garlic

1 tablespoon seeded and minced jalapeño chile

1 teaspoon chopped fresh thyme

1 teaspoon chopped fresh sage

1 teaspoon ground cumin

Salt

Freshly ground pepper

6 cups rich chicken stock or nonfat,
    low-sodium chicken broth

3 tablespoons cornstarch dissolved
    in 3 tablespoons cold water

2 cups whole milk

2 cups finely diced peeled potatoes

1 cup stemmed, peeled, seeded, and diced
    roasted poblano chile (see page 15)

Fresh lime juice

Tabasco sauce

Shrimp Hush Puppies, for garnish (recipe follows)

Using a sharp knife and holding the cob vertically, slice the kernels from each corn cob, cutting only to half of their depth. With the back of the knife or using a box grater, scrape the cobs up and down to remove all the pulp. The corn should resemble scrambled eggs. Set aside.

Place the bacon in a large soup pot over medium-high heat. Cook, stirring frequently, for about 5 minutes, or until the fat has been rendered out and the bacon is crisp.

Add the onion and celery and cook, stirring constantly, for 3 minutes. Stir in the leek, garlic, chile, thyme, sage, and cumin and cook, stirring constantly, for 2 minutes more.

Stir in the reserved corn and continue to cook, stirring constantly, for 5 minutes. Season to taste with salt and pepper.

Stir in the chicken stock, and bring to a boil. Lower the heat and cook at a gentle simmer for 20 minutes.

Stirring constantly, add the cornstarch mixture in a slow, steady stream and cook for about 5 minutes, or until thickened. Immediately add the milk, along with the potatoes and chile, and bring to a boil; then lower the heat and cook at a gentle simmer for 10 minutes, or until the potatoes are tender.

Remove from the heat and season to taste with lime juice and Tabasco. Taste again and, if necessary, add additional salt and pepper.

Ladle an equal portion into each of four large warm shallow soup bowls. Garnish each serving with 3 hush puppies and serve immediately.

SHRIMP HUSH PUPPIES

MAKES 12 HUSH PUPPIES

1 cup all-purpose flour

½ cup cornmeal

1 teaspoon baking powder

1 teaspoon salt, plus more as needed

2 large eggs, beaten

1 cup whole milk

4 poached large shrimp, finely diced

½ cup minced scallions

½ cup minced white onion

6 cups vegetable oil, for frying

Combine the flour, cornmeal, baking powder, and salt in a medium bowl.

Whisk the eggs and milk together in a separate small bowl, slowly add to the dry ingredients, and stir gently to just combine. Do not overmix; the mixture can be slightly lumpy.

Fold in the shrimp, scallions, and onion and season with salt.

Heat the oil in a deep-fat fryer over high heat until it registers 350°F on a candy thermometer.

Drop the batter by the teaspoonful into the hot oil, taking care not to crowd the fryer. Fry for about 2½ minutes, or until golden brown.

Using a slotted spoon, lift the hush puppies from the oil and transfer to a double layer of paper towels to drain.

Lightly season with salt and serve immediately.

CELERY ROOT *and* APPLE SOUP
with JALAPEÑO VENISON SAUSAGE   SERVES 6 TO 8

This is a wonderful fall soup. Since it is easy to make, it is a great addition to the holiday table. I turn it into a Texas soup by adding a slice of nicely browned game sausage from Broken Arrow Ranch in Ingram, Texas, to the bottom of the bowl. The sausage adds a surprise as well as an interesting flavor note. If you can't find venison sausage, almost any artisanal-quality meat sausage will do.

2 cups celery root, peeled, rinsed,
 and cut into large chunks

6 tablespoons olive oil

2 large Granny Smith apples, peeled, cored,
 and halved

2 tablespoons sliced shallots

½ cup leeks, white part only, roughly chopped

2 teaspoons finely chopped fresh thyme

8 cups rich turkey stock or nonfat,
 low-sodium turkey broth

½ cup heavy cream, warmed

Juice of 1 lemon

Salt

Freshly ground pepper

1 cup sliced venison sausage (see page 129)

1 tablespoon snipped fresh chives

Preheat the oven to 350°F.

Put the celery root in a baking pan large enough to hold it in a single layer. Add about 4 tablespoons of the oil and toss to lightly coat all of the pieces. Transfer to the preheated oven and roast, stirring occasionally, for about 20 minutes, or until light brown on the edges. Remove from the oven and set aside.

Put the apples, cut side down, in a small nonstick baking pan. Transfer to the preheated oven and roast for about 12 minutes, or until softened and lightly colored. Remove from the oven, roughly chop, and set aside.

Place the remaining 2 tablespoons of the oil in a soup pot over medium-low heat. Add the shallots, leeks, and thyme and sauté for about 5 minutes, or until very soft. Stir in the reserved celery root and apple and continue to sauté for 5 minutes.

Add the stock, raise the heat, and bring to a simmer. Lower the heat and cook at a gentle simmer for 30 minutes.

Remove from the heat, transfer to a blender, and, holding the lid down with a folded kitchen towel, process to a smooth puree. This is best done in small batches; you don't want to overfill a blender with hot liquid, as the steam might pop the lid. The soup should be very, very smooth. If not, pour through a fine-mesh sieve into a clean saucepan to remove any lumps.

Place the pan over low heat and slowly stir in the cream. Season the soup with lemon juice, salt, and pepper, to taste. Cook until just heated through.

When hot, ladle an equal portion of the soup into six shallow soup bowls. Place an equal portion of the sausage on top of each bowl, sprinkle with chives, and serve.

3

SALADS

Farm-to-Fearing's Vegetable Salad *with* Sherry Vinaigrette *and* Paula's Goat Cheese Croquettes   SERVES 4

This is a real big Texas salad. We won't settle for just a few leaves of lettuce in a simple vinaigrette; we want the whole enchilada! In this salad we mix all kinds of veggies with the lettuces and then garnish the plate with some great little croquettes made with Paula Lambert's (see page 209) wonderful goat cheese.

4 cups mixed baby lettuces, well washed and dried

1 cup halved cherry tomatoes

½ cup golden beets (see sidebar at right)

½ cup 1-inch pieces blanched green beans

½ cup 1-inch pieces blanched asparagus

½ cup thinly sliced carrots

½ cup thinly sliced fennel

½ cup sliced fresh hearts of palm

2 tablespoons cold-smoked pecan pieces (see sidebar, page 139; and page 177)

½ cup Sherry Vinaigrette (page 38)

Salt

Freshly ground pepper

¼ cup Creamy Basil Dressing (page 36)

12 Paula's Goat Cheese Croquettes (page 209)

Combine the lettuce with the tomatoes, beets, green beans, asparagus, carrots, fennel, hearts of palm, and pecans in a large bowl. Add the sherry vinaigrette and toss gently to coat all of the salad ingredients. Season with salt and pepper to taste.

Place an equal portion of the salad on each of four chilled plates. Around the outside of the salad, using a tablespoon of the basil dressing, drop 3 spots of dressing. Then top each spot of dressing with 3 croquettes. Serve immediately.

Cooking Beets

I was not always a fan of beets. I grew up eating earthy red beets, and their flavor reminded me of dirt, so I understand that they can be a difficult veggie to like. However, once I learned to cook them properly, I began to like them, particularly for their natural sweetness. Now, with the wide variety of vibrantly colored beets available, I love them, both for their flavor and for their decorative abilities on the plate.

To boil beets, begin with beets of the same size. Trim off the tip of the root end and cut the stems down to about an inch. Scrub well under cold running water. Keep the skin on, as this will ensure that the beets maintain their color when cooking. Place the beets in a large saucepan with cold water to cover. Add salt to taste; I use about a teaspoon for every 2 quarts of water. Place over high heat and bring to a boil. Immediately lower the heat and cook at a gentle simmer for about 30 minutes (for fairly large beets), or until tender when pierced with the point of a small, sharp knife. The cooking time will vary depending on the size and freshness of the beets. Remove the beets from the heat and drain in a colander. Set aside until cool enough to handle. Using a small knife, cut off the root tips and stems and rub off the skin with a clean, damp towel. Leave the beets whole, or cut crosswise into slices or as required by a specific recipe.

Red Chile Caesar Salad *with* Grilled Radicchio *and* Romaine Hearts   SERVES 4

This is not a typical Caesar salad, but it sure is a good one! The smokiness of the dressing hints of the anchovy in the classic while the chile defines it as Texan. It is a very modern take on the original, with a marvelous blend of smoke, spice, and the bite of lime. You can use almost any dry, crumbly cheese if you can't find Cotija, a Texas favorite. Among your choices would be queso fresco, Mexican (or other) farmer's cheese, or even an Italian cheese, such as ricotta salata.

1 head radicchio, washed well, trimmed, and cut in half lengthwise

2 tablespoons olive oil

Salt

Freshly ground pepper

2 large heads romaine lettuce, well washed, trimmed, outer leaves removed, and cut into 1-inch pieces

¾ cup **Smoked Chile Aioli** (page 35)

½ cup crumbled **San Pedro cheese**

½ cup diced tomatoes

½ cup julienned fresh hearts of palm

½ cup pomegranate seeds (optional)

Preheat the grill, taking care that the grates are very clean and brushed with oil.

Using a pastry brush, lightly coat the radicchio with olive oil and season with salt and pepper.

Place the seasoned radicchio, cut side down, on the hot grill. Grill for 2 minutes, then, using tongs, turn it about 90 degrees. Grill for 2 minutes and, using tongs, transfer to a cutting board.

Using a sharp knife, slice the grilled radicchio into thin shreds. Transfer to a plate, lightly cover, and refrigerate.

Put the romaine in a large salad bowl and toss with just enough aioli to lightly coat all the lettuce. Season to taste with salt and pepper. Add the reserved radicchio along with half the cheese and toss again to coat; the salad ingredients should just be touched with the dressing.

Place an equal portion of the salad on each of four salad plates. Sprinkle each portion with an equal amount of the remaining cheese along with the tomatoes, hearts of palm, and pomegranate seeds, if using.

Wilted Spinach and Arugula Salad with Blue Cheese and Warm Smoked-Bacon Dressing

SERVES 4

What's there to say about a spinach salad with warm smoky dressing? Easy to make and even easier to eat, this spinach salad has a wonderful combination of textures and flavors that combine to make it a lunchtime favorite. The addition of arugula adds just the perfect bite to the otherwise soft and gentle mix.

½ pound baby spinach leaves,
    washed well and trimmed

½ pound baby arugula, washed well and trimmed

6 to 8 large button mushrooms, stemmed,
    washed, and cut lengthwise into thin slices

1 cup Mustard Dressing (recipe follows)

6 slices cooked smoked bacon,
    cut into 1-inch pieces

Salt

Freshly ground pepper

1 cup crumbled blue cheese

Put the spinach and arugula in a large salad bowl. Sprinkle the mushroom slices over the top. Set aside.

Combine the dressing with the bacon in a small frying pan over low heat. Cook, stirring constantly, for about 3 minutes, or until very warm. Do not boil, or the dressing will separate. Season to taste with salt and pepper.

Pour the warm dressing over the salad and gently toss to coat. Taste and, if necessary, adjust the seasoning.

Place an equal portion of the salad mixture on each of four salad plates. Sprinkle each plate with an equal portion of the cheese and serve immediately.

MUSTARD DRESSING

MAKES 2 CUPS

1 cup mayonnaise

2 tablespoons Dijon mustard

1 tablespoon red wine vinegar

1 tablespoon pure maple syrup

½ cup olive oil

Fresh lemon juice

Salt

Combine the mayonnaise with the mustard, vinegar, and maple syrup in a small bowl. Whisking constantly, add the oil in a slow, steady stream. When well blended and thick, whisk in the lemon juice. Taste and, if necessary, season with salt.

Use as directed in the recipe.

TEXAS COBB SALAD SERVES 4

In Texas we don't cotton to any of that fancy "composed" salad business—we just take all of those delicious traditional salad ingredients and toss 'em all together in a pretty bowl. Then we sprinkle the good stuff with even better stuff—toasty pepitas and salty cheese. Now you know that a Texas Cobb Salad runs rings around the fancy original. A terrific addition to this salad is "Chicken-Fried" Texas Quail (page 147), which gives it a real Texas flavor.

2 romaine lettuce hearts, washed,
    trimmed, and cut into 1-inch pieces

2 cups diced smoked skinless chicken breast

1 cup diced cooked smoked bacon

1 cup chopped hard-boiled eggs

1 cup peeled, seeded, and chopped tomatoes

1 cup corn kernels, cut from 2 grilled
    ears of corn (page 189)

1 cup diced avocado

1 cup Pickled Red Onions (page 43)

½ cup grated asadero cheese

2 tablespoons chopped fresh cilantro

Smoked Chile Aioli (page 35)

2 tablespoons coarsely ground Barbecue
    Spiced Pepitas (page 39)

¼ cup grated Cotija cheese

4 fresh cilantro sprigs, for garnish

Put the romaine in a large bowl. Add the chicken, bacon, hard-boiled eggs, tomatoes, corn, avocado, pickled red onion, asadero cheese, and cilantro and toss to blend.

Drizzle on the dressing and toss to very lightly coat the salad.

Place an equal portion of the salad in the center of each of four chilled luncheon plates. Generously sprinkle pepitas and the Cotija cheese over the top of each and garnish with a sprig of cilantro.

MANGO-PICKLED RED ONION SALAD

MAKES ABOUT 6 CUPS

This is a terrific salad to use as a garnish for almost any grilled fish or meat. The tanginess of the pickled onions meets its match in the sweetness of the mango. The crunchiness of the cabbage and jicama, along with the pungent vinaigrette, creates a parade of flavors and textures that highlight a simple grill. If you want to liven up some tacos, this is the perfect garnish to use.

2 ripe mangoes, peeled and julienned

1 recipe Pickled Red Onions (page 43)

3 cups shredded rib-free cabbage

1 cup finely diced jicama

½ cup toasted pecans

¼ cup finely sliced fresh cilantro leaves

⅓ cup Smoky Cumin-Lime Vinaigrette (page 38)

Salt

Combine the mangoes with the pickled onion, cabbage, jicama, pecans, and cilantro in a medium bowl. When well blended, slowly add the vinaigrette and toss to coat lightly. Season with salt and serve immediately.

If not serving immediately, do not add the vinaigrette until a few minutes before you are ready to serve, as the salad will lose its crispness.

FIESTA SALAD MAKES ABOUT 2 CUPS

Light and crunchy, Fiesta Salad brings a celebration to the plate. A perfect side for grilled meats, fish, or poultry, this is an easy salad to put together at the last minute to add to a party on the table.

1 cup shredded rib-free cabbage

½ cup Pickled Red Onions (page 43)

½ cup julienned jicama

¼ cup finely sliced fresh cilantro leaves

¼ cup Lime Vinaigrette (page 38)

Salt

½ cup fried tortilla threads (see Note)

Combine the cabbage with the onions, jicama, and cilantro in a medium bowl. Drizzle in the vinaigrette and stir to just coat lightly. Season with salt and serve immediately, garnished with the tortilla threads.

NOTE: Tortilla threads are made by frying thin slivers of tortilla in 365°F oil until crisp and golden brown. They add a nice crunchy texture to vegetable salads, or make a lively garnish for soups.

JICAMA-CARROT SLAW SERVES 4

It takes a bit of time to julienne the vegetables, but once that's done, this is a quick and easy salad to put together. If you want to make it in advance, mix all of the vegetables together early in the day, cover, and refrigerate. Just before serving, toss in the tortilla strips and add the vinaigrette. This will keep the tortillas from getting soggy. It goes with absolutely everything, so it is a great party salad.

½ cup thinly julienned red bell pepper

½ cup julienned jicama

½ cup julienned carrot

¼ cup julienned seeded and minced jalapeño chile

¼ cup julienned Fried Tortilla Strips (page 161)

¼ cup finely sliced fresh cilantro leaves

1 cup Lime Vinaigrette (page 38)

Salt

Combine the bell pepper, jicama, carrot, chile, tortilla strips, and cilantro in a medium bowl. Add the vinaigrette and toss to coat. Season with salt. Serve immediately.

FIRECRACKER SLAW MAKES ABOUT 6 CUPS

This is certainly not your typical creamy cole-slaw. Although it begins with the usual cabbage, I add a mix of colorful vegetables and top it off with a good dose of jalapeño and a tongue-tingling dressing. I dreamed it up for a Fourth-of-July party thinking that with fireworks in the sky I'd like to put some fireworks in the mouth, and this sure does. It is a terrific slaw to accent Tex-Mex tamales, enchiladas, and tacos, and brings some zest to all kinds of barbecues and grills.

2 cups julienned rib-free green cabbage

1 cup julienned rib-free red cabbage

½ cup thinly julienned red bell pepper

½ cup thinly julienned yellow bell pepper

½ cup julienned jicama

½ cup julienned carrot

½ cup julienned zucchini, outer green skin only

½ cup Pickled Red Onions (page 43)

¼ cup julienned seeded and minced jalapeño chile

¼ cup finely sliced fresh cilantro leaves

Salt

Freshly ground pepper

1 cup Firecracker Dressing (page 36)

Combine the green and red cabbage in a large bowl. Add the red and yellow bell pepper along with the jicama, carrot, zucchini, pickled onions, chile, and cilantro and toss to blend completely. Season to taste with salt and pepper.

Add the dressing and toss to coat well. Set aside to marinate for 10 minutes before serving.

East Texas Field Pea Salad *with* Barbecued Thousand Island Dressing *and* Heirloom Tomatoes   SERVES 4

Purple hull and lady cream peas are both cowpeas and much loved throughout the South (see sidebar at right). Arkansas even has a purple hull pea festival, and it is through migration from the Southern states that Texans got to know and love these summertime favorites. Almost any type of field pea could replace either of the two I use here, but if you can find them, try the lady creams—they are the real "ladies" of the group. This is one salad that really shines only in the summer, when the peas are fresh from the field and the tomatoes are ripe on the vine.

Salt

1 cup purple hull peas

1 cup lady cream peas

1 teaspoon olive oil

¼ pound applewood-smoked bacon, cut into small dice

¼ cup finely diced celery root

¼ cup finely diced carrot

1 tablespoon minced shallot

1 tablespoon finely diced onion

1 tablespoon seeded and minced jalapeño chile

1 teaspoon finely chopped fresh thyme

2 cups baby arugula, stems removed

½ cup Barbecued Thousand Island Dressing (page 34)

Freshly ground pepper

2 medium heirloom tomatoes, peeled, cored, and cut crosswise into ½-inch-thick slices

8 fresh basil leaves

Fill a medium saucepan with enough cold water to fill the pan halfway. Stir in a pinch of salt and place over medium-high heat. Bring to a boil and add both the purple hull and the lady cream peas. Boil for about 5 minutes, or just until the peas are tender. Remove from the heat and drain well. Set aside.

Heat the oil in a medium frying pan over medium heat. Add the bacon and fry for about 4 minutes, or until just crisp.

Add the celery root, carrot, shallot, onion, and chile and cook, stirring constantly, for about 3 minutes, or just until the vegetables soften. Remove from the heat and stir in the thyme. Set aside to cool.

Combine the reserved peas and bacon mixture with the arugula. Add the dressing, season to taste with salt and pepper, and stir to combine.

Place 2 tomato slices in the center of each of four large salad plates. Spoon an equal portion of the field pea salad on top of the tomatoes. Tear the basil leaves into random pieces and distribute evenly among the plates. Serve immediately.

Field Peas

Field peas, or cowpeas, were introduced to the American South by slaves who carried the seeds in the holds of the ships that transported them to the Americas. The name *cowpea* comes from the fact that the landowners (and slaveholders) grew the peas as forage for their cattle. However, slaves (and all poor folks) valued the lowly plant as a nutritious and filling meal when seasoned with little scraps of meat or fat available to them. The combination of peas and seasoned liquid, known as *pot likker*, traveled from the eastern seaboard through all of the Southern states and into the Southwest as settlement spread. This is no longer a poor man's meal; Texans still enjoy this simple dish, particularly when served with a zesty chile-flavored cornbread.

BLACK-EYED PEA SALAD
on FRIED GREEN TOMATOES   SERVES 4

Rather than the traditional New Year's black-eyed pea dish, Hoppin' John, I prefer this garden-fresh salad. It is a wonderful blend of tender, earthy peas with the crunch of tiny diced vegetables. When it's spooned over tangy, crisp Fried Green Tomatoes (page 208), you will find summer singing on the plate.

3 bacon slices, diced

2 garlic cloves, chopped

½ cup diced onion

2 cups fresh black-eyed peas

1 cup chicken stock or nonfat, low-sodium chicken broth

2 tablespoons finely diced carrot

2 tablespoons finely diced zucchini

2 tablespoons finely diced tomato

2 tablespoons finely diced yellow squash

2 teaspoons chopped fresh cilantro

1 teaspoon seeded and minced jalapeño chile

⅓ cup Mustard-Sage Vinaigrette (page 37)

Salt

Fried Green Tomatoes (page 208)

1 bunch watercress, well washed and dried, tough stems removed

In a medium saucepan over medium heat, fry the bacon, stirring occasionally, for about 4 minutes, or until most of the fat has rendered out. Add the garlic and onion and cook, stirring occasionally, for another 4 minutes, or until the onions are translucent. Add the black-eyed peas and enough chicken stock to cover by 3 inches and bring to a boil. Lower the heat and simmer for about 10 minutes, or until tender. Remove from the heat, drain well, and set aside to cool.

When the peas are cool, transfer them to a medium bowl. Add the carrot, zucchini, diced tomato, yellow squash, cilantro, and chile and stir to combine. Stir in the vinaigrette and season to taste with salt.

Place 2 fried tomatoes, slightly overlapping, in the center of each of four luncheon plates. Spoon a generous portion of the black-eyed pea salad over the top, nestle a little bundle of watercress against the salad, and serve immediately.

Apricot Barbecue Sauce–Glazed Bobwhite Quail on Iceberg Wedge *with* Point Reyes Blue Cheese Dressing *and* Cider-Braised Bacon   SERVES 4

Quail has a long culinary history in Texas. With a huge population on the prairies and in the forests, it was a sustenance food for Native Americans as well as for early settlers. But because their habitat has been diminished over time through increased agriculture and deforestation, quail is now mostly farm-raised. Occasionally we do get the opportunity to go hunting, but that, too, is now done most reliably on game farms. If quail is not readily available, you could use small chicken legs with the thighs attached, but these will take quite a bit longer to cook; I'd say about 15 minutes or so.

The quail turns this salad into the most modern take on the classic wedge salad—and who doesn't love the crunch of a crisp wedge of iceberg lettuce? Rather than the crumbled bacon, the warm braised bacon kicks the salad forward. The sweetness of the apricot blends with the earthiness of the blue cheese to make an unbelievably all-around delicious mix.

3 tablespoons olive oil

Four 5-ounce semiboneless quail, wings removed

Salt

Freshly ground pepper

½ cup Apricot Barbecue Sauce (page 19)

Four 4-ounce slices Cider-Braised Bacon (page 192)

1 head baby iceberg lettuce, well washed, trimmed, and cut into 4 wedges

2 cups Point Reyes Blue Cheese Dressing (page 34)

1 cup halved cherry tomatoes

1 packed cup baby arugula

¼ cup snipped fresh chives

Heat 2 tablespoons of the oil in a medium frying pan over medium-high heat.

Season the quail with salt and pepper and place them, skin side down, in the pan. Sear for 3 minutes. Turn and sear for an additional 3 minutes.

Remove from the heat and, using a pastry brush, lightly coat the birds with the barbecue sauce. Set aside and keep warm.

Place the remaining 1 tablespoon oil in a clean medium frying pan over medium-high heat. Add the bacon to the hot pan and sear for 3 minutes, or until a golden crust forms. Turn and sear for another 3 minutes, or until both sides are crisp.

Remove from the pan and keep warm.

Place a lettuce wedge on each of four luncheon plates. Drizzle ½ cup of the dressing over each wedge. Using a sharp knife, cut each quail in half lengthwise, then rest the 2 halves against the lettuce on each plate. Place a slice of bacon opposite the quail on each plate and then garnish with tomatoes, arugula, and chives. Serve immediately.

LUCIAN'S CRAB SALAD SERVES 4

This salad is named after Lucian LaBarba, president of American Food Service, now Freshpoint, a fourth-generation purveyor of produce throughout Texas. As the main supplier of produce to Fearing's, Lucian has become a lunch regular, and I can guarantee that he will always order crab salad. That being the case, I decided to honor him by renaming the plate "Lucian's Crab Salad."

½ cup mayonnaise

1 tablespoon snipped fresh chives

Fresh lemon juice

Pinch cayenne pepper

Salt

Freshly ground black pepper

2 tablespoons finely diced carrot

2 tablespoons finely diced celery root

1 tablespoon finely diced shallot

1 pound Gulf or Jonah crab leg meat, picked clean of all cartilage and shell (see sidebar, page 56)

½ cup Carrot-Cumin Vinaigrette (page 37)

1 large avocado, pitted, peeled, and cut lengthwise into thin slices

1 roasted red bell pepper, stemmed, peeled, seeded, and julienned

Combine the mayonnaise with the chives, lemon juice, and cayenne in a small bowl. Season with salt and black pepper.

Stir in the carrot, celery root, and shallot and, when just blended, fold in the crabmeat. Taste and, if necessary, adjust the seasoning.

Using a 3-inch round ring mold, form a tower of crabmeat in the center of each of four chilled luncheon plates. Spoon an equal portion of the vinaigrette around the tower. Garnish each plate with an equal portion of the avocado and bell pepper. Serve immediately.

4

MAIN COURSES

Wood-Grilled Pork Chops Glazed *with* "D1" Sauce *on* Poblano-Pepita Pesto *and* Heirloom Tomatoes *with* Crispy Sweet Onion Rings   SERVES 4

I love the flavors in this dish. The garlicky hint underneath the vinegary glaze just seems to be the perfect Texas grill. Top the chops off with garden-fresh tomatoes and the poblano pesto, and you've got a summertime barbecue straight off the range. Then add those crisp, slightly salty onion rings, and you are ready for a hoedown.

Four 12-ounce center-cut pork chops, trimmed of silverskin and excess fat

Fearing's Garlic Salt (page 41)

Sea salt

Freshly ground pepper

1 cup "D1" Sauce (page 21)

2 medium heirloom tomatoes, cored and cut crosswise into ½-inch slices

1 tablespoon olive oil

¼ cup Poblano-Pepita Pesto (page 28)

Crispy Sweet Onion Rings (page 201)

Preheat the grill, taking care that the grates are very clean and brushed with oil.

Season the chops with garlic salt, salt, and pepper. Place on the hottest section of the grill without crowding. Grill for 3 minutes, rotate a half-turn, and grill for 3 minutes more. Turn the chops over and repeat the grilling steps on the opposite sides. About 1 minute before removing the chops from the grill, using a pastry brush, generously coat both sides with the sauce, turning the chops to glaze both sides nicely. This grilling time should yield chops cooked to medium.

Remove from the heat and let rest for 5 minutes. The internal temperature will rise to 145°F for the desirable medium degree of doneness.

Season the tomatoes with salt and pepper and drizzle with a touch of the olive oil.

Spoon 1 tablespoon of the pesto into the center of each of four warm dinner plates. Place an equal number of tomato slices, slightly overlapping, around the pesto. Place a chop against the tomatoes and lay 2 onion rings behind the pork. Serve immediately.

"D1" Sauce

"D1" Sauce really makes this dish. It came about when I was noodling around in the kitchen thinking "This really needs some A1," so my crew and I set out to try to make our own version of that famous commercial sauce. When we succeeded in cooking up something that made our taste buds say WOW, one of the cooks said "Why don't we name it after yourself—'D1' for Dean's sauce." So the name stuck, and it has become one of my favorite go-to sauces to zip up any grilled meat.

Pork Tenderloin *with* Watermelon-Jalapeño Glaze on Yellow Tomato-Pozole Stew SERVES 4

This recipe makes a terrific entertaining menu. The hot 'n' sweet glaze adds big flavor to the mild taste of the pork. The stew can be made in advance and reheated just before serving. Since the pork cooks quickly, your guests won't have a clue that you've spent much time in the kitchen.

Four 6-ounce pork tenderloin fillets, trimmed of all fat and silverskin

Salt

Freshly ground pepper

1 tablespoon canola oil

Watermelon-Jalapeño Glaze (page 29)

Yellow Tomato–Pozole Stew (page 167)

4 fresh cilantro sprigs

Season the pork with salt and pepper.

Place the oil in a large frying pan over medium-high heat. Add the seasoned pork without crowding the pan, and sear for 3 minutes. Turn and continue to sear on the opposite sides for another 2 minutes, or until you reach the desired degree of doneness. (My recommendation is for medium rare, which this amount of time should achieve.)

Remove the meat from the pan and, using a pastry brush, generously coat both sides with the glaze. Keep warm.

Spoon an equal portion of the stew into the center of each of four warm dinner plates. Lay a glazed pork fillet on top. Garnish with a cilantro sprig and serve immediately.

PORK MILANESA *with* MEXICAN RELISH   SERVES 4

The first time one of my Mexican cooks handed me a Milanesa torta (sandwich), I couldn't believe my taste buds. The word *Milanese* meant Italian veal to me. But here it was a crisply fried pork, rather than veal, scallopini stuffed into a roll called a *bolillo* and stacked up with jalapeños, Mexican pickles, avocado, onion, and tomato. It was delicious, and I knew I had to take the pork from a sandwich filling to a fancy plate. And here it is—simple yet fancy, with the zesty Mexican Relish adding some color and flavor to the delicate crisp meat.

1½ pounds boneless pork loin, trimmed of all fat, cut ½ inch thick, pounded thin

½ cup fresh lime juice

Salt

Freshly ground pepper

1½ cups all-purpose flour

2 large eggs, at room temperature

½ teaspoon ground cumin

3 tablespoons cold water

1½ cups bread crumbs

1½ cups ground crisply fried corn tortillas

Vegetable oil, for frying

2 cups Mexican Relish (page 44)

8 lime wedges, for garnish

4 large fresh cilantro sprigs

2 tablespoons crumbled Cotija cheese

Using a sharp knife, cut the pork crosswise into 8 slices. Working with one piece at a time, place the meat between 2 pieces of waxed paper and, using a mallet or a cleaver, pound to flatten. The scallops should be very thin.

When all of the meat has been pounded flat, put it in a shallow dish. Add the lime juice and toss to coat well. Cover with plastic wrap and refrigerate for 1 hour.

Remove from the refrigerator, uncover, and season with salt and pepper.

Place 3 shallow bowls in a line on the countertop. Put the flour in the first bowl. Whisk together the eggs and cumin with the cold water in the second bowl. Combine the bread crumbs and ground tortillas in the third bowl.

Working with one piece at a time, coat the pork in the flour, shaking off the excess. Dip the flour-coated pork into the eggs, and finally into the bread crumbs, taking care that all sides are well coated.

Heat ½ inch of oil in a large cast-iron skillet over medium heat. When very hot but not smoking, add the pork, working in small batches if necessary and being careful not to crowd the pan. If the oil darkens, pour it out and start again with fresh oil.

Fry the pork scallops for 3 minutes, or until golden brown and crisp. Carefully turn and fry the remaining sides for about 3 minutes, or until golden brown, crisp, and cooked through. Transfer to a double layer of paper towels to drain. Season to taste with salt.

When all of the pork has been fried, place 2 pieces on each of four warm plates. Spoon an equal portion of the relish in a neat pile at the side of the pork. Garnish each plate with 2 wedges of lime and a sprig of cilantro and sprinkle the cheese over the top. For a striking presentation, the lime can be cut in half and grilled. The sugars in the lime naturally caramelize. Serve immediately.

DUBLIN DR PEPPER–BRAISED SHORT RIBS *with* QUESO FRESCO–CORN WHIPPED POTATOES *and* CRISPY TOBACCO ONIONS SERVES 4

When I first made this dish, the Dublin Bottling Works still sold Dr Pepper all across the state, but when the Dr Pepper folks got word of this, no more Dublin Dr Pepper could be found in Dallas (see sidebar, facing page). But since we can still get Dr Pepper made with pure cane sugar, this recipe lives on. I think that it combines old-fashioned Texas goodness with some extraordinary Texas beef to make the ultimate home-style Texas dish.

Four 8-ounce beef short ribs, cut into 2 by 2-inch pieces

Salt

Freshly ground pepper

¼ cup diced celery

¼ cup diced carrot

¼ cup diced onion

2 dried ancho chiles, stemmed and seeded

¼ cup diced tomato

¼ cup diced cold-smoked onion (see page 177)

1 teaspoon roughly chopped seeded and minced jalapeño chile

1 small bunch fresh thyme

1 bay leaf

1 teaspoon smoked paprika

1 teaspoon ground dried sage

½ teaspoon ground cumin

½ teaspoon ground coriander

1 cup red wine

3 cups Dr Pepper soda

6 cups chicken stock or nonfat, low-sodium chicken broth

Queso Fresco–Corn Whipped Potatoes (page 204)

Crispy Tobacco Onions (page 202)

Preheat the oven to 300°F.

Place the short ribs in a large frying pan over medium-high heat. Season with salt and pepper, and sear for 3 minutes. Turn and sear the opposite sides for 3 minutes. Remove from the pan and set aside.

With the pan still on medium-high heat, add the celery, carrot, and onion and sauté for about 5 minutes, or until nicely colored. Stir in the ancho chiles, tomato, smoked onion, and jalapeño. When blended, add the thyme, bay leaf, paprika, sage, cumin, and coriander and cook, stirring occasionally, for 5 minutes. Add the wine and cook, scraping up the browned bits from the bottom of the pan, for about 5 minutes, or until the liquid has reduced by half.

Add the Dr Pepper and bring to a simmer. Simmer, stirring occasionally, for about 15 minutes, or until the liquid has again reduced by half.

Add the stock along with the reserved short ribs, cover, and braise in the preheated oven for about 5 hours, or until the meat is very tender—almost falling off the bone.

Remove from the oven and, using tongs, remove the short ribs from the braising liquid. Set aside and keep warm.

Pour the braising liquid through a fine-mesh sieve into a clean saucepan. Discard the solids.

Place the saucepan over medium-high heat and bring to a boil. Boil for about 10 minutes, or until reduced by half. Taste and, if necessary, season with salt and pepper.

Spoon an equal portion of the potatoes into the center of each of four warm dinner plates. Nestle a short rib in the center of the potatoes. Spoon about 2 tablespoons of the reduced braising liquid over the top of the meat and top with an equal portion of the onions.

Dublin Bottling Works

Texans far and wide covet the extraordinary old-fashioned sodas made exclusively with cane sugar at the Dublin Bottling Works, a tiny plant in Dublin, Texas. It is a family-owned company that has been bottling sodas for more than 120 years. Dr Pepper, the drink, was introduced in Waco, Texas, in 1885, and the plant, originally called Dublin Dr Pepper Bottling Works, began the production of the cane sugar–sweetened Dr Pepper soda in 1891. In 2012, after a dispute with the Dr Pepper Snapple Group, the parent company of the Dr Pepper brand, the Dublin soda works eliminated the Dr Pepper from its name and, although it continued to make the cane sugar–sweetened drink, its distribution was limited to a 44 mile radius around the town of Dublin. Besides Dr Pepper, the plant makes a number of old-time flavored sodas, such as root beer, orange, and grape. The bottling works, with its ancient equipment, runs only once a week, bottling about 2,000 refillable and recirculated bottles. To purchase soda, the buyer has to do an even exchange, offering a crate of empty bottles for filled ones. You feel just like you're sitting up at a drugstore soda fountain, the flavor is so pure!

BONE-IN RIB EYE GRILLED *over* LIVE MESQUITE *with* WEST TEXAS "MOP" SAUCE *and* CREAMY CORNBREAD PUDDING SERVES 4

Texas is cattle ranching and farming; in fact, it produces more beef than any other state in this wonderful country of ours and most of it on family-run farms and ranches. All of our wide-open spaces allow cattle to roam and develop into premier stock. We use a terrific Wagyu beef at the restaurant (see sidebar, facing page) and, if you can get it, I highly recommend that you try it. You'll thank the stars over Texas!

Mop Sauce

The "mop" comes from the old days when whole towns got together to pit-roast half a steer. This was a long process, eighteen hours or so, and the meat had to be doused with a sauce to keep it from drying out. Since it was such a large piece of meat, the roasters used a mop to continuously coat it in a mixture of molasses, beer, and vinegar. I have found recipes for mop sauces in almost every old Texas cookbook I've come across. I like to think that they are Texas' first barbecue sauces, as they are the perfect mix of sweet, savory, and tangy.

Four thick 12-ounce center-cut rib eye steaks, cleaned of all fat and silverskin

Salt

Freshly ground pepper

1½ cups Fearing's Mop Sauce (see page 20 and sidebar at left)

4 cups Creamy Cornbread Pudding (page 198)

Preheat the grill, taking care that the grates are very clean and brushed with oil.

Season the steaks with salt and pepper and place them on the hot grill without crowding. Grill for 4 minutes, or just until nicely charred with grill marks. Turn and grill the remaining sides for 4 minutes, or until medium rare: 135°F on an instant-read thermometer.

Just about a minute before you think the meat is done, using a pastry brush, generously coat the steaks on both sides with the sauce to glaze nicely.

Place a steak in the center of each of four warm dinner plates. Spoon an equal portion of the pudding next to the bone and serve immediately.

Texas Wagyu

The word *Wagyu*, from the Japanese words *Wa*, or "cattle," and *gyu*, or "beef," is the name of the cattle made famous by Kobe beef, the most expensive beef in the world. The meat is extremely tender and beautifully marbled, and is a chef's dream to cook. For centuries, this beef was available only in Japan, but much to my delight, in recent years it has been raised in the United States. The name "Kobe" comes from the city in Japan where the cattle were first bred more than 170 years ago. In 1976, two pairs of Japanese cattle, two Tottori Black Wagyu and two Kumamoto Red Wagyu bulls, were imported to the United States. The resulting breed now has a stronghold in Texas, represented by the Texas Wagyu Association.

Prime Rib Roast *with* Natural Jus *and* Fresh Horseradish Cream   SERVES 4

Is there anything better than a Sunday supper with a big juicy prime rib roast at the center of the table? I don't think so, nor do most Texans. Although cattle ranching throughout the state has been sorely tested during the past few years of drought, we remain committed beef eaters. This is a classic Sunday-supper dish with a real good dose of Texas barbecue spice.

One 4-rib prime beef rib roast

Salt

Freshly ground pepper

¼ cup Fearing's Barbecue Spice Blend (page 39)

2 garlic cloves, sliced

½ cup roughly chopped onion

½ cup roughly chopped celery

½ cup roughly chopped carrot

1 tablespoon chopped fresh thyme

2 cups beef stock or nonfat, low-sodium beef broth

1 tablespoon cornstarch dissolved in 1 tablespoon cold water

1 cup Horseradish Cream Sauce (page 28)

Preheat the oven to 450°F.

Generously season the beef with salt, pepper, and the spice blend.

Place the seasoned roast, fat side up and bone side down, in a roasting pan that is slightly larger than the roast. Transfer to the preheated oven and roast for 15 minutes.

Reduce the oven temperature to 325°F. To assess the total cooking time, allow 13 to 15 minutes per pound for rare and 15 to 17 minutes per pound for medium rare. The actual cooking time will depend on the shape of the roast and your particular oven. A flatter roast will cook more quickly than a thicker one. Use an instant-read meat thermometer to gauge the correct internal temperature:

115°F to 120°F for rare or 125°F to 130°F for medium. Begin checking the internal temperature about 30 minutes before you expect the meat to be done. For example, a 10-pound roast should take about 2½ hours, so you would begin checking after 2 hours of roasting.

Remove from the oven and allow the roast to rest for 15 minutes before carving into 4 equal portions.

While the meat is resting, prepare the natural jus. Pour the pan juices from the roasting pan through a fine-mesh sieve into a clean container, leaving about 2 tablespoons in the pan. Reserve the strained juices.

Place the roasting pan on the stovetop over medium heat. Add the garlic, onion, celery, carrot, and thyme and cook, stirring constantly, for about 5 minutes, scraping up all the browned bits on the bottom of the pan.

Add the stock along with the reserved pan juices and bring to a boil. Boil for about 5 minutes, or until reduced by half.

Whisking constantly, add the cornstarch mixture to the boiling liquid. Cook, whisking, for a couple of minutes, just to cook the starch taste out. A natural jus should not be as thick as a gravy or sauce so, if necessary, add a bit more water to achieve the proper consistency. Season to taste with salt and pepper and remove from the heat.

The meat can be carved away from the bones in one solid piece and then cut into individual ½-inch-thick slices, or cut down next to the bone to make individual servings including the rib bone (see Note). Serve with the jus spooned over the meat and a generous dollop of the horseradish cream alongside.

NOTE: For ease of carving, ask your butcher to cut the bones away from the roast and then tie them back onto the roast with butchers' twine. Follow the steps above for roasting. This will make it much easier to carve the roast into equal bone-free slices, while still allowing you to stand the roast on the rib bones while cooking.

BARBECUE SPICED BEEF TENDERLOIN SERVES 4

This simple preparation stars in my Texas Surf and Turf (page 141), but it also is a great stand-alone steak, which can be served with a great side of Roasted Asparagus with Smoked Texas Pecans (page 209). Beef tenderloin is such a tender, mild-flavored meat that it needs a little spice to accent the tenderness. My spice blend does the job and then some! It's a terrific mix to keep in your pantry to accent plain grilled meats and poultry.

Four 5-ounce beef tenderloin medallions

¼ cup Fearing's Barbecue Spice Blend (page 39)

Salt

Freshly ground pepper

1 tablespoon olive oil

Season the beef with the spice blend and salt and pepper.

Heat the oil in a large frying pan over medium-high heat. When very hot, but not smoking, add the meat and sear for about 4 minutes, or until nicely charred. Turn and continue to sear for an additional 4 minutes on the opposite sides, or until both sides are charred and the meat is medium rare: 130°F on an instant-read thermometer.

Remove the beef from the pan and let rest for 5 minutes before serving.

GRILLED LAMB CHOPS *with* BAKED CHUCK WAGON BLACK BEANS *and* SWEET POTATO RAJAS SERVES 4

Although not much lamb can be found on Texas ranches, Texans sure do love it. I always add a hint of heat and some tradition to the plate. In this recipe, some chuck wagon beans do the trick. If you don't have the urge to make the beans and rajas, you can just grill the chops with the barbecue spice to take you to the chuck wagon table.

½ cup Fearing's Barbecue Spice Blend (page 39)

Two 8-ounce (see Note) 8-rib racks of lamb, trimmed of all fat and silverskin, and cut in half; remove all but one end-bone

Salt

Baked Chuck Wagon Black Beans (page 194)

Sweet Potato Rajas (page 205)

Preheat and generously oil the grill, taking care that the grate is very clean.

Place the spice mix in a large shallow bowl and dredge each chop in it, making sure that the chops are well coated. Season with salt.

Place the chops on the hot grill and grill for 3 minutes, or just until one side is nicely charred with grill marks. Turn the chops and grill on the opposite sides for 2 minutes more, or until cooked to medium rare. (If you like, add some wet wood chips to the fire to add a hint of smokiness to the meat.)

Remove from the grill and place 4 chops on each of four warm dinner plates, crisscrossing each pair of rib bones pointing toward the inside of the plate. Spoon the beans and the rajas in back of the chops and serve immediately.

NOTE: A rack of lamb is the complete section of one-half of the ribs, usually comprised of 7 to 8 ribs. It can be fabricated or cooked a number of ways: grilled or roasted whole racks or cut into various-sized single or 2-bone chops. A "frenched" rack is one from which all meat and fat have been scraped from the long bone "handle" of the rib. Frenched racks are available, vacuum-sealed, from many supermarkets or freshly cut from quality butchers.

Maple-Black Peppercorn Buffalo Tenderloin *on* Jalapeño Grits *and* Crispy Butternut Squash Taquitos

SERVES 4

This is a pretty fancy dish with lots of Texas cowboy-style flavors that takes some doing to put together. However, you can just as easily serve the meat (even exchange the buffalo meat for a Texas beef) without some or even all of the accompaniments. The maple glaze adds not only great flavor, but also a subtle hint of tenderness.

All parts of the dish are great on their own, and the taquitos are particularly good as a snack or a treat with a bottle of Lone Star beer. If you choose to make only one of the components, try the grits—they are a perfect match to the sweet-spicy meat.

1 cup pure maple syrup

2 garlic cloves, finely chopped

1 large shallot, finely chopped

2 tablespoons freshly cracked black pepper

1 teaspoon finely chopped fresh sage leaves

1 teaspoon finely chopped fresh thyme

Crushed red pepper flakes

One 24-ounce buffalo tenderloin, trimmed of all fat and silverskin

Salt

Freshly ground black pepper

2 tablespoons vegetable oil

Jalapeño Grits (page 200)

Tangle of Greens (page 206)

4 Butternut Squash Taquitos (recipe follows) (optional)

Yellow Tomato Pico de Gallo (page 31)

Smoked Chile Aioli (page 35)

4 fresh cilantro sprigs

Combine the maple syrup with the garlic, shallot, cracked black pepper, sage, thyme, and red pepper flakes in a large resealable plastic bag. Seal the bag and squeeze to mix.

Open the bag and add the buffalo. Again, seal and squeeze to coat the meat well. Place in the refrigerator and marinate, turning every 2 hours, for 8 hours or overnight.

Remove the tenderloin from the bag and, using a sharp knife, cut it crosswise into four 6-ounce steaks. Season with salt and black pepper.

Heat the oil in a large cast-iron skillet over medium-high heat. When very hot, but not smoking, add the steaks. Sear for 4 minutes; then turn and sear on the opposite sides for an additional 3 minutes for medium rare. Remove from the pan and let rest for a couple of minutes.

Spoon an equal portion of the grits into the center of each of four warm dinner plates.

Using a sharp chef's knife, cut each steak crosswise on the diagonal, through the middle. Crisscross the meat over the grits. Place an equal portion of the greens next to the meat on the side of each plate. Lay a taquito, if using, between the steak and the greens. Sprinkle with the pico de gallo and spoon a pool of the aioli toward the front of the plate. Garnish the top with a cilantro sprig and serve.

BUTTERNUT SQUASH TAQUITOS

3 teaspoons vegetable oil, plus 2 cups for frying

1 pound butternut squash, cut in half lengthwise and seeded

Salt

Freshly ground pepper

2 fresh rosemary sprigs

1 tablespoon minced shallot

½ tablespoon minced garlic

½ cup Cotija cheese

8 corn tortillas, warmed

Preheat the oven to 350°F.

Using 2 teaspoons of the vegetable oil, rub each cut side of the squash. Season with salt and pepper to taste and place a sprig of rosemary in each cavity. Place the squash, cut side down, on a rimmed baking sheet. Transfer to the preheated oven and roast for about 45 minutes, or until tender when pierced with the point of a small, sharp knife. Remove from the oven and set aside to cool.

When the squash is cool enough to handle, scoop the pulp from the skin using a large soup spoon.

Put the pulp in a food processor fitted with the metal blade and process, using 3 to 4 quick on-and-off turns, or until evenly chopped. Scrape the squash into a medium bowl and set aside.

Heat the 2 cups vegetable oil in a deep-fat fryer over high heat until it registers 350°F on a candy thermometer.

Heat the remaining 1 teaspoon oil in a medium frying pan over medium-high heat. Add the shallot and garlic and sauté for about 2 minutes, or just until the aromatics have sweat some of their liquid. Remove from the heat and scrape into the reserved squash along with the cheese.

Place about 2 tablespoons of the squash mixture in the center of each warm tortilla and roll up, cigar-fashion. Skewer closed with a toothpick so that the taquito will stay closed when fried. Set aside. The taquitos may be made early in the day and fried just before serving.

When the oil has reached the desired temperature, add the taquitos and fry for about 4 minutes, or until golden brown and crisp.

Remove from the heat and transfer to a double layer of paper towels to drain. Serve warm.

South Texas Nilgai Antelope *with* Cactus Pear Glaze, Chile-Braised Rabbit Enchiladas, Jicama-Carrot Salad, *and* Two Chile Sauces

SERVES 4

You can use any steak you like for this recipe, but in Texas we love the nilgai antelope from the Broken Arrow Ranch in Ingram, Texas. This is a very ornate recipe combining many favorite Texas flavors and foods. However, there is nothing wrong in grilling up the steaks on their own. Just don't forget the glaze—it absolutely gives the Texas stamp to the dish. If you don't serve the enchiladas along with the antelope, you will miss both the red and the green chile sauces.

2 cups cactus pear juice (see Note)

1 tablespoon dark rum

1 teaspoon peeled and grated fresh ginger

1 tablespoon cornstarch dissolved in 1 tablespoon cold water

1 tablespoon pure maple syrup

Fresh lime juice

Sea salt

Four 6-ounce antelope sirloin (or any steak), trimmed of all fat and silverskin

2 tablespoons Fearing's Garlic Salt (page 41)

Freshly ground pepper

Chile-Braised Rabbit Enchiladas with Roasted Green Chile Sauce (page 170) (optional)

Jicama-Carrot Slaw (page 101) (optional)

2 tablespoons crumbled Cotija cheese

4 fresh cilantro sprigs, for garnish (optional)

Combine the cactus pear juice, rum, and ginger in a small saucepan over medium-high heat and bring to a boil. Immediately lower the heat and simmer for 15 minutes, or until reduced by half.

Whisking constantly, add the cornstarch mixture in a slow, steady stream. Continue to simmer for 5 minutes, or until thickened.

Remove from the heat and whisk in the maple syrup. Season to taste with lime juice and salt and set aside.

Preheat the grill, taking care that the grates are very clean and heavily brushed with oil.

Generously season the antelope with the garlic salt and pepper. Place on the hot grill and grill for 3 minutes, or just long enough to mark the meat. Turn and grill on the opposite sides for about 2 minutes, or until the remaining sides are marked and the steaks are rare: 130°F to 135°F on an instant-read thermometer.

Using a pastry brush, generously coat both sides of the steaks with the reserved glaze, and grill, turning once, for an additional minute, or just long enough to set the glaze. Remove from the grill.

If serving with the enchiladas, spoon a pool of their red chile cooking sauce in the center of each of four warm dinner plates. Place a steak in the center of each pool of sauce. Again, if using, place 2 enchiladas along with their green sauce on one side, top with the slaw, and garnish with a nice sprinkle of cheese and a sprig of cilantro.

If not serving with the enchiladas, simply nestle an equal portion of the slaw next to the steaks on each plate. Garnish with a sprig of cilantro, but eliminate the sprinkle of cheese.

NOTE: Cactus pear juice is juice extracted from the fruit of the paddle cactus and is available from Hispanic markets, at some specialty food stores, and online. Paddle cactus, also known as nopales, provides a vegetable dish also called nopales in Mexican and Tex-Mex cooking. Nopales are the young tender paddles that are usually harvested in the spring to use in pickles or are eaten cooked, with eggs, in fillings for tortillas, or as a vegetable side dish.

South Texas Antelope

Nilgai, or South Texas antelope, originated in India and Nepal and were introduced into Texas in the 1930s on the famous King Ranch. They are large animals that thrive in the semi-arid inland areas of South Texas. The name nilgai means "blue bull" in certain East Indian dialects, and the antelope is sometimes referred to as "blue deer." These are real wild antelope, not those that are pen-raised. The meat is mild-flavored, richly textured, and very lean. Low-calorie and low-fat equal excellent health benefits.

JALAPEÑO VENISON SAUSAGE
on CAMPFIRE BARBECUE BEANS   MAKES 12 PATTIES

This is one of my favorite family-style dishes. I like to serve it on platters in the center of the table with Sweet Potato Spoonbread (page 206) on the side. All the components can be made ahead of time, so the complete dish is a perfect one for entertaining, Texas-style. Venison backstrap is the filet mignon of the deer, but it can easily be replaced with lean pork, turkey, or chicken. If you have a sausage-making attachment for your stand mixer, use it to both grind the meat and stuff the sausage into links.

2 pounds boneless venison backstrap, cleaned of all fat and silverskin and cut into ½-inch cubes (or lean pork, turkey, or chicken)

1 pound pork belly, skinned and cut into ½-inch cubes

2 tablespoons seeded and minced jalapeño chiles

1 tablespoon minced shallot

2 teaspoons salt

1 teaspoon minced garlic

1 teaspoon ground cumin

1 teaspoon ground coriander

1 teaspoon ground fennel seed

1 teaspoon crushed red pepper flakes

1 teaspoon Fearing's Barbecue Spice Blend (page 39)

1 teaspoon smoked paprika

1 teaspoon freshly ground black pepper

2 cups grated smoked cheddar cheese

2 cups cornmeal

1 cup vegetable oil

4 cups **Campfire Barbecue Beans** (page 193)

Combine the venison and pork belly in a large bowl. Add 1 tablespoon of the jalapeño along with the shallot, salt, garlic, cumin, coriander, fennel, red pepper flakes, spice mix, paprika, and black pepper and stir to blend very well. Cover lightly and transfer to the freezer.

Freeze for about 1 hour, or just until partially frozen.

Prepare a meat grinder, fitting it with the fine grinding plate. Remove the meat mixture from the freezer and begin to slowly feed it through the grinder into a large clean bowl.

When all of the meat has been ground, stir in the remaining 1 tablespoon jalapeño along with the cheese and mix until thoroughly blended.

Using wet hands, form the sausage into 12 patties of equal size.

Place the cornmeal in a large shallow bowl. Working with one at a time, dredge each patty in the cornmeal. (The sausage may be made up to this point and stored, tightly wrapped and refrigerated, for 1 day or frozen for up to 3 months. Thaw before using.)

Heat the oil in a large cast-iron skillet over medium-high heat. Add the sausage patties without crowding the pan. Fry for about 3 minutes, turn, and fry the remaining sides for 3 minutes, or until nicely browned. Transfer the sausage to a platter and serve immediately along with the beans.

BARBECUED VENISON FAJITAS   MAKES 4 FAJITAS

Fajitas in all forms are a big Texas favorite. Although the meat of choice is usually skirt steak, I like to use venison, as we have so many hunters in Texas who enjoy it. In fact, hunters come from all over the world to engage in the sport on game ranches all over the state. But if you don't have venison on hand, use any other meat you like. The fajitas will still be tasty.

1½ teaspoons olive oil

1 poblano chile, stemmed, seeded, and cut lengthwise into thin strips

1 medium red onion, peeled and cut lengthwise into thin strips

½ pound venison loin, trimmed of all fat and silverskin, cut into thin strips

Salt

Freshly ground pepper

½ cup Texas-Style Barbecue Sauce (page 19) or your favorite barbecue sauce

¼ cup grated jalapeño Jack cheese

Four 6-inch corn tortillas, warmed

Heat the oil in a medium frying pan over medium-high heat. Add the poblano and onion and sauté for 1 minute. Add the venison and season with salt and pepper. Continue cooking for another minute or so, or just until the meat is barely cooked and the onion is still crunchy.

Stir in the barbecue sauce and remove from the heat. Immediately add the cheese and stir to incorporate.

Transfer the venison mixture to a bowl. Serve with a stack of warm tortillas to fill with venison.

A word about these fajitas: Although they really are the "icing on the cake," I particularly like these fajitas when they are used as a side garnish to one of my favorite dishes, Pork Tenderloin with Watermelon-Jalapeño Glaze on Yellow Tomato–Pozole Stew (page 113). It is a true Texas treat.

Fajitas

Although not an absolute certainty, it is thought that fajitas began as a meal for Mexican cowboys (*vaqueros* in Spanish) working on cattle roundups in South and West Texas in the early 1900s. During roundups, cattle were slaughtered to feed the crews, and the least desirable meat, such as the skirt (now known as the not-inexpensive skirt steak), was handed off to the vaqueros. They, in turn, grilled it over an open campfire, cut it into strips (*fajas* in Spanish), and probably wrapped the succulent meat in tortillas. It is also thought that the first commercial fajita was sold in Kyle, Texas, in 1969, but there are also those who think that the locale was Georgetown, Texas. Whatever the history, it is clear that fajitas are a Texas invention. But you can now find every possible combination of meats, fish, and poultry served on a sizzling platter along with guacamole, pico de gallo, sour cream, chiles, fried onions, and peppers in restaurants all across the world.

GRILLED BARBECUE CHICKEN BREASTS
with WATERMELON PICO DE GALLO   SERVES 4

This is a simple barbecue—low-fat, low-calorie, and simply delicious. When those big, fat, juicy Texas watermelons aren't stacked up at the farm stand, use any other pico de gallo you like to accent the tender chicken.

4 boneless, skinless chicken breast halves

2 tablespoons peanut oil

Salt

Freshly ground pepper

**1 cup Smoky Bacon Barbecue Sauce (page 20)
    or your favorite barbecue sauce**

Watermelon Pico de Gallo (page 31)

Preheat the grill, taking care that the grates are very clean and brushed with oil.

Using a pastry brush, lightly coat the chicken with peanut oil. Season with salt and pepper.

Lay the breasts on the hot grill and grill for 5 minutes, frequently basting with the barbecue sauce. Turn and grill the opposite sides, basting frequently, for another 5 minutes, or until the juices run clear when the meat is pricked with the point of a sharp knife.

Serve hot or at room temperature with the pico de gallo on the side.

Granny Fearing's Paper Bag-Shook Fried Chicken   SERVES 4 TO 6

This is my granny's recipe, and I can still see her shaking a big ole brown paper bag with the A&P logo on the side. I find it a little easier and neater to use a resealable plastic bag, but feel free to paper-bag it if you wish. I have been eating and serving this chicken for Sunday dinner my entire life, and once you taste it, I guarantee it will become a lifetime favorite for you, too.

I always serve it family-style with a big bowl of "Loaded" Mashed Potatoes (page 202), a boat of Smoked Tomato Gravy (page 27), and All-Day Green Beans (page 208), but find your family favorites to make Granny's chicken your own Sunday supper.

6 cups apple juice

2 cups plus 1 tablespoon salt

One 1-inch piece peeled and thinly
    sliced fresh ginger

1½ quarts ice

2 fryer chickens, well washed and cut into
    8 pieces (2 each breast, thigh, leg, wing)

4 cups all-purpose flour

½ cup Fearing's Barbecue Spice Blend (page 39)

1 tablespoon freshly ground pepper

2 cups vegetable oil

"Loaded" Mashed Potatoes, for
    serving (page 202) (optional)

Smoked Tomato Gravy, for serving
    (page 27) (optional)

All-Day Green Beans, for serving
    (page 208) (optional)

Combine the apple juice with the 2 cups of salt in a large saucepan over medium-high heat. Add the ginger and bring to a boil. Immediately remove from the heat and add the ice.

When the ice has melted and the brine has cooled, transfer it to a container large enough to hold all of the chicken and still fit in the refrigerator. Add the chicken, making sure that all of the pieces are submerged in the brine. (This can also be done in an extra-large resealable plastic bag.)

Transfer the chicken to the refrigerator and marinate for 24 hours.

Preheat the oven to 300°F.

Combine the flour with the spice blend and pepper along with the remaining 1 tablespoon salt in a resealable plastic bag and shake to blend well.

Fill a large cast-iron skillet with oil to the depth of ½ inch. Heat the oil over medium heat until it registers 300°F on a candy thermometer.

Remove the chicken from the refrigerator. Lift from the brine, shaking off any excess liquid.

Working with a few pieces at a time, dredge the chicken in the flour mixture, seal the bag, and toss to coat well.

Place the chicken, skin side down, in the hot oil. Cook the chicken in batches (or in 2 skillets) to avoid crowding the pan.

Fry, turning occasionally, for about 20 minutes, or until crisp, golden brown and cooked through. Continue frying until all of the chicken has been cooked. Remember that since each piece of chicken is a different size, each one will require a different cooking time.

Transfer the chicken pieces, as fried, to a large rimmed baking sheet. When all of the chicken has been fried, transfer it to the preheated oven and bake for 10 minutes.

Remove from the oven and transfer to a large platter. Serve immediately with a big dish of the mashed potatoes, a boat of the gravy, and green beans, just like I do.

ERIC'S RANCH CHICKEN ENCHILADA CASSEROLE *with* ROASTED GREEN CHILE SAUCE SERVES 6

Made famous by the cooks at the King Ranch (one of South Texas' most historically significant ranches), some version of this casserole can be found in almost any home kitchen across Texas. From oil baron to stay-at-home mom, each Texan has a favorite version. This version comes from Eric Dreyer, the chef de cuisine at Fearing's, a good ole Texas boy.

To speed the making of this recipe, don't hesitate to use prepared rotisserie chicken. Just be sure to remove all the skin and to pull the meat off in shreds.

2 teaspoons vegetable oil, plus
    more for oiling the pan

1 cup julienned onion

2 pounds shredded cooked chicken

1 pound jalapeño Jack cheese, grated

2 cups sour cream

½ cup roasted, stemmed, peeled, seeded,
    and julienned poblano chile

½ cup **Charred Tomato Salsa (page 32)**

1 tablespoon **Fearing's Barbecue Spice Blend
    (page 39)** or a favorite chile powder

Salt

Freshly ground pepper

6 corn tortillas, warmed

3 cups **Roasted Green Chile Sauce (page 24)**

¼ cup finely chopped fresh cilantro

Preheat the oven to 350°F.

Lightly oil a 9 by 13-inch baking pan. Set aside.

Heat the oil in a medium frying pan over medium heat. Add the onion and fry, stirring frequently, for about 7 minutes, or until well caramelized. Remove from the heat and set aside to cool.

Place the chicken in a large bowl. Add half the cheese along with the sour cream, chile, salsa, spice blend, and reserved cooled onions and fold together to evenly combine. Season to taste with salt and pepper.

Working with one at a time, place an equal portion of the chicken mixture in the center of each of the 6 warm tortillas and roll the tortilla up and around the chicken to make a neat package. Place, tightly packed, in the prepared baking pan, seam side down.

Spoon the green chile sauce over the top and evenly coat with the remaining cheese. Transfer to the preheated oven and bake for 20 minutes, or until bubbling.

Remove from the oven, sprinkle with cilantro, and serve immediately.

NOTE: If you want to make shredded chicken from scratch, here's what you do: Place a big fat chicken in a large pot with a cup of chopped onions and about ½ cup each of chopped carrots and celery. Add some herb stems and cold water to cover by at least 2 inches and bring to a boil over high heat. Lower the heat to a gentle simmer. Simmer for about 45 minutes, or until the chicken is beginning to fall off the bone. Remove from the heat and transfer the chicken to a platter to cool. Strain the cooking liquid through a fine-mesh sieve and cool it down in an ice-water bath. You now have a good amount of chicken stock for a rainy day. When the chicken is cool enough to handle, remove the skin and pull the meat off in shreds.

Pan-Roasted Gulf Snapper on Lump Crabmeat–Sweet Corn Cream Succotash with Smoked-Bacon Gastrique and Sweet Potato Ribbons SERVES 4

Although I use Gulf snapper in this recipe, you can use almost any sweetly flavored, firm-fleshed fish. Because Gulf red snapper is becoming increasingly difficult to get due to overfishing and, thus, stronger restrictions, a large percentage of fish labeled "red snapper" is actually blackfin snapper or Pacific rockfish Gulf snapper. If you have concerns, check the eyes: a red snapper has bright red irises.

Four 7-ounce red snapper fillets

¼ cup Fearing's Barbecue Spice Blend (page 39)

Salt

Freshly ground pepper

2 tablespoons vegetable oil

Sweet Corn Cream Succotash (page 196)

6 ounces jumbo lump Gulf crabmeat

½ cup Smoked-Bacon Gastrique (page 29)

Sweet Potato Ribbons, for serving
   (recipe follows) (optional)

Preheat the oven to 350°F.

Generously season the fish with the spice blend, salt, and pepper.

Heat the oil in a large frying pan over medium-high heat. Add the fish, flesh side down, and cook for 4 minutes, or until golden brown. Turn and transfer to a rimmed baking sheet and into the preheated oven.

Roast for 5 minutes. Remove from the oven, but keep warm.

Place the succotash in a large saucepan over medium heat. Cook for just a couple of minutes to warm. Fold in the crabmeat. Taste and, if necessary, season with salt and pepper.

Spoon an equal portion of the succotash into the center of each of four warm dinner plates. Place a fillet on top and drizzle the gastrique around the edge to create a tight circle. If using, scatter some Sweet Potato Ribbons over the fish and serve.

SWEET POTATO RIBBONS

I like to garnish dishes with what I call Sweet Potato Ribbons. They are easy to make and add elegance to the plate.

1 large sweet potato, peeled

Vegetable oil, for frying

Using a vegetable peeler, peel off "ribbons" of the potato into a bowl of ice water.

Heat oil in a deep-fat fryer until it registers 225°F on a candy thermometer.

Working with a few ribbons at a time, pat them very dry with paper towels. Drop the ribbons into the hot oil and fry for a couple of minutes, or until bright orange and crisp. Watch them carefully as they fry or they will quickly burn to a dark brown.

Using a slotted spoon, transfer the ribbons to a double layer of paper towels to drain.

SMOKED PECAN-CRUSTED GROUPER on LOBSTER-SWEET CORN GRAVY with CRISPY TABASCO OYSTERS   SERVES 4

Due to overfishing, there is not as much Gulf grouper available as there once was. However, management policies are making good inroads into bringing the fish back. Anglers from all over flood the Texas Gulf region in the late fall to catch the few weeks that fishing for grouper is allowed. In this recipe, I combine the sweet grouper with even sweeter lobster-corn gravy and then highlight the sweetness with crisp and spicy oysters.

- 4 tablespoons olive oil
- 1 cup small-dice onion
- 2½ cups fresh corn kernels (or thawed frozen)
- 1 teaspoon chopped fresh thyme
- 2 cups chicken stock or nonfat, low-sodium chicken broth
- ¼ cup heavy cream
- Fresh lemon juice
- Salt
- ½ cup diced cooked smoked bacon
- ¼ cup crumbled cooked breakfast sausage
- ¼ cup diced roasted poblano chile
- 1 tablespoon seeded and minced jalapeño chile
- 1 teaspoon minced garlic
- Four 6-ounce Gulf grouper fillets, trimmed of skin and bones
- Freshly ground pepper
- ½ cup Roasted Garlic Mayonnaise (page 33)
- ¾ cup cold-smoked pecan pieces (see sidebar at right)
- 1 cup large-dice cooked lobster meat
- Crispy Tabasco Oysters (recipe follows)

Heat 1 tablespoon of the olive oil in a large saucepan over medium-high heat. Add the onion and cook, stirring, for 1 minute. Stir in 2 cups of the corn kernels and the thyme and sauté for 2 minutes more.

Add the stock and bring to a boil. Immediately add the cream and reduce the heat to a simmer. Cook for 20 minutes, or until the corn is very tender and the liquid has thickened.

Remove from the heat and pour into a blender. Process to a smooth puree. Season with lemon juice and salt and set aside.

Heat 1 tablespoon of the remaining oil in a large frying pan over medium-high heat. Add the bacon, sausage, poblano, jalapeño, and garlic and cook, stirring occasionally, for 2 minutes.

Stir in the remaining ½ cup of corn and bring to a boil. Remove from the heat and keep warm.

Preheat the oven to 350°F.

Season the grouper with salt and pepper.

Heat the 2 remaining tablespoons of oil in a large ovenproof skillet over medium heat. Carefully lay the fish in the hot pan, flesh side down. Sear for 1 minute. Turn and sear the opposite sides for an additional minute.

Using a pastry brush, generously coat the top of each fillet with the mayonnaise. Sprinkle a thick layer of the pecans over the mayonnaise on each fillet.

Transfer the pan to the preheated oven and roast for 4 minutes per each ½ inch of thickness (measuring from the thickest section). Do not overcook, as the fish should still be very moist. Remove from the oven and keep warm.

Return the corn gravy to medium heat, fold in the lobster, and cook, stirring occasionally, for about 3 minutes, or just until the lobster is hot.

Spoon an equal portion of the gravy into the center of each of four warm dinner plates. Place a grouper fillet in the center of the gravy and then place 3 oysters on top of the fish. Serve immediately.

About Cold-Smoked Pecans

Following the instructions for cold smoking on page 177, you will need to smoke the pecans for 10 or 15 minutes. When you do, make a batch. They are an addictive snack but also add subtle flavor to all sorts of dishes, from salads to soups to desserts.

CRISPY TABASCO OYSTERS

MAKES 12 OYSTERS

12 large shucked and drained Gulf or other high-quality oysters

2 tablespoons Tabasco Chipotle sauce

1 cup buttermilk

4 cups all-purpose flour

¼ cup Fearing's Barbecue Spice Blend (page 39)

Vegetable oil, for frying

Salt

Combine the oysters and Tabasco in a small bowl and toss gently to coat well. Cover and refrigerate for 1 hour.

Remove the oysters from the refrigerator. Uncover, add the buttermilk, and stir to blend.

Combine the flour and spice blend in a medium bowl.

Heat the oil in a deep-fat fryer over medium-high heat until it registers 350°F on a candy thermometer.

Working with a few at a time, lift the oysters from the buttermilk mixture and dredge completely in the flour mixture.

When the oil has reached the desired temperature, quickly, but carefully, drop the oysters into the hot oil and fry for about 2 minutes, or until golden brown and crisp.

Using a slotted spoon, transfer to a double layer of paper towels to drain. Season with salt and serve hot.

CAST-IRON SKILLET CATFISH *with* EAST TEXAS SEAFOOD JAMBALAYA *and* CRISPY TEXAS OKRA

SERVES 4

Catfish are found in every body of water throughout Texas, and hooking them is the most popular sportfishing expedition. Blue, channel, and flathead catfish, ranging in size from just a pound or two to trophy fish well over one hundred pounds, are not only great sport, but terrific eating. In this dish, we combine the familiar but delicious catfish with two other traditional Texas dishes, Gulf jambalaya and country okra.

Four 6-ounce boneless, skinless catfish fillets

Salt

Freshly ground pepper

1 cup yellow cornmeal

¼ cup all-purpose flour

1 tablespoon Fearing's Barbecue
    Spice Blend (page 39)

1 cup vegetable oil

2 cups hot East Texas Seafood
    Jambalaya (page 162)

16 to 20 pieces Crispy Texas Okra (page 207)

Season both sides of the fish with salt and pepper.

Combine the cornmeal, flour, and spice blend in a large shallow bowl.

Place the seasoned catfish in the cornmeal mixture and turn to coat evenly. Press the fish into the mix to make sure the coating adheres.

Heat the oil in a large cast-iron skillet over medium heat until it registers 350°F on a candy thermometer. Add the catfish in a single layer without crowding the pan. Fry for 3 minutes and then turn and fry on the opposite sides for an additional 3 minutes, or until the fish is golden brown and cooked through.

Using a slotted spatula, transfer to a double layer of paper towels to drain.

Spoon about ½ cup of the jambalaya into the center of each of four warm dinner plates. Place a catfish fillet on top of each serving and tuck 4 to 5 pieces of the okra beside the fish. Serve immediately.

Texas Surf *and* Turf: Chicken-Fried Lobster *and* Barbecue Spiced Beef Tenderloin *on* "Loaded" Whipped Potatoes, *and* Spinach Enchilada *with* Smoked Tomato Gravy SERVES 4

Holy Moly! That's my favorite expression to say "WOW!" This is truly a Texas "Wow" recipe. Steak, lobster, potatoes, enchiladas, smoked tomatoes, pickled onions—could you want anything more? I know it sounds like a lot, but I'm telling you, if you do it all, you are going to be serving one unforgettable Texas-size meal—and, come on, who doesn't love a good surf-and-turf dinner?

Four 5-ounce lobster tails, cut in half lengthwise

1 cup buttermilk

2 cups all-purpose flour

¼ cup Fearing's Barbecue Spice Blend (page 39)

Salt

Freshly ground pepper

Vegetable oil, for frying

2 cups "Loaded" Mashed Potatoes (page 202)

4 Spinach Enchiladas (page 154)

1 cup Smoked Tomato Gravy (page 27)

Barbecue Spiced Beef Tenderloin (page 121)

½ cup Pickled Red Onions (page 43)

Place the lobster tail halves in a medium bowl. Add the buttermilk and toss to coat. Transfer to the refrigerator and let marinate for 30 minutes.

Combine the flour, spice blend, salt, and pepper in a medium bowl and stir to blend well.

Heat the oil in a deep-fat fryer over medium-high heat until it registers 350°F on a candy thermometer.

Remove the lobster from the refrigerator. Working with one piece at a time, lift the lobster from the buttermilk, shaking off excess liquid. Press the marinated lobster into the flour mixture, taking care that all sides are well coated.

Transfer the lobster to the hot oil and fry for 3 minutes, or until golden brown. Carefully transfer to a double layer of paper towels to drain. Season with salt.

Spoon ½ cup of the potatoes into the center of each of four warm dinner plates. Place an enchilada at one side and then spoon an equal portion of the gravy over each enchilada. Place a tenderloin medallion on top of the potatoes and tuck 2 lobster tail halves next to the beef. Place a small mound of the onions between the beef and the enchilada and serve.

COWBOY SHRIMP ON JALAPEÑO GRITS SERVES 4

Here you have my version of the Southern classic shrimp and grits with a little Texas jump start. Even if you don't live on the Gulf, this dish will transport you there. Of course, you can use any shrimp; we're just partial to ours. The sauce is spilling over with deep-in-the-heart-of-Texas flavor—a little heat, a little sweet, and a little spice. Piled on a mess o' grits, you've got one perfect meal.

Texas Shrimp

Texas shrimp are caught wild out in the deep waters of the Gulf, and nothing can compare to their sweet flavor. The two main commercial species harvested from the Gulf of Mexico and South Atlantic Ocean are typed by color. White shrimp are the most predominant catch and are the standard by which all other shrimp are measured. They are very sweet and firm-textured and can grow to about 8 inches in length. The bulk of the annual harvest comes directly from the Gulf. Mostly concentrated in the waters off Texas and Louisiana, brown shrimp are somewhat smaller with firmer flesh. When cooked, both result in red shells with pinkish-white meat and have the same nutritional value and about the same flavor. Brown shrimp often have a slightly higher iodine flavor. In Texas, shrimping generates more than $800 million in sales and provides almost 15,000 jobs.

12 large (16–20 per pound) Gulf shrimp or other high-quality shrimp, peeled and deveined

Salt

3 tablespoons olive oil

¼ cup minced red onion

2 tablespoons minced garlic

2 tablespoons seeded and minced jalapeño chile

1 teaspoon ground cumin

2 cups Thickened Chicken Stock (page 29) or thickened nonfat, low-sodium chicken broth

¼ cup crumbled cooked bacon

¼ cup chopped tomato

2 tablespoons chopped fresh cilantro

Fresh lime juice

Tabasco sauce

2 cups Jalapeño Grits (page 200)

¼ cup crumbled Cotija cheese

Fresh cilantro sprigs, for garnish (optional)

Season the shrimp with salt. Set aside.

Heat the oil in a large heavy-bottomed saucepan over high heat. When very hot but not smoking, add the seasoned shrimp and sauté for 2 minutes. Stir in the onion, garlic, chile, and cumin and cook for another 2 minutes. Stir in the stock, bacon, tomato, and chopped cilantro and bring to a simmer. Simmer for about 3 minutes, or just until the shrimp are cooked through.

Remove from the heat and season with lime juice and Tabasco. Taste and, if necessary, season with salt.

Spoon about ½ cup of the grits into the center of each of four warm dinner plates. Place 3 shrimp on top of the grits on each plate. Spoon an equal portion of the shrimp cooking sauce over the top of the shrimp, and sprinkle each plate with a tablespoon of the cheese. Garnish with a cilantro sprig, if desired.

SHRIMP DIABLO "TAMALES" SERVES 4

Although this recipe has many of the components of a traditional tamale, it has a more contemporary look on the plate. The husks normally used to enclose the filling become little "boats" to hold it instead. The tails-up shrimp add an extra bit of fun to the design. However, the dish could also be made with almost any meat or fish cooked in the Diablo Sauce.

5 large dried corn husks (see sidebar at right)

4 ears fresh yellow corn, shucked and cleaned

1 teaspoon pure maple syrup (optional)

Fresh lime juice

Salt

1 tablespoon olive oil

16 large Gulf shrimp, peeled and
    deveined, with tails attached

Salt

Freshly ground pepper

1 cup Diablo Sauce (page 25)

2 flour tortillas, warmed

¼ cup crumbled Cotija cheese

¼ cup Pueblo dried corn (see Note) (optional)

2 tablespoons Pumpkin Seed
    Powder (page 40) (optional)

¼ cup Pico de Gallo (page 30)

About 3 hours before you are ready to cook, submerge the corn husks in hot water to cover and set aside to soak until very soft and flexible.

When ready to cook, drain and pat the husks dry. Beginning at one end, pull one of the husks into thin strips. Using 2 strips per husk, tie each end of each of the remaining husks closed. Pull each tied husk open to form a boat (see photo).

Using a box grater, grate the corn on the large holes until all of the pulp is extracted. In a cast-iron skillet over low heat, cook the corn, stirring, for about 7 minutes, or until it is thoroughly cooked and quite thick.

If the corn is not naturally sweet, add a bit of maple syrup. Season to taste with lime juice and salt. Set aside, but keep warm.

Heat the oil in a large heavy-bottomed skillet over medium-high heat. Add the shrimp in a single layer and season with salt and pepper. Sear for 1 minute; turn and sear the opposite sides for another minute.

Add the sauce and cook for about 3 minutes, or until the sauce thickens a bit and coats the shrimp. Remove from the heat.

Cut each tortilla in half and form each half into a cone shape. Set aside.

Spoon an equal portion of the corn puree into the center of each corn husk "boat," spreading it out to cover. Stand 4 shrimp, tails up, in the corn. Transfer one tamale to each of four warm dinner plates. Sprinkle each tamale with a tablespoon of the cheese and with equal portions of the dried corn and pumpkin seed powder, if using. Garnish each plate with a tablespoon of pico de gallo and a tortilla cone. Serve immediately.

NOTE: Pueblo dried corn, or dehydrated freeze-dried corn, is available from some Hispanic or specialty food markets or online.

Dried Corn Husks

In traditional Mexican cooking, dried corn husks are used to wrap tamales. They must be soaked for a few hours in either hot or cold water to become flexible enough to wrap around and enclose a filling. Traditionally a soaked husk is torn into strips for tying the ends of the filled husk together. In this recipe, I tie the ends of the husk together before filling and then pull the husk open to form a "boat" to hold the filling, creating an open tamale. Dried corn husks can be purchased from Latin markets, at specialty food stores and some supermarkets, or online.

"Chicken-Fried" Texas Quail
on Bourbon-Jalapeño Creamed Corn   SERVES 4

Texans love quail! If I hadn't been tartly informed that the mockingbird was the state's official bird, I would have put money on it being quail. Although tiny, the birds pack a wallop of flavor, somewhere between the mildness of chicken and the gaminess of a wild bird. Served on top of the rich creamed corn, this is an elegant but easy-to-prepare dish. To complete the restaurant main course, I always garnish the plate with a mound of Mango–Pickled Red Onion Salad (page 100). If you don't have time to make the salad, place a little bundle of watercress on the plate to add a touch of color. And if you can't find quail, you can use halved small Cornish game hens, which will take about 20 minutes to fry.

3 cups all-purpose flour

6 large eggs

1 cup buttermilk

½ cup Fearing's Barbecue Spice Blend (page 39) or your favorite barbecue spice blend

4 semiboneless quail, wings removed and cut in half lengthwise

2 cups safflower oil

Salt

Freshly ground pepper

Bourbon-Jalapeño Creamed Corn (page 197)

Mango–Pickled Red Onion Salad (page 100), for serving (optional)

Place 3 medium bowls in a line. Place 1½ cups of the flour in the first bowl. Whisk the eggs and buttermilk together in the second bowl. Then combine the remaining 1½ cups of flour with the spice blend in the third bowl, taking care that they are well blended.

Working with a half bird at a time, first dredge in the plain flour and shake off any excess. Then dip into the egg mixture to fully coat. Dredge each egg-battered quail half in the spiced flour mixture, pressing to coat evenly.

Heat the oil in a large cast-iron frying pan over medium-high heat. Add the quail, skin side down, and fry for 2 minutes, or until golden brown. Lower the heat, if necessary, to keep the birds from burning. Turn and fry the opposite sides for 2 minute more, or until just cooked through.

Transfer to a double layer of paper towels to drain. Season with salt and pepper.

Spoon an equal portion of the corn into the center of each of four warm dinner plates. Place 2 quail halves on top of the corn and serve with a mound of the salad, if using.

Hunting Quail

Bobwhite, the most common species of quail, is the premier game bird in Texas, where the perfect combination of field, weed, brush, and forest create the ideal habitat. Although there remains a wide expanse of this habitat in South Texas, most hunting is now done on game farms throughout the state. The birds are released just before the hunters go to the field, with trained dogs to flush the wary little creatures from the brush. This is because Texas has had such severe periods of drought that quail populations have sometimes failed to thrive due to the lack of rain. However, in good rainfall years, when flocks increase, hunters by the thousands can be found tracking the cagey birds in the wild.

Roasted Pheasant *with* Natural Gravy *on* Sweet Corn–Sage Pan Stuffing, Gun Barrel City Collard Greens, *and* Crispy Pheasant Tenders *with* Honey-Mustard Dressing   SERVES 4

This is Emeril Lagasse's favorite recipe. In fact, a version of it appeared on his television show from time to time. Whenever he is in town, he will always stop by to check if it is still on the menu. Besides Emeril, hunters from all over the state say this is their favorite dish also. Guess it will have to stay on my menu, and now on yours, if you want Emeril to stop by.

You don't have to make the tenders, but they sure are a terrific add-on. In the restaurant, we try to use every bit of the bird. The tenders make excellent use of the thigh meat.

Two 3-pound fresh pheasants (or chicken)

Salt

Freshly cracked pepper

1 tablespoon olive oil

Sweet Corn–Sage Pan Stuffing (page 199)

Gun Barrel City Collard Greens (page 207)

Natural Gravy (recipe follows)

Crispy Pheasant Tenders, for garnish
    (recipe follows) (optional)

Honey-Mustard Dressing (page 37) (optional)

Using a sharp knife, cut off the legs and thighs and trim the 2 smaller wing bones from each pheasant, leaving just the body with the large wing bones attached. Reserve the trimmings for use in the gravy.

Prepare a smoker for cold smoking (see page 177).

Place the pheasant bodies on a perforated pan. Transfer to the smoker and smoke for 20 minutes. (This is a good time to begin making the gravy.)

Preheat the oven to 400°F. Place a rack in a roasting pan. Set aside.

Season both the exterior and the cavity of the pheasant bodies with salt and pepper.

Heat the oil in a large frying pan over medium-high heat. Add the pheasant and sear, turning occasionally, for about 4 minutes, or until all sides are golden brown.

Transfer to the rack in the roasting pan and into the preheated oven. Roast for 10 minutes.

Remove from the oven and set aside to rest for 5 minutes.

Using a very sharp knife, carefully cut each breast half from the pheasant. The meat should be medium rare or rosy pink. Cut each breast crosswise, slightly on the diagonal, into ½-inch slices.

Spoon an equal portion of the stuffing and the greens into the center of each of four warm dinner plates. Place a breast on top of the stuffing, slightly fanning out the slices. Ladle a generous portion of the gravy over the meat. If using, garnish the plate with the pheasant tenders, and drizzle a bit of the dressing over the top of them, if desired. Serve immediately.

NATURAL GRAVY

MAKES 2 CUPS

Bones, legs, wing tips, and thighs from two 3-pound fresh pheasants (or chickens)

1 tablespoon olive oil

1 large onion, chopped

1 large carrot, trimmed, peeled, and chopped

1 celery stalk, trimmed and chopped

2 quarts chicken stock or nonfat, low-sodium chicken broth

2 fresh thyme sprigs

1 bay leaf

1 teaspoon peppercorns

2 tablespoons unsalted butter

2 tablespoons all-purpose flour

Fresh lemon juice

Salt

Freshly cracked pepper

Preheat the oven to 400°F.

Place the pheasant parts on a rimmed baking sheet. Transfer to the preheated oven and roast for about 10 minutes, or until golden brown.

Remove from the oven and set aside.

Heat the oil in a large stockpot over medium heat. Add the onion, carrot, and celery and sauté for 5 minutes, or until the onion is translucent. Stir in the reserved pheasant bones along with the chicken stock, thyme, bay leaf, and peppercorns. The liquid should cover the bones and vegetables completely. Bring to a boil; lower the heat and simmer, skimming off surface fat as necessary, for 1 hour.

Remove from the heat.

Place a fine-mesh sieve over a container large enough to hold the pheasant stock. Pour the stock through the sieve and discard the solids. Reserve the stock.

Melt the butter in a medium saucepan over medium heat. When completely melted, stir in the flour and cook, stirring constantly, for 4 minutes, or until the mixture begins to brown. This is a roux.

Whisking constantly, slowly add the reserved stock to the roux. When all the stock has been added, lower the heat and cook, stirring occasionally, for 20 minutes.

Remove from the heat and season to taste with lemon juice, salt, and pepper. Use as directed in the recipe.

CRISPY PHEASANT TENDERS

1 cup buttermilk

2 cups all-purpose flour

2 tablespoons Fearing's Barbecue Spice Blend (page 39)

4 boneless, skinless pheasant thighs, cut into long strips

2 quarts safflower oil, for frying

Salt

Place the buttermilk in a large shallow bowl. Combine the flour and spice blend in a separate large shallow bowl and set it next to the buttermilk.

Working with one piece at a time, dip the pheasant strips into the buttermilk and then into the flour mixture, taking care to coat them completely. Transfer the coated pheasant pieces to a rimmed baking sheet as they are coated.

Heat the oil in a deep-fat fryer over high heat until it registers 350°F on a candy thermometer. When all the pheasant has been coated and the oil has reached the desired temperature, fry the pheasant tenders, a few at a time, for 3 minutes, or until golden brown and cooked through.

Transfer to a double layer of paper towels to drain. Season with salt and serve.

MOLASSES-TABASCO DUCK *with* SMOKED VEGETABLE DRESSING *and* PEAR CHUTNEY   SERVES 4

One of the most popular outdoor pastimes is duck hunting in the Texas Coastal Bend, and even in northeastern Texas, less than an hour from Dallas, waterfowl hunting is supreme. Because duck hunting is so popular, Texas cooks always have a favorite recipe for cooking it. I love this one 'cause it produces the almost-Chinese lacquer look while carrying some spice and sweetness to accent the rich duck.

3 cups molasses

⅓ cup Tabasco sauce

Two 5-pound ducks, cleaned and rinsed

Salt

Freshly ground pepper

Smoked Vegetable Dressing (page 200)

Pear Chutney (page 45)

Preheat the oven to 325°F.

Combine the molasses and Tabasco in a medium bowl. Set aside.

Generously season the exterior and cavity of the ducks with salt and pepper. Place the ducks on a rack in a large roasting pan. Transfer to the preheated oven and roast for 2 hours. Do not turn off the oven.

Remove the pan from the oven and pour off all of the fat.

Using a pastry brush, generously coat the exterior of each duck with the reserved molasses mixture, taking care that all the skin is covered.

Return the pan to the oven and roast for an additional 40 minutes, brushing the ducks with the molasses mixture every 8 minutes; you want to achieve a lacquer on the skin. Remove the pan from the oven and let the ducks rest on the rack.

When cool enough to handle, using a sharp knife, carefully remove the breast halves and legs from each duck. Take care that the molasses-glazed skin remains intact.

Spoon an equal portion of the dressing into the center of each of four warm dinner plates. Place a duck breast half and a leg beside the dressing. Place an equal portion of the chutney on each breast and serve immediately.

JALAPEÑO CORNBREAD-STUFFED DOVE BREASTS SERVES 4

In Texas, dove season opens on Labor Day weekend, and I can tell you, hunters are more than ready to go. Unfortunately, dove is not easy to purchase, so if you're not a hunter and dove is not a local favorite, quail can easily be substituted.

12 boneless dove breasts (or quail breasts)

Salt

Freshly ground pepper

2 cups Jalapeño-Cornbread Stuffing (page 199)

8 thin strips smoked bacon

Gun Barrel City Collard Greens (page 207) and your favorite barbecue sauce, for serving (optional)

Preheat the oven to 375°F.

Generously season the dove breasts with salt and pepper. Place the seasoned breasts, skin side down with the longest side facing you, on a clean, flat work surface.

Spoon about 1 tablespoon of the stuffing onto the meat and, working with one at a time, roll the breast meat up and over the stuffing to make a tight cylinder. Take care that all the stuffing remains inside the flesh.

Place the bacon in a single layer on a rimmed baking sheet, making sure that each piece is flat. Transfer to the preheated oven and bake for 3 minutes, or just until the fat has melted slightly.

Remove from the oven and let rest until cool enough to handle. Do not turn the oven off.

Working with one at a time, place a rolled dove breast at one end of a bacon strip; then tightly roll the bacon up and around the breast to make a tight cigar shape. The bacon should completely encase the breast. Use a toothpick to secure the bacon, if necessary.

Place the bacon-wrapped breasts on the baking sheet, leaving about 2 inches between breasts.

Transfer to the preheated oven and roast for 12 minutes, or until the bacon has browned and the dove is cooked through.

Remove from the oven and let rest for 5 minutes.

Transfer to a serving platter, or cut in half crosswise and serve on four individual warm dinner plates, with collard greens and your favorite barbecue sauce for dipping.

TEX-MEX BAKED POTATO ENCHILADAS
with RANCHERO SAUCE SERVES 4

This is a very tasty vegetarian dish that will please meat eaters as well. The enchiladas also can be a spicy garnish to a simple meat or poultry grill or a great accompaniment to a juicy grilled Texas-size steak. Sure beats a steak-house baked potato and sour cream!

2 large Idaho potatoes, scrubbed clean

1 tablespoon olive oil

Salt

½ cup sour cream

2 tablespoons grated jalapeño Jack cheese

2 tablespoons minced scallions

1 tablespoon seeded and minced jalapeño chile

2 teaspoons shredded fresh cilantro leaves

1 teaspoon Fearing's Barbecue
　　Spice Blend (page 39)

Fresh lime juice

Eight 6-inch flour tortillas, warmed

1 cup warm Ranchero Sauce (page 23)

2 cups Fiesta Salad (page 100)

Preheat the oven to 400°F.

Lightly rub the skin of the potatoes with the oil and season with salt. Place in the preheated oven and bake for 45 minutes.

Remove the potatoes from the oven and split in half lengthwise. Scoop out the pulp into a medium bowl; discard the skins. Roughly chop the pulp in the bowl.

Add the sour cream, cheese, scallions, chile, cilantro, and spice blend and toss gently. Season to taste with lime juice and salt and stir to blend.

Lay the tortillas out on a clean, flat work surface. Spoon an equal portion of the potato mixture into the center of each one. Roll into a tight cylinder, completely enclosing the potato mixture.

Spoon about ¼ cup of the Ranchero Sauce into the center of each of four warm dinner plates. Place 2 enchiladas on top of the sauce. Nestle ½ cup of the salad on top of the enchiladas and serve immediately.

Mexican Sampler Platter—Spinach Enchiladas, Butternut Squash Taquitos, Mexican Corn Gratin, Avocado Fries, Guacamole Tostada *with* Yellow Tomato Pico de Gallo SERVES 4

Other than the simple spinach enchiladas, this really isn't a recipe, but a suggestion of recipes throughout the book that can be brought together to make a vegetarian feast. You can pick and choose which ones you might like to combine. You could make separate platters of each dish, or create beautiful dinner plates with each item having its special place. This is just an idea to make vegetarians feel special, particularly in Texas, where meat really does seem to be the thing.

To make the guacamole tostada, all you have to do is crisp up a tortilla, mound it with Guacamole (page 30), and then drizzle the pico de gallo (page 31) over the top.

SPINACH ENCHILADAS

1½ cups cooked (about 1 pound raw) spinach, squeezed dry

½ cup grated jalapeño Jack cheese

1 tablespoon minced shallot

1 teaspoon minced garlic

Salt

Freshly ground pepper

Four 6-inch corn tortillas, warmed

Your favorite sauce or salsa for dipping

SAMPLER PLATTER ADD-ONS

Butternut Squash Taquitos (page 125) (optional)

Mexican Corn Gratin (page 197) (optional)

Avocado Fries (page 203) (optional)

Guacamole Tostada (see headnote) with Yellow Tomato Pico de Gallo (page 31) (optional)

Make the spinach enchiladas: Combine the spinach, cheese, shallot, and garlic in a medium bowl. Season with salt and pepper.

Spoon an equal portion of the spinach mixture into the center of each warm tortilla and roll the tortilla up, cigar-fashion.

Place the tortillas, seam side down, on a microwave-safe platter.

Transfer to the microwave and cook on high for 1 minute, or just until heated through.

Serve hot as is or with almost any sauce or salsa in this book for dipping.

5

CHILIES,
BRAISES,
and
STEWS

TEXAS-STYLE CHILI SERVES 4 TO 6

This is my take on the classic, bean-free Texas chili. (Now, you do know that only Yankees would put beans in chili.) It's good and spicy with a hint of cinnamon. You'll need a couple of bottles of ice-cold brew to complete the experience. The chili gets better as it mellows, so make it in advance and you'll be able to relax with your guests.

4 dried pasilla chiles, stemmed and seeded

2 dried ancho chiles, stemmed and seeded

1 dried chile de árbol, stemmed and seeded

2 cups cold water

Two 6-inch corn tortillas, cut into quarters

6 tablespoons vegetable oil

1½ pounds coarsely ground beef

Salt

Freshly ground pepper

2½ cups small-dice onions

4 tablespoons seeded and minced jalapeño chile

2 tablespoons minced garlic

1 tablespoon ground cumin

4 cups chicken stock or nonfat, low-sodium chicken broth

1½ cups dark beer

8 fresh cilantro sprigs, tied in a bundle

1 cinnamon stick

Fresh lime juice

½ cup grated queso fresco

Combine the pasilla, ancho, and árbol chiles with the cold water in a medium saucepan over high heat and bring to a boil. Lower the heat and simmer, stirring twice, for 10 minutes, or until the chiles are very soft. Remove from the heat and set aside to cool slightly.

Pour the cooled chiles and some of the cooking liquid into a blender. You may not need all the liquid; just enough to make a thick puree. Add the tortillas and process to a smooth puree. If the mixture does not puree easily, add additional cooking liquid or, if necessary, water. Set aside.

Heat the oil in a large frying pan over medium-high heat. Add the beef, season with salt and pepper, and fry, stirring frequently, for 5 minutes, or just until browned.

Using a slotted spoon, transfer the meat to a bowl. Leave the frying pan on the heat.

To the hot pan, add 2 cups of the onions and 2 tablespoons of the jalapeño along with the garlic and cumin and cook, stirring frequently, for about 3 minutes, or until light brown. Add the reserved chile puree and cook, stirring frequently, for about 4 minutes, or until very dark and quite thick. Take care that the mixture does not scorch on the bottom of the pan.

Stir in the reserved beef along with the stock and beer and bring to a boil. Lower the heat and simmer for 1 hour, or until it has reduced by half and is very thick.

Remove from the heat and stir in the cilantro bundle and cinnamon stick. Let stand for 15 minutes without stirring.

Remove the cilantro and cinnamon stick and discard. Stir in the lime juice. Taste and, if necessary, season with salt and pepper.

Pour the chili into a soup tureen. Serve with small bowls filled with the queso fresco and the remaining ½ cup onion and 2 tablespoons jalapeño.

The Origins of Chili

Where, oh where did chili originate? This is a question that can lead to a barroom brawl, as everyone has a theory. Rather than depend upon any one person's sense of history, I will place a bet down that chili was a stew that evolved from all kinds of cooks using the products they had on hand to create a filling meal. But here's just a bit of the history that is based on fact: As early as the mid-1700s, a small group of Spanish immigrants to the area now known as San Antonio were making a chile-spiced stew that resembled the mix that we now call "chili." (Historians believe that the original chiles used were chile piquin, which, early on in Texas, grew wild throughout the state.) It seems that this stew spread throughout the state so that by the early 1800s, Catholic priests were warning their flocks about the passion caused by eating foods as hot as hell's brimstone made with chiles, claiming them to be aphrodisiacs. Like all forbidden fruit, this probably caused an increase in the popularity of chile-spiced stews.

By the 1850s, records show that "chili bricks"—pounded, dried meat; fat; chiles; and seasonings formed into dense rectangles—were carried by cowboys and thrill seekers as they traveled around Texas and out to the California gold fields. Reconstituted in boiling water, these bricks were an easy fix for hunger on the range or trail. Around the same time, another group of Texans known as *Lavanderas* (washerwomen who followed the traveling Texas army around the state) made a stew of goat meat or wild game, wild herbs, and chile peppers. Most interesting of all tales is that a type of chili made from the toughest meat, chiles, and water was the main food of the Texas prison system beginning sometime in the mid-1800s. The race to make good chili became a game throughout the system, with prisoners rating the prison based on its chili. It is said that many prisoners were recidivists simply so they could enjoy a bowl of great chili.

In 1895, a gentleman in Corsicana, Lyman Davis, developed a signature recipe he called Wolf Brand Chili, which he sold from a wagon. He was so successful that he opened a meat market where he sold his chili in brick form as Lyman's Famous Home Made Chili. By 1921, he was operating a canning business and distributing canned chili throughout the region, again as Wolf Brand Chili (in honor of his pet wolf). Although Mr. Davis sold the company, it continued in operation until purchased by the Quaker Oats Company in 1957, still using the original recipe. It was the owners of Wolf Brand who were the driving force behind lobbying the Texas legislature to proclaim chili the official state food, which occurred in 1977. By 1985 the original Wolf plant had closed and the company operations merged with Stokely-Van Camp in Dallas.

Chili had its first national exposure when a San Antonio Chili Stand was featured at the 1893 Columbian Exposition in Chicago. And the rest, as they say, is history.

COS' CHILI SERVES 6

About twenty years ago when I was chef at the Mansion on Turtle Creek, I got a call in the kitchen from a guest whose voice sounded pretty familiar...said he was a chili expert and was hankering for a bowl. Could I oblige? I said, "Mr. Cosby, I think that I make the best bowl of chili in the country and I'd be happy to send one up." "Better be with a bowl of white rice, a stack of saltines, and a bottle of Tabasco," he said, "and I'll sure let you know if you're right." I sent that bowl of chili with its accompaniments up to his suite, and I guess I did something right, 'cause I've been serving bowls of chili to Bill Cosby every year (and often more than once a year) for the past twenty years. This is the recipe that sold my expertise to Mr. Cosby. I can't guarantee that he'll stop by for a bowl, though.

CHILI BASE

- 10 dried ancho chiles, stemmed and seeded
- 2 dried pasilla chiles, stemmed and seeded
- 1 tablespoon vegetable oil
- 1 cup roughly chopped carrots
- 1 cup roughly diced onions
- ½ cup celery, trimmed and chopped
- 2 tablespoons peeled and smashed garlic
- 2 tablespoons roughly chopped shallot
- 2 tablespoons toasted cumin seeds
- 2 tablespoons toasted coriander seeds
- 1 bottle Shiner Bock beer
- 2 cups fresh orange juice
- Fried Tortilla Strips (recipe follows)
- ¼ cup toasted unsalted peanuts

CHILI

- 1 tablespoon vegetable oil
- 1¾ pounds lean sirloin, finely diced
- Salt
- Freshly ground pepper
- 1 cup small-dice onions
- 3 cups chile base
- Juice of 1 lime
- 1 tablespoon Aleppo pepper (see Note)
- 1 teaspoon Tabasco sauce
- 1 tablespoon pureed chipotle chiles (optional)
- Hot cooked rice, for serving (optional)
- Saltines, for serving (optional)
- Tabasco sauce, for serving (optional)

Preheat the oven to 375°F.

To make the base, place the dried chiles on a baking sheet in the preheated oven and toast for 1 minute, or just until slightly softened. Set aside.

Heat the oil in a medium sauté pan over medium-high heat. Add the carrots, onions, celery, garlic, and shallot, and cook, stirring frequently, for about 5 minutes, or until the vegetables begin to color and caramelize.

Stir in the reserved chiles along with the cumin and coriander. When blended, add the beer and orange juice, scraping up the browned bits from the bottom of the pan, and bring to a simmer. Lower the heat and cook at a gentle simmer for 5 minutes.

Raise the heat, add the tortilla strips and peanuts, and bring to a boil. Lower the heat and cook at a gentle simmer for about 10 minutes, or until the liquid has reduced by three-quarters.

Remove from the heat and pour into a blender. Process to a smooth puree. Strain the puree through a fine-mesh sieve into a clean container. Set aside.

To make the chili, heat the oil in a large saucepan over medium heat. Add the meat, season with salt and pepper, and cook, stirring frequently, for 3 minutes, or until lightly browned. Add the onions and cook, stirring frequently, for about 4 minutes, or until translucent. Add the reserved chili base and cook, stirring occasionally, for about 1 hour.

Stir in the lime juice, Aleppo pepper, and Tabasco. Taste and, if necessary, season with additional salt and pepper. If you would like the chili to be hotter, add chipotle puree until you reach the desired degree of heat.

Serve hot over a bowl of rice with saltines and Tabasco sauce, if desired.

Dean's Frito Pie

Place a good handful of Fried Tortilla Strips (or Frito-Lay Corn Chips) in the center of each of four warm large shallow soup bowls. Spoon an equal portion of Cos' Chili over the top of the tortillas. Sprinkle with as much grated cheddar cheese, sliced fresh or pickled jalapeño chiles, and diced red onions as you like. This is the best of the best Texas dishes!

NOTE: Aleppo pepper is a Middle Eastern spice with a gentle "kick," which I often use because of its hint of cumin and slight sweetness combined with its heat. It is available from Middle Eastern markets, at specialty food stores, online, and at some quality supermarkets.

FRIED TORTILLA STRIPS

4 cups vegetable oil

5 yellow corn tortillas, cut into short, thin strips

Salt

Heat the oil in a medium frying pan until it registers 350°F on a candy thermometer. Add the tortilla strips and fry for about 2 minutes, or until lightly colored and crisp.

Using a slotted spoon, transfer the tortilla strips to a double layer of paper towels to drain.

Season with salt and use as directed. Or just snack away!

East Texas Seafood Jambalaya   SERVES 6 TO 8

Jambalaya says "Creole" or "Cajun" to most people, but in East Texas it says "down-home cooking." This is simply because locally grown rice is a source of great pride, and it shines as it meets Gulf seafood and a little hit of chile that the original recipe lacks. Jambalaya is a terrific party dish accompanied by one of the great Texas craft beers, such as Shiner Bock, or one from our own local Dallas brewery, Deep Ellum.

2 tablespoons bacon fat

½ pound lean pork, cut into ½-inch pieces

Salt

Freshly ground black pepper

½ pound andouille sausage, cut into
    ½-inch pieces (see sidebar at right)

1 cup small-dice onions

1 cup small-dice celery

½ cup small-dice green bell pepper

2 tablespoons seeded and minced jalapeño chile

1 tablespoon minced garlic

8 cups chicken stock or nonfat,
    low-sodium chicken broth or fish stock

1 bay leaf

1 teaspoon cayenne pepper

1 teaspoon Old Bay Seasoning

3 cups Texas long-grain white rice

1 cup small-dice peeled and seeded tomatoes

1 cup shucked oysters

1 cup peeled, deveined, and halved
    (lengthwise) shrimp

1 cup jumbo lump crabmeat

1 tablespoon chopped fresh flat-leaf parsley

1 tablespoon sliced scallions

Fresh lemon juice

Tabasco sauce

Heat the bacon fat in a large soup pot over medium-high heat. Add the pork and season with salt and black pepper. Fry, turning frequently, for about 10 minutes, or until well browned on all sides.

Stir in the sausage and cook, stirring occasionally, for 4 minutes. Add the onions, celery, bell pepper, chile, and garlic and cook for another 3 minutes. Stir in the chicken stock along with the bay leaf, cayenne, and Old Bay and bring to a boil.

Add the rice and tomatoes and stir to combine. Lower the heat, cover, and cook for about 30 minutes, or until the rice is thoroughly cooked.

Remove from the heat. Remove and discard the bay leaf. Add the oysters, shrimp, and crabmeat along with the parsley and scallions. Cover and let sit for 15 minutes, or until the seafood has cooked.

Season with lemon juice and Tabasco and, if necessary, additional salt and black pepper, and serve steaming hot.

Andouille Sausage

Andouille sausage made its way into Texas via Louisiana, where it is a mainstay in Cajun cooking. Originally, it was made with the internal organs of the pig, seasoned with hot chiles, and stuffed into pig intestine. Nowadays it is usually made from pork shoulder and stuffed into synthetic casings; however, it is still smoked and heavily seasoned with chiles and spices. You can't make a true jambalaya without it!

Texas Rice

According to the Texas State Historical Society, rice farming in Texas began as early as the late 1600s, when rice was first brought to the United States from Madagascar. Throughout the centuries, rice production evolved to be a major Texas agricultural product grown primarily in the southeastern part of the state.

EAST TEXAS GUMBO SERVES 4 TO 6

This dish crawled over the border into East Texas from Louisiana. It is a classic gumbo that utilizes some of the great Gulf seafood. It is a terrific party dish as it can be made in advance, with the seafood and filé powder added just before serving.

1 cup bacon fat or 2 sticks unsalted butter

2 cups diced boneless, skinless chicken thigh meat

1 cup diced pork butt

Salt

Coarsely ground black pepper

1 cup diced green bell pepper

1 cup diced celery

1 cup diced onions

1 cup all-purpose flour

2 tablespoons minced garlic

2 teaspoons dried basil

2 teaspoons dried thyme

2 teaspoons dried rosemary

2 teaspoons crushed red pepper flakes

1 teaspoon Old Bay Seasoning

1 bay leaf

6 cups chicken stock or nonfat,
    low-sodium chicken broth

½ pound smoked sausage, cut
    crosswise into thin slices

1 cup ½-inch sliced okra

1 cup peeled, seeded, and diced tomatoes

½ pound shrimp, cleaned and deveined

12 shucked oysters

½ pound Gulf jumbo lump crabmeat

1 tablespoon chopped fresh flat-leaf parsley

1 teaspoon filé powder (see Note)

Fresh lemon juice

Lemon wedges, for serving

Saltine crackers, for serving

Tabasco sauce, for serving (optional)

Heat the bacon fat (or unsalted butter) in a large stockpot over medium-high heat. Add the chicken and pork and season lightly with salt and black pepper. Cook, stirring occasionally, for about 5 minutes, or until nicely browned.

Add the bell pepper, celery, and onions and cook, stirring, for 1 minute. Stir in the flour and cook, stirring frequently, for about 5 minutes, or until the roux is almond colored and has a distinct nutty aroma.

Stir in the garlic, basil, thyme, rosemary, red pepper flakes, Old Bay, and bay leaf and cook, stirring, for 1 minute.

Stir in the stock, 1 cup at a time, and continue to cook, stirring, until all the stock has been added and the mixture has thickened. Bring to a boil, then lower the heat to a simmer and cook, stirring occasionally, for 45 minutes. The gumbo may be made up to this point and stored, tightly covered and refrigerated, for up to 3 days. Reheat before adding the remaining ingredients.

Add the sausage, okra, and tomatoes and continue to cook for 10 minutes. Remove and discard the bay leaf.

Add the shrimp, stirring to combine, and continue to cook for 5 minutes.

Add the oysters, crabmeat, parsley, and filé powder, and remove from the heat. Let rest for 5 minutes. Add the lemon juice. Taste and, if necessary, season with salt and black pepper.

Serve piping hot with lemon wedges, a heap of saltines, and a bottle of Tabasco sauce on the side, if desired.

NOTE: Equal portions of onion, celery, and green pepper are known as the "holy trinity" in gumbo parlance.

Filé powder (also known as gumbo filé) is ground from dried leaves of the sassafras tree. The spicy herb was first used by the Choctaw Indians, indigenous to the American South, as a thickening agent for stews. It is now primarily used in Creole and Cajun cooking to both thicken and season stews and soups. It has an earthy, woody taste that some liken to root beer. It is always added after the cooking is completed, as it turns stringy and tough when cooked.

MEXICAN GREEN CHILE-POZOLE STEW   SERVES 4

We have some chilly nights in Texas, and this stew is a perfect antidote to the cold. Rich and spicy, filling and warming—what more could you need? A few tortillas for dipping and getting that last bit of sauce from the bowl and some great Texas beer wouldn't hurt!

1 tablespoon olive oil

2 cups ½-inch-dice pork butt

¼ cup chorizo sausage

1 cup small-dice onions

½ cup small-dice roasted, peeled,
    and seeded poblano chiles

¼ cup small-dice celery

¼ cup small-dice carrot

2 tablespoons minced garlic

2 tablespoons seeded and minced jalapeño chile

1 tablespoon ground cumin

2 dried ancho chiles, stemmed, seeded,
    and cut into thin strips

4 cups chicken stock or nonfat,
    low-sodium chicken broth

2 cups canned white hominy,
    rinsed and well drained

¼ cup small-dice tomato

2 tablespoons chopped fresh cilantro

Fresh lime juice

Salt

Freshly ground pepper

1 tablespoon crumbled Cotija cheese

Eight 6-inch corn tortillas, warmed, for serving

Heat the oil in a medium saucepan over medium heat. Add the pork and chorizo and cook, stirring frequently, for about 5 minutes, or until nicely browned.

Add the onions, poblano, celery, and carrot and cook, stirring frequently, for 3 minutes. Stir in the garlic along with 1 tablespoon of the jalapeño and the cumin. Cook for 1 minute.

Add the anchos, stock, hominy, and tomato and bring to a boil. Lower the heat and simmer for about 40 minutes, or until the liquid has reduced slightly, the meat is tender, and the mixture is as thick as a rich stew. Stir in the cilantro and season to taste with lime juice, salt, and pepper.

Transfer to a large bowl and sprinkle the top with the cheese and the remaining 1 tablespoon jalapeño. Serve hot with warm tortillas on the side.

About Pozole

Pozole is a classic Mexican home-style stew or soup made with dried corn kernels that are also often referred to as pozole, dried nixtamal, or *maiz pozolero*. In the United States, corn kernels prepared in this fashion are known as hominy. The kernels are prepared by cooking them briefly in slaked lime in a process called nixtamalization, which removes the pedicel (the nodule that connects the kernel to the cob), loosens the hull, and softens the corn. It also enhances the flavor and releases niacin, making it healthier than other plain dried corn and/or cornmeal. When cooked, it opens up like a flower at the top. The dried corn has to be presoaked and then cooked in water or broth to further soften for eating. Dried corn for pozole is available from Hispanic markets. It is also available frozen. Frozen pozole does not have to be presoaked.

If you can't find dried corn for pozole, you can substitute hominy, which is available dried from many farmers' markets. Canned hominy is more readily available but lacks real flavor and texture.

YELLOW TOMATO-POZOLE STEW SERVES 4

This is a rich, nourishing stew that has hints of both Mexico and the American South along with a real hit of Texas spice. Lovely colors invite the diner to dive in, particularly with some warm tortillas to dip into the delicious broth. I often use this stew as a base for grilled or barbecued pork dishes.

4 large yellow tomatoes, cored but left whole

2 tablespoons olive oil

1 poblano chile, stemmed, seeded,
    and cut into large dice

1 large onion, cut into large dice

1 cup large-dice celery

3 garlic cloves, minced

1 jalapeño chile, stemmed, seeded,
    and cut into small dice

2 teaspoons ground cumin

2 teaspoons ground coriander

½ cup beer

¼ cup gold tequila

2 cups rich chicken stock or nonfat,
    low-sodium chicken broth

4 fried corn tortillas, broken into pieces

Fresh lime juice

Salt

Freshly ground pepper

¼ cup finely diced country ham

1 cup fresh corn kernels (or thawed frozen)

¼ cup finely diced red onion

¼ cup finely diced celery

1 tablespoon seeded and minced jalapeño chile

1½ cups cooked pozole corn or hominy
    (see sidebar, facing page)

¼ cup finely diced yellow tomato

¼ cup finely diced red tomato

2 tablespoons chopped cilantro

Warm tortillas, for dipping

Preheat the oven to 375°F.

Place the tomatoes on a baking pan and roast in the preheated oven for 15 minutes, or just until soft.

Remove the tomatoes from the oven and transfer to a blender. Process to a smooth puree, and set aside.

Place 1 tablespoon of the oil in a heavy-bottomed saucepan over medium-high heat. Add the poblano, onion, and celery and cook, stirring, for about 3 minutes, or just until the onion is translucent.

Stir in the garlic, diced jalapeño, cumin, and coriander and continue to sauté for 1 minute more. Add the beer and tequila and, using a heatproof spatula, scrape up any browned bits from the bottom of the pan. Cook for about 2 minutes, or until the pan is nicely deglazed and the liquid has reduced by half.

Add the reserved tomato puree along with the stock. When combined, add the tortillas and bring to a boil. Lower the heat and cook, stirring occasionally, for about 20 minutes, or until it has a thick sauce-like consistency.

Remove from the heat and transfer to a blender. Process to a smooth puree. Strain through a fine-mesh sieve into a clean container. Season with lime juice and salt and pepper and set aside.

Heat the remaining 1 tablespoon oil in a heavy-bottomed saucepan over medium-high heat. Add the ham and fry for about 2 minutes, or until lightly browned.

Add the corn, onion, celery, and minced jalapeño and continue to fry for about 3 minutes, or until the onion is translucent.

Add the pozole along with the yellow and red tomato and cook, stirring, for about 1 minute, or until just heated through.

Stir in the reserved tomato mixture and the cilantro; cook for another couple of minutes, or until hot.

Serve as is with tortillas for dipping, or as directed in a specific recipe. The stew may be made in advance and stored, tightly covered and refrigerated, for up to 3 days.

PANHANDLE VEGETABLE STEW   SERVES 4

The northernmost part of Texas is known as the Panhandle, just 'cause that's exactly what it looks like. It is made up of beautiful, flat plains with deep canyons and rivers. I don't know why I call this stew after the area, except that there can be cold nights, and lots of hunters spend time out in the elements, and this seems like a hearty meal that would satisfy chilled bones and is easy enough to put together at a campsite.

1 tablespoon olive oil

¼ cup small-dice smoked country ham

1 cup small-dice onion

½ cup small-dice celery

2 garlic cloves, minced

1 jalapeño chile, stemmed, seeded, and minced

2 cups fresh corn kernels (or thawed frozen)

1 cup finely chopped tomatoes

½ cup hominy or pozole

½ cup small-dice roasted poblano chiles, stemmed, seeded, and peeled

2 cups Thickened Chicken Stock (page 29)

1 tablespoon chopped fresh cilantro

Fresh lime juice

Salt

Tortilla chips, for serving (optional)

Heat the oil in a large saucepan over medium-high heat. Add the ham and cook, stirring frequently, for 2 minutes, or until nicely colored. Stir in the onion and celery and continue to cook, stirring, for about 1 minute, or just until softened. Stir in the garlic and jalapeño and cook, stirring, for 30 seconds. Add the corn and cook, stirring occasionally, for about 3 minutes, or just until the corn begins to cook.

Add the tomatoes, hominy, and poblanos and stir to combine. Stir in the stock and bring to a boil. Immediately remove from the heat and add the cilantro and lime juice. Taste and season with salt. Serve hot with tortilla chips, if desired.

CHILE-BRAISED RABBIT ENCHILADAS
with ROASTED GREEN CHILE SAUCE   SERVES 4

This is another recipe that utilizes one of the many meats that Texas hunters particularly like. If rabbit is not a favorite, you could easily use chicken to make these classic enchiladas. The braising liquid yields a delicious red chile sauce that adds deep flavor to the enchilada filling, while the Green Chile Sauce is the accent.

1 rabbit, quartered

Salt

Freshly ground pepper

2 tablespoons olive oil

1 jalapeño chile, stemmed, seeded, and chopped

½ cup large-dice onion

½ cup chopped carrot

½ cup chopped celery

4 cups Dean's Tortilla Soup with South-of-the-Border Flavors (page 86)

2 dried ancho chiles, stemmed and seeded

1 dried pasilla chile, stemmed and seeded

1 small bunch fresh thyme

1 bay leaf

2 cups shredded jalapeño Jack cheese

1 cup julienned caramelized onions (see page 62)

8 corn tortillas, warmed

1 cup Roasted Green Chile Sauce (page 24)

2 tablespoons grated Cotija cheese

Season the rabbit generously with salt and pepper.

Heat the oil in a large, wide, heavy-bottomed pot with straight sides (known as a rondeau in the restaurant kitchen) over medium-high heat. Place the rabbit in the pan, skin side down, and sear for 4 minutes, or until the skin is golden brown. Turn and add the jalapeño, onion, carrot, and celery to the pan. Continue to cook, stirring the vegetables occasionally, for another 4 minutes.

Add the soup along with the ancho and pasilla chiles, thyme, and bay leaf and bring to a boil. Lower the heat, cover, and cook at a gentle simmer for 1 hour, or until the meat gently pulls away from the bone.

Using a slotted spoon, remove the rabbit from the broth and set aside to cool.

Raise the heat and bring to a boil. Then lower the heat to a simmer and cook for 20 minutes, or until the liquid has reduced by half. Remove and discard the bay leaf.

Transfer the liquid to a blender and process to a smooth puree. Pour into a clean saucepan and keep warm.

When the rabbit is cool enough to handle, remove and discard the skin and pull the meat from the bones, breaking it into bite-size pieces.

Transfer the rabbit to a large bowl. Add ½ cup of the warm cooking liquid along with the Jack cheese and caramelized onions. Season with salt and pepper and stir to blend.

Lay the warm tortillas out on a clean work surface. Working with one at a time, spoon an equal portion of the rabbit mixture into the center of each tortilla and then roll up, cigar-fashion. Spoon the green chile sauce over each rolled tortilla, and sprinkle with the Cotija cheese. Serve immediately.

Hunting Game

Texans like to hunt, and although we have many game farms and large landholdings that allow hunters to spend luxurious time in the outdoors, the Texas Parks and Wildlife Department sponsors a public hunting program that offers hunters the opportunity to hunt in various parts of the state for only a small license fee. Rabbit and hare and dove abound all over the state, as do deer and wild hog. Pheasant is found in the Panhandle, quail in South Texas, blue quail in the west, and turkey in the east and in San Angelo.

STEPHAN PYLES' SON-OF-A-BITCH STEW

SERVES 8 TO 10

As you might be able to tell by the name, a version of this stew was a frequent meal for cowboys on early Texas cattle drives. We don't really know how "popular" it was, but it was extremely important because it was made with nutrient-rich organ meats (like liver and kidneys), which helped the cowboys stay in good health on the trail. Stephan Pyles, an old friend of mine and one of the pioneers of "Southwest cooking," has updated it quite a bit, turning it from a necessary "evil" to a rich and very tasty veal stew. However, making it is quite a big project with a lot of different techniques for preparing a lot of unusual proteins. He has broken it down so that you can spread out the preparation over three days.

1 calf's heart

1 calf's tongue

Handful of coarse salt, plus
   3 tablespoons and more as needed

½ pound veal sweetbreads

2 quarts whole milk

½ pound calf's liver, cut into ½-inch cubes

5 bay leaves

6 cloves

4 celery stalks, trimmed and chopped

2 large onions, peeled and cut into quarters

2 large carrots, trimmed, peeled,
   and cut into large pieces

1 garlic head, cut in half lengthwise

2 tablespoons peppercorns

3 fresh thyme sprigs

2 quarts heavy cream

1 tablespoon chipotle powder, or as needed

24 pearl onions, peeled and trimmed

16 baby carrots, trimmed, peeled, and
   cut crosswise into thin slices

16 Brussels sprouts, trimmed and quartered

4 tablespoons (½ stick) unsalted butter

Freshly ground black pepper

2 cups all-purpose flour

1 teaspoon garlic powder

White pepper

1 cup buttermilk

2 pounds veal tenderloin butt, trimmed
   and cut into ½-inch cubes

About 2 quarts vegetable oil, for frying

1 cup pickled onions

Three days before you want to serve the stew, begin the preparation.

On the first day, rinse the heart under cold running water until the water runs clean. Then combine the heart and tongue in a container large enough to hold them easily with cold water to cover. Add a good handful of salt and add enough cold water to cover completely. Cover and refrigerate for at least 1 hour or, preferably, overnight.

Put the sweetbreads in a small bowl with 1 quart of the milk, making sure that it covers the sweetbreads completely. Cover and refrigerate for 8 hours or overnight.

Put the liver in a small bowl with the remaining 1 quart milk, making sure that it covers the liver completely. Cover and refrigerate for 8 hours or overnight.

On the second day, drain the heart and tongue well and put them in a large saucepan. Add 4 of the bay leaves along with the cloves, celery, onions, carrots, garlic, and peppercorns. Cover with cold water by at least 2 inches and add 3 tablespoons of salt. Place over high heat and bring to a simmer, skimming off any foam that rises to the surface. Lower the heat to a gentle simmer and simmer, adding water as necessary to keep the heart and tongue covered, for 2 hours, or until the meat is tender when pierced with a fork. Remove from the heat and set aside to cool to room temperature.

When cool, remove the heart and tongue from the liquid, reserving the cooking liquid. Place the meat in a bowl, cover, and refrigerate.

Fold a large piece of cheesecloth into thirds and place it in a large strainer, taking care that all the holes are covered by the cheesecloth. Set the strainer over a large clean bowl.

Pour the cooking liquid through the cheesecloth into the bowl. Discard the cheesecloth and reserve the strained liquid. Do not stir; let any sediment remain at the bottom of the bowl. You should have about 3 quarts of almost clear liquid. Measure out 4 cups of the strained liquid and cover and refrigerate the remaining 2 quarts.

Remove the sweetbreads from the milk and rinse them under cold running water. Place them in a medium saucepan along with the 4 cups of the strained liquid, 1 sprig of thyme, and the remaining bay leaf. Place over medium-high heat and bring to a simmer. Immediately lower the heat and cook at a gentle simmer for about 10 minutes, or until the sweetbreads are springy to the touch. Remove from the heat and set aside to cool to room temperature in the broth.

Using a slotted spoon, remove the sweetbreads from the poaching liquid and discard the liquid. Transfer the sweetbreads to a small bowl, cover, and refrigerate.

Remove the heart and tongue from the refrigerator.

Using a sharp knife, peel the textured, outer skin from the tongue. Cut the veins away from the bottom and cut the resulting meat into ½-inch cubes. Transfer to a small container, cover, and refrigerate.

Remove any fat and cartilage from the exterior of the heart. Cut into ½-inch cubes, transfer to a small container, cover, and refrigerate.

On the third day, pour the remaining 2 quarts of strained liquid into a large soup pot, taking care that none of the sediment that has settled to the bottom is poured out. Place over high heat and bring to a boil. Boil for about 20 minutes, or until reduced by half.

Preheat the oven to 400°F.

While the liquid is reducing, remove the liver from the refrigerator. Strain it through a fine-mesh sieve and discard the milk. Rinse under cold running water and pat dry with paper towels. Set aside.

Remove the sweetbreads from the refrigerator, uncover, and peel off the thin skin that covers them. Using your fingertips, break the sweetbreads into bite-size nuggets.

When the strained liquid has reduced by half, stir in the heavy cream and chipotle powder and continue to cook until the liquid has reduced a bit more and is thick enough to coat the back of a spoon.

While the mixture is reducing, combine the pearl onions, carrots, and Brussels sprouts in a large bowl. Add 2 tablespoons of the butter along with the remaining 2 thyme sprigs. Season with salt and black pepper and spread the vegetables out in an even layer on a large rimmed baking sheet.

Place in the preheated oven and roast for about 20 minutes, or until lightly browned and slightly crunchy. Remove from the oven and set aside.

Combine the flour with the garlic powder and white pepper in a large shallow bowl. Place the buttermilk in a large shallow bowl next to the seasoned flour.

Working with a few pieces at a time, dredge the liver and sweetbreads in the seasoned flour, shaking off excess. Dip the floured meat into the buttermilk, allowing the excess to drain off, and then again dredge the meat in the seasoned flour. Set aside to rest on a double layer of paper towels while you continue to prepare the other elements of the dish.

Melt the remaining 2 tablespoons butter in a large saucepan over medium heat. When melted, season the veal with salt and place in the hot butter. Sear, turning occasionally, for about 5 minutes, or until light brown on all sides. Do this in batches if necessary to avoid crowding the pan.

Using a slotted spoon, remove the meat from the pan and set aside.

While the veal is searing, place the vegetable oil in a deep-fat fryer over high heat and heat the oil until it registers 325°F on a candy thermometer.

Place the heart and tongue in the reduced cream mixture and bring to a simmer. Simmer for 5 minutes.

When the oil has reached the desired temperature, place the floured sweetbreads and liver in the deep-fat fryer and fry for 3 minutes, or until golden brown. Transfer to a double layer of paper towels to drain.

Add the reserved vegetables along with the veal to the creamy broth and bring to a simmer. Taste and, if necessary, adjust the seasoning with salt and white pepper.

Pour an equal portion of the stew into each of 8 to 10 (or however many you are serving) large shallow soup bowls. Garnish each bowl with an equal portion of fried sweetbreads and liver along with pickled onions. Serve immediately.

Stephan Pyles is an old buddy of mine. We have been promoting Texas cooking around the world for years. Stephan is a fifth-generation Texan and one of the founding chefs/fathers of Southwestern cuisine. He has created fifteen restaurants in four cities over the past twenty-six years, including his famous Routh Street Cafe, Baby Routh, and Star Canyon in Dallas. *Texas Monthly* named one of his most recent ventures, the eponymous restaurant Stephan Pyles, "Best New Restaurant" in Texas in 2005. Stephan continues to be one of the brightest stars in Dallas.

6

WORKING *the* SMOKER *and the* GRILL

★ ★ ★ ★ ★ ★ ★

So much of the flavor in Texas cooking comes from both smoking and grilling. Smoking, in particular, has been used for centuries as a method to cook and preserve foods, and throughout the Southwest it has been continuously done for generations, particularly among the indigenous peoples.

Traditionally, only meats were "cooked" through the smoking process. In recent years, Texas cooks have treated vegetables in the same way; however, with vegetables, the smoking is done just to flavor, not to cook. It takes days or sometimes weeks to "cook" meat and fish through smoking, but I now often treat meat just like vegetables, reducing the smoking time to offer only a faint hint of flavoring smoke. Vegetables are, for the most part, smoked for just a few minutes.

GENERAL SMOKING INSTRUCTIONS

The preparation, temperature, and time required to "cook" with smoke is quite different from that required for flavoring. "Cooking" requires that the product be brined and then held over (or in) very low, but measurable heat for a long period of time. Flavoring is done by cold smoking for minutes.

COOKING WITH SMOKE

You can cook using smoke in as many ways as you can imagine, from a primitive hole in the ground right up to custom-built commercial machines. However, most hardware and big-box stores sell many different styles of outdoor cookers, ranging from inexpensive to very, very expensive, for home use. These may be called either smokers or water smokers. Some may even be a combination smoker and grill. They can be powered by wood pellets, charcoal, gas, or electricity, but I believe that true smoking or grilling is best done on a wood- or wood charcoal–fired cooker. To me, hickory wood or mesquite wood charcoal is the preferred fuel to give foods an authentic Texas flavor. I do not recommend charcoal briquettes or liquid starter, both of which infuse an unnatural flavor into the smoke. I, personally, use a Hasty-Bake Smoker/Grill that I believe works magic every time. I cannot recommend it more highly.

A charcoal-fired water smoker is usually a rather tall (about 3 feet), narrow metal canister with a bottom pan that holds the charcoal. A second pan set between the coals and the upper cooking rack (there might also be two cooking racks) holds the water (or other flavoring liquid) and lowers the internal temperature. A lid is always used to trap the smoke. All smokers are sold with explicit instructions for appropriate use, and I recommend that you follow them to a T. However, my general rule is to allow 30 minutes of smoking time per pound of product being smoked.

Smoking is not difficult, but it does require an almost constant control of temperature to fully cook the product being smoked. The temperature should remain between 200°F and 220°F for smoking meat, game, and fowl. It is a good idea to have two thermometers—one to take the internal temperature of the product being smoked and one to test the temperature inside the smoker. A constant low, even temperature allows the time necessary to tenderize the product completely and allow the smoke flavor to permeate the flesh.

To be fully cooked, meats should be smoked to an internal temperature of 145°F and poultry to 165°F. For falling-off-the-bone meats, such as pulled pork or brisket, the internal temperature should be around 180°F to reach the degree of tenderness required. It is good to remember that often smoking is nothing more than long, slow cooking that will result in an extremely tender, flavorful end to a very tough piece of meat.

I use a large amount of wood charcoal to start the process, as this tends to create a slow-burning fire. To create the desired smoke, once the fire is hot and burned down, wood chips or pieces, such as those from hickory, apple, pecan, or cherry, which have been presoaked in water, are placed on top of the gray ash. If the wood is very green, it does not have to be soaked, as its inherent moisture will create smoke rather than fire. Dry wood must always be soaked; otherwise, it will simply burn, not smoke. Soaked or green wood is added frequently to keep a constant level of smoke.

Almost all smokers can hold small pieces of meat or fish as well as whole birds or roasts. The flavor is usually more intense when the product has a thin layer of natural fat to keep the meat moist as it slow cooks. Therefore, skin should be left on poultry or wild birds as well as fish, while lean meats should either be wrapped in fat or have pieces of fat inserted into the flesh. Often poultry and game need to be brined before smoking and/or grilling. If necessary, use my Texas Brine on page 178.

COLD-SMOKE METHOD

Place about 2 cups of wood chips or pieces (such as hickory, pecan, apple, or cherry) in cold water to cover. Soak for at least 30 minutes, or until very wet. Do not remove them from the water until ready to use, as they must be thoroughly soaked in order to smoke rather than burn. You can also use very green pieces of wood, which do not have to be soaked. It is these wet pieces that will produce the aromatic flavoring smoke. You can also soak a few branches of a woody herb, such as rosemary, to introduce an herbal hint to the smoke.

Place 6 to 8 pieces of hardwood charcoal (or charcoal briquettes) in a smoker or a grill with a lid. For small amounts to be smoked, the standard Weber Kettle Grill will work just fine. Ignite the charcoal; a chimney-style starter that uses newspaper to ignite the coals is an excellent fire-starting tool.

Once lit, mound the hot coals in the bottom of the smoker or grill and allow them to burn down to gray ash. The bottom damper should be closed and the top vent (in the lid) should be open just a crack to draw the smoke upward. This process lowers the heat of the coals to "cold smoke."

Remove the soaked wood chips or pieces from the water, shaking off any excess. Lay the wet wood or, if using, green wood over the ash. Place the item to be smoked in an aluminum pie pan, then place the pan on the grate to the side, not directly over, the coals, and smoke for 20 minutes. If the soaked wood burns down, add more soaked wood to keep a constant stream of smoke going.

Gas grills can also be used to cold smoke as follows:

Preheat one side of the grill for about 10 minutes, or until the thermostat registers "low." Turn off the heat.

Place soaked or green wood chips or pieces on the preheated grill rocks.

Place the item to be smoked in an aluminum pie pan, then place the pan on the grate to the side, not directly over, the coals, and smoke for 20 minutes. If the soaked or green wood burns down, add more soaked or green wood to keep a constant stream of smoke going.

Texas Brine *for* Smoking Meat, Game, *or* Fowl   MAKES 1 GALLON

2 garlic cloves, peeled

2 serrano chiles, stemmed, seeded, and chopped

1 large onion, peeled

1 celery stalk, trimmed and chopped

1 carrot, trimmed, peeled, and chopped

1 fresh thyme sprig

1 fresh basil sprig

1 fresh cilantro sprig

1 fresh flat-leaf parsley sprig

1 bay leaf

1 gallon cold water

¼ cup dry white wine

½ cup white wine vinegar

1 cup salt

Put the garlic, chiles, onion, celery, carrot, thyme, basil, cilantro, parsley, and bay leaf in a large stockpot. Add the cold water along with the wine and vinegar. Stir in the salt, place over high heat, and bring to a boil. Lower the heat and simmer for 20 minutes.

Remove the brine from the heat and set aside to cool completely.

When cool, strain through a fine-mesh sieve and discard the solids.

Depending on the size of the meat (or fowl or game) that you are going to smoke, place the brine either in a resealable plastic bag large enough to hold the meat, or in a nonreactive container of the appropriate size. Submerge the meat in the brine and soak for 30 minutes per pound.

When brined, remove the meat from the brine, shaking off the excess. Season the meat, place in the prepared smoker, and smoke according to the manufacturer's directions.

The brine may be frozen and reused up to 3 times. If you do so, *always reboil* before using.

SMOKED BRISKET SERVES 4 TO 6

Smoked brisket has Texas written all over it. I've eaten my share across the state and certainly have some favorites, but this method will bring you as close as I can take you to the real thing right in your own backyard. When buying brisket, allow about 3 servings per pound of trimmed meat. If the meat has not been trimmed, calculate about 2 servings per pound.

2 cups Fearing's Barbecue Spice Blend (page 39)

One 10- to 12-pound beef brisket, fat trimmed to a thickness of ¼ inch

Using your hands, generously massage the spice mix into all sides of the meat; it should be well coated. Wrap in plastic wrap and refrigerate for 12 hours.

Prepare the smoker as directed by the manufacturer.

When the fire is gray and ashy, add your soaked or green wood pieces (the wood should begin to smoke almost immediately) and cover.

Open both the top and the bottom vents and, once the smoke has settled, take the interior temperature. It needs to be at least 220°F and no more than 250°F.

Insert the bottom grill grate and place a pan of water on it, opposite the coals.

Insert the top grill grate and lay the brisket on it directly over the water. Cover and smoke, replenishing your coals as needed, for about 5 hours, or until the internal temperature registers 160°F.

Keeping the fire/smoke going, remove the brisket and wrap it tightly in aluminum foil. You can, if desired, coat it in a barbecue sauce or additional spice mix before wrapping. If it seems dry, you can pour about a cup of beer or stock over it before wrapping, taking care that all the liquid stays within the wrap.

Return the brisket to the smoker and smoke for an additional 2 hours, or until the internal temperature registers 190°F. Uncover and let the fire die out, leaving the wrapped brisket on the grate for another hour.

Unwrap and place on a cutting board to catch the juices as you carve.

NOTE: Here's a little tip I learned from old-time Texas pitmasters: When you want to know if your brisket is cooked to perfection, take a meat fork and stick it down into the center of the meat and give it a twist. If it twists easily, the meat is ready to eat.

SONNY BRYAN'S-STYLE RIBS SERVES 4

When I moved to Dallas in 1978, the first question I asked one of my cohorts was "Where is the best barbecue in town?" His reply was Sonny Bryan's barbecue spot over on Inwood. I headed right over and, let me tell you, the Sonny Bryan experience was life changing. When I took one taste of the sauce on his pork ribs, I knew that I had finally found the flavor that I had been searching for.

Sonny and I became good friends, and I tried like the devil to get his "secret" sauce recipe. He wouldn't part with it until he was coming to the end of his time here, and then he decided to entrust me with the "secret." But you know what? I stopped making my own barbecue sauce because it never tasted like his, so to this day Sonny Bryan's supplies the sauce to my restaurant.

I can't imagine how many times I have eaten these ribs over the years. This recipe is my homage to this legendary king of the Texas smoke pit.

2 racks St. Louis–cut pork ribs

Salt

Coarsely ground pepper

3 quarts Texas-Style Barbecue Sauce (page 19) or your own favorite sauce

Prepare the smoker for hot smoking, about 250°F.

Generously season all sides of the ribs with salt and pepper. Place the ribs in the smoker and smoke for 5 hours. The ribs should be cooked when they register 185°F but are not falling off the bone. Remove the ribs from the smoker.

Combine the hot ribs with 2 quarts of the sauce in a large nonreactive container; the sauce should cover the ribs. Cover and refrigerate for 8 hours or overnight.

When ready to grill, preheat and oil the grill.

Using a chef's knife, cut the ribs parallel to the bone into single portions.

Place the ribs on the grill and grill, turning once or twice, for about 3 minutes, or until heated through and lightly charred. Serve with extra barbecue sauce for dipping, if desired.

NOTE: When you decide to cook ribs, you will need to decide what kind of ribs to use. Sonny used St. Louis–cut pork ribs, which are meatier. They are taken from the whole spareribs of the hog and have had the rib tips removed so the cut appears more rectangular in shape. If you like a more tender rib, baby back ribs will do the trick, and they will cook faster. Allow 5 to 6 hours for St. Louis–cut ribs and 3 to 4 hours for baby backs.

Mr. B's Pork Shoulder Butt
with Apple Cider Injection   SERVES 8 TO 10

Mr. B works in the kitchen at Fearing's. He is a rising star and is active in barbecue competitions all over the state. I can't tell you how many ribbons he has won. This is one of his prizewinning recipes that he has shared with our crew. You do need a flavor injection syringe to get the full apple flavor that gives the meat its special goodness.

3 cups apple cider

¼ cup packed light brown sugar

2 tablespoons Worcestershire sauce

2 tablespoons soy sauce

2 tablespoons salt

1 tablespoon Fearing's Garlic
    Powder (page 41)

1 pork butt, about 8 pounds

2 cups Dry Rub Seasoning (recipe follows)

¾ cup Butter Wrap Mix (recipe follows)

Combine the apple cider with the brown sugar, Worcestershire sauce, soy sauce, salt, and garlic powder in a medium bowl. Stir until the mixture is lump-free and the sugar has dissolved.

Place the pork butt, fat side down, in a deep casserole.

Fill a flavor injection syringe with the apple cider mixture and insert the syringe about three-quarters into the depth of the meat and randomly inject the mixture into spots all over the pork butt. Pour the remaining apple cider mixture over the meat, cover with plastic wrap, and refrigerate for at least 2 hours, or up to 12 hours; you want the flavor to permeate the meat.

One hour before you are ready to grill, place 2 cups of applewood chips or chunks in cold water to cover and soak for 1 hour.

Preheat a grill to 275°F. Add the applewood and prepare the grill for indirect heat.

Remove the meat from the refrigerator. Drain off excess liquid and pat dry with a towel. Season the pork with dry rub seasoning to taste, making sure you cover the sides.

Transfer the seasoned meat to the grill, fat side down. Grill/smoke for 3 to 4 hours, or until the pork registers 160°F on an instant-read thermometer.

Lay 2 sheets of heavy-duty aluminum foil, long enough to wrap the pork completely, on a flat work surface. Place the hot pork in the center of the foil. Do not turn off the grill.

Using your hands (you might need to put on heavy rubber gloves to protect them from the heat), completely cover the pork with the butter wrap. Pull the foil up and over the meat to completely enclose it. Check to make sure all seams are sealed.

Place the pork in a disposable roasting pan and return to the grill. Grill for about 3 hours, or until the pork registers 193°F on an instant-read thermometer.

Remove the pork from the grill and let rest for 45 minutes. Remove the foil and transfer to a serving platter. Serve hot, warm, or at room temperature.

DRY RUB SEASONING

MAKES ABOUT 2¼ CUPS

½ cup packed light brown sugar

½ cup granulated sugar

½ cup paprika

¼ cup granulated garlic

¼ cup coarse sea salt

1 tablespoon chile powder

1 teaspoon granulated onion

1 teaspoon ground cumin

1 teaspoon cayenne pepper

1 teaspoon freshly ground black pepper

½ teaspoon dry mustard powder

Combine the sugars with the paprika, granulated garlic, salt, chile powder, granulated onion, cumin, cayenne, black pepper, and mustard powder in a small bowl and stir to blend completely.

Use as directed in the recipe, or store, tightly covered, in a cool spot for up to 1 month.

BUTTER WRAP MIX

MAKES ABOUT ¾ CUP

4 tablespoons (½ stick) unsalted butter

¼ cup packed light brown sugar

2 tablespoons apple cider vinegar

2 tablespoons seeded and sliced jalapeño chile

1 tablespoon fresh lemon juice

1 teaspoon salt

Combine the butter with the sugar, vinegar, chile, lemon juice, and salt in a small nonreactive saucepan over low heat. Cook, stirring, for about 2 minutes, or until the butter has melted and the sugar has dissolved.

Remove from the heat and keep warm until ready to use.

GENERAL GRILLING INSTRUCTIONS

When Texans talk about grilling, they are talking about cooking over live coals, not gas heat. Perhaps this comes from the deeply held traditions of cowboys on the trail, when all meals were cooked on open fires. Grilling as we now know it is a form of quick cooking involving high, dry heat that effectively seals the exterior of the food being grilled while rapidly cooking the interior. The food is placed on a rack or grill with the heat directly radiating from below or above the grill rack. Grilling is often referred to as barbecuing, but barbecue also implies pre-marination or mopping with a sauce during the grilling process. Meats cooked by grilling acquire a toasty exterior that accentuates caramelization, resulting in a very desirable richness.

Although grilling can be done on a stovetop grill pan, this method does not achieve the same high quality of caramelization that is realized when grilling over hot coals. In Texas, the standard is high heat, and outdoor grilling is the method of choice, with the frequent addition of mesquite, hickory, or fruitwoods to heighten flavor. The heat should be hot enough to immediately char grill marks into the meat (or poultry, fish, or vegetable). In addition, it should be hot enough to seal the grill side of the exterior and cook the product about halfway through. This should take only a few minutes; the time will vary depending upon the food being grilled. The food should then be turned to allow the opposite side to seal and finish cooking. The heat is adjusted by moving the food away from or closer to direct heat, not by allowing the fire itself to wax and wane.

The grill is ready when the flames have died down and the coals are burning red. If the coals have gone beyond red, the heat will not be high enough, and you will have to add more coals and wait for them to turn red. I recommend partially opening the bottom vent, as I think it helps keep the fire hot. Opening and closing the vent is one way to control the temperature. For instance, if the flames are burning high, closing the vent slightly will calm them.

If using a gas grill, it should be preheated for at least 10 minutes. Many gas grills now have a thermostat to gauge the internal temperature; and remember, you want it to be hot. If hot enough, the food should cook as quickly as it would on a wood- or charcoal-fired grill. Move the food away from the direct heat when necessary to ensure even grilling.

No matter the type of grill used, remember that all grilling should take no more than a few minutes. You should stand by the grill, ready to take action immediately should flare-ups occur. Simply move the food away from the flame and wait for it to die down. Do not spray with water or lower the lid. Water spray can cause the ash to rise and contaminate the food, and lowering the lid can cause the food to overcook.

Many cooks worry about undercooking foods on a grill, but it is more likely that meats, particularly, will be overcooked, as the high heat works its magic quickly. And overcooking is the killjoy of great grilling; it dries out the natural juices, destroying both flavor and texture. Even the best sauce cannot fix overgrilled meat.

Fuel for the Grill

Wood and charcoal are the fuels of choice. I do not recommend charcoal briquettes, especially those presoaked with lighter fluid, as they impart an undesirable flavor to the food during grilling. Texans particularly love mesquite wood charcoal for the delicate Lone Star flavor it infuses into meat. For open-fire cooking, large pieces of wood can be used, but grilling is a bit tricky, as the wood tends to flare up in spots and the temperature is uneven. Foods grilled over wood charcoal take on a subtle flavor of the wood being used. Add a piece or two of aromatic wood on the rock bed above the heat source of a gas grill to achieve a similar effect.

Deep-in-the-Heart-of-Texas Barbecue Chicken SERVES 4

This is my go-to barbecued chicken, and I think it will quickly be yours. In fact, I'll bet that you may find one chicken is just not enough to satisfy a big Texas-style appetite. Friends coming for a weekend backyard feast at my house always know that this chicken will be on the menu. I always serve my barbecue with some type of cornbread stuffing and Jalapeño-Peach Chutney (page 45) and, if they're right from the field, ears of grilled corn on the cob.

One 3- to 4-pound chicken, quartered, well rinsed, and patted dry

1 tablespoon vegetable oil

Salt

Freshly ground black pepper

Dried thyme

Crushed red pepper flakes

3 cups Texas-Style Barbecue Sauce (page 19) or your own favorite barbecue sauce

If using, soak about 2 cups hickory chips in cold water to cover.

Preheat the grill, taking care that the grates are very clean and brushed with oil.

Lightly coat the chicken pieces with the oil and season with salt, black pepper, thyme, and red pepper flakes.

When the charcoal has burned to white ash, or when the gas grill is very hot, add the chicken quarters, skin side down. You now want to render as much grease as possible from the skin without burning the skin or causing the grease to flare up on the fire and burn the skin. Take your time and watch carefully.

Right after the chicken has settled down on the grill, add water-soaked hickory chips, a small handful at a time, to the edge of the fire. This will start the smoking process. Cover the grill to seal in the smoke.

After about 8 minutes, uncover the grill and check to see if the skin is crisping but not burning. If the smoke has died down, add another handful of hickory chips. Continue to smoke and grill, turning frequently, for another 15 minutes, taking care that both sides of the chicken are evenly cooked.

Using a mop or pastry brush, begin generously coating the chicken with the sauce. Don't be afraid to swipe the barbecue sauce on heavily while frequently turning each piece to prevent burning.

Remove from the grill, transfer to a platter, and serve family-style.

NOTE: Remember, a clean grill is a happy grill! Make sure old ashes are long gone and the grates are brushed clean. Add wood charcoal and ignite—and not with charcoal lighter fluid!

ROBERT DEL GRANDE'S GRILLED RIB EYE STEAKS
with BACKYARD STEAK SAUCE SERVES 4

Chef Robert Del Grande is one of my best friends and a true genius in the kitchen. Robert says, "In the category called 'Nothing could be better than,' I would include a thick, charcoal-grilled rib eye steak—nice and caramelized and crusty on the outside and rosy pink and succulently tender on the inside. Some things you never get tired of, and this is one of those things. This recipe combines the two—a thick grilled rib eye steak with a grilled steak sauce. The steak mop is simple and facilitates the rich browning of the steak."

Two 18-ounce thick-cut rib eye steaks

3 tablespoons extra-virgin olive oil

1 tablespoon pure maple syrup

1 tablespoon balsamic vinegar

¼ teaspoon salt

¼ teaspoon freshly ground pepper

Few drops Tabasco sauce

Extra-virgin olive oil, for drizzling

Coarse sea salt, for sprinkling

Backyard Steak Sauce (recipe follows)

Remove the steaks from the refrigerator and let them come to room temperature.

Move the grill grates at least 12 inches away from the fire. Preheat and oil the grill, first making sure it is clean as a whistle.

Combine the oil, maple syrup, vinegar, salt, pepper, and Tabasco in a small bowl and whisk to blend completely.

Using a pastry brush or a barbecue mop brush, generously coat the steaks with the maple "mop."

Place the steaks directly over the hot coals (or fire) for 3 minutes. Turn and grill the opposite sides for 3 minutes. Again brush with the "mop."

Rotate the steaks 90 degrees, turn, and grill for 3 minutes. Again brush with the "mop." Turn and brush again. At this point the steaks should be nicely browned but still rare.

Move the steaks to the side of the grill that is not directly over the hot fire. Lower the lid and finish grilling off the fire, brushing occasionally, for 5 to 10 minutes more, depending on the thickness of the steaks and the desired degree of doneness. Among the several different ways to tell if a steak is done, two can be very helpful: An instant-read thermometer inserted into the center of the steak should register approximately 125°F for medium rare. Alternatively, when small beads of juice begin to appear on the surface of the steak, the steak will be medium rare. The more juice that appears on the surface of the steak, the more cooked the steak is.

Transfer the steaks to a cutting board and let rest for 10 minutes. The resting will allow the hot juices in the steak to be reabsorbed back into the meat rather than flow out onto the board when sliced.

Using a sharp knife, carve the steak into thick slices and arrange on a platter. Drizzle with a little extra-virgin olive oil and sprinkle with coarse sea salt.

Serve with the Backyard Steak Sauce on the side.

Robert Del Grande,
Kitchen Genius and Musician

Houston-based Robert Del Grande is one of Texas' finest culinary stars. In fact, I think he is a genius in the kitchen. Trained as a scientist, Robert has taken that precision and developed his own take on the flavors and ingredients that have evolved into the new Southwestern cooking. If his restaurants were in Dallas, I'd sure be a regular. That he also happens to be a great buddy and fellow musician is the icing on the cake. We have a little band we call the "Barbwires" that plays at charity events and such around the state, but it is mostly for fun and relaxation. However, we are serious enough about it to record our efforts, and we have a few enthusiastic followers. Don't think we'll take on the Rolling Stones, but what the heck, we're happy to be just a good ole Texas band.

BACKYARD STEAK SAUCE

MAKES 2 CUPS

4 garlic cloves

4 pitted prunes (dried plums)

2 bacon slices, cut crosswise into 4 equal pieces

2 dried ancho chiles, stemmed and seeded

2 plum tomatoes, cut in half lengthwise

Two 1-ounce brown mushrooms, stems removed

½ medium onion, cut in half lengthwise

1 cup water

2 tablespoons white wine vinegar

2 tablespoons light brown sugar

½ teaspoon salt

¼ teaspoon freshly ground pepper

Robert's Thoughts on His "Sauce on a Stick"

Several years ago, I started a series of sauces called "sauce on a stick" or "sauce skewers." The basic idea is that you skewer all the vegetable ingredients for a sauce or salsa and grill them over a charcoal fire. When all the flavors have developed from the grilling process, you transfer the ingredients to a blender and puree them into a sauce or salsa. Skewering the ingredients means you don't have to chase the ingredients, particularly the smaller ones, around the grill. It's simple and efficient as well as very tasty. For this recipe, the sauce is made on the backyard grill, therefore a Backyard Steak Sauce.

If using wooden skewers, soak them in cold water to cover for at least 30 minutes before using.

Skewer the garlic, prunes, bacon, chiles, tomatoes, mushrooms, and onion on wood or metal skewers, alternating the smaller ingredients with the larger ones. The objective is to get the larger pieces of tomato and onion to nicely char without burning the smaller ingredients.

To one side of a grill, prepare a charcoal fire.

When the fire is hot, place the skewers directly over the fire, turning frequently to evenly brown all sides. The skewers are done when the tomato and onion are well cooked and all of the vegetables are lightly charred. If the ingredients begin to burn before they are well cooked, move the skewers to the side of the grill without the charcoal. Lower the lid and roast until everything is tender and lightly charred.

Remove the skewers from the grill and push everything into a medium bowl. Add the water along with the vinegar, brown sugar, salt, and pepper and stir to blend. Set aside for 30 minutes.

Transfer to a blender and process to a smooth consistency. If the sauce is too thick, add a bit of water, a tablespoon at a time, to thin.

Use the sauce immediately or store, tightly covered and refrigerated, for up to 1 week.

SIMPLE GRILLED VEGETABLES

MAKES AS MANY AS YOU LIKE

Once you've got the grill going, throw on some veggies and dinner is complete. You can either grill up one type of veggie, or mix and match colors and textures. All this is to say, cook whatever vegetables you like. Just make sure to season them with a great olive oil and, if you're in a real Texas mood, a good dose of pure chile powder, and, of course, salt and pepper. I generally allow 5 or 6 pieces per person, except for corn, where one ear usually does it.

Here are some hints for specific vegetables:

Corn on the Cob: Leave the husks on and soak in cold water to cover for about 30 minutes before you are ready to grill. Shake off excess water and pull back the husks a bit so you can remove the silk. Discard the silk and push the husks closed around the cob. You can, if you like, pull the husks all the way back and brush the corn with oil, and season with Tabasco and lime juice, then pull them back up to enclose the cob and, if needed, tie them shut with a strip of husk. Place the corn directly over the coals and grill, turning frequently, for about 4 minutes, or until nicely charred. Move to a cooler part of the grill, cover, and grill for about 10 minutes, or until tender. Use oven mitts to handle and remove the husks, as they will be very hot.

Big Fat Red Onions: Peel and cut some fat red onions crosswise into thick slices. Place a skewer or extra-long toothpick through the rings to hold them in place as they grill. Generously brush with olive oil, season with salt and pepper, and grill, turning frequently, over direct coals for about 5 minutes, or until charred and still crisp-tender.

Potatoes: Parboil halved potatoes for 7 or 8 minutes, or until just barely cooked. Drain and pat dry. Brush with oil, season with chile powder, salt, and pepper, and grill, turning frequently, for about 10 minutes, or until nicely marked and cooked through.

Other Veggies: Try sliced summer squashes, bell peppers, or asparagus. Season with oil, salt, and pepper and grill over hot coals, turning frequently, for about 6 minutes, or until lightly charred and cooked through.

7

SIDES

CIDER-BRAISED BACON SERVES 4

Rather than use prepared smoked bacons in some of my dishes, I go back to the old days and make my own "bacon." Cider braising adds the sweetness of fruitwood smoking and turns fatty pork belly into a delicious treat. The braising liquid can be strained and used as a rich stock for cooking beans or making soups or gravies.

3 tablespoons olive oil

2 pounds center-cut pork belly

Salt

Freshly ground pepper

2 garlic cloves, chopped

1 cup peeled and chopped Granny Smith apples

1 cup chopped onions

1 cup chopped celery

½ cup chopped carrot

1 cup white wine

2 fresh thyme sprigs

1 bay leaf

4 cups chicken stock or nonfat, low-sodium chicken broth

2 cups apple cider

Line a small baking sheet with parchment paper. Heat the oil in a Dutch oven over high heat.

Season the pork belly with salt and pepper and when the oil is very hot but not smoking, place the pork belly in the pan. Sear for 4 minutes, or until a golden crust forms.

Turn the pork belly and add the garlic, apple, onion, celery, and carrot and cook for 4 minutes, or until the vegetables begin to color.

Add the wine, thyme, and bay leaf and continue to cook for about 3 minutes, or until almost all of the liquid has evaporated.

Stir in the stock and cider and bring to a boil. Immediately lower the heat, cover, and cook at a gentle simmer for 2½ hours, or until the pork is fork-tender. Check occasionally to make sure that there is enough liquid to cover the pork belly in the pan. If not, add more stock.

Using tongs, transfer the cider-braised bacon to the prepared baking sheet. Place a sheet of parchment paper on top of the bacon. Place another pan on top of the parchment paper–covered bacon and then place a weight (a heavy frying pan works well) directly on top of the bacon to press it down. Refrigerate for 12 hours.

Use as directed in a specific recipe, or tightly wrap and store, refrigerated, for up to 5 days.

CAMPFIRE BARBECUE BEANS SERVES 4 TO 6

The deep, rich flavor of these beans will take you straight outdoors, with a tin plate on your lap. This is a true Texas side dish—smoky, spicy, and complex, yet simple to pull together. It's a terrific picnic, barbecue, or party dish!

1 tablespoon vegetable oil

1 cup diced smoked bacon

½ cup small-dice onion

¼ cup seeded and minced jalapeño chile

1 tablespoon minced garlic

2 teaspoons cracked black pepper

1 teaspoon chopped fresh sage

1 teaspoon chopped fresh thyme

1 teaspoon ground cumin

1 teaspoon crushed red pepper flakes

1 cup cooked pinto beans

1 cup cooked white beans

1 cup cooked black beans

1 cup cooked red beans

2 cups Texas-Style Barbecue Sauce (page 19) or your favorite barbecue sauce

2 cups chicken stock or nonfat, low-sodium chicken broth

1 bay leaf

Salt

Heat the oil in a large saucepan over medium-high heat. Add the bacon and sauté for about 3 minutes, or until golden. Stir in the onion, chile, and garlic and cook, stirring, for 1 minute. Add the black pepper, sage, thyme, cumin, and red pepper flakes and stir to blend. Add the pinto, white, black, and red beans along with the barbecue sauce, stock, and bay leaf and bring to a boil. Immediately lower the heat and cook at a simmer for 45 minutes, or until the liquid has been absorbed and the mixture is very thick. Taste and, if necessary, season with salt. Remove and discard the bay leaf.

Serve warm as directed in a specific recipe, or as a side dish for any grilled meat, game, poultry, or fish.

Baked Chuck Wagon Black Beans   SERVES 4 TO 6

This is a version of classic baked beans. It has many of the traditional flavors, but the black beans add their own subtle twist, as does the veal demi-glace. I know that the chuck wagon cook didn't have any demi-glace, but I just love the richness that it gives to the finished dish.

4 cups cooked black beans, well drained

1 large onion, finely chopped

1½ cups ketchup

1¼ cups packed brown sugar

¼ cup molasses

1 tablespoon prepared yellow mustard

1 tablespoon sweet pickle juice

1 tablespoon apple cider vinegar

Salt

Freshly ground pepper

¼ pound thickly sliced smoked bacon

1 cup veal demi-glace (see Note)

Preheat the oven to 350°F.

Combine the beans with the onion, ketchup, brown sugar, molasses, mustard, pickle juice, and vinegar in a 2-quart casserole. Season to taste with salt and pepper.

Crisscross the bacon strips over the top of the beans. Cover tightly with aluminum foil, transfer to the preheated oven, and bake for 1 hour.

Remove the foil from the beans and continue to bake for another 30 minutes.

Remove from the oven. Lift the bacon from the beans and coarsely chop it. Return the chopped bacon to the beans along with the demi-glace, and stir to blend well. Serve warm.

NOTE: Veal demi-glace, a rich reduction of veal stock, is available from fine butchers, at specialty food stores, and online.

Mashed Black Beans   MAKES ABOUT 4 CUPS

Mashed black beans work well as a side dish, a filling for burritos or enchiladas, a topping for tostadas, or a dip for chips. They are a terrific multipurpose staple to keep on hand.

1 tablespoon vegetable oil

3 slices hickory-smoked bacon, cut into small pieces

3 garlic cloves, minced

1 small onion, chopped

1 jalapeño chile, stemmed, seeded, and minced

4 cups cooked black beans (see page 14), well drained

6 cups rich chicken or ham stock or nonfat, low-sodium chicken broth

Fresh lime juice

Salt

Heat the oil in a large saucepan over medium heat. Stir in the bacon and fry for about 4 minutes, or until most of the fat has rendered out. Add the garlic, onion, and chile and continue to cook, stirring frequently, for about 3 minutes, or until softened slightly.

Stir in the beans, add the stock, and bring to a boil. Lower the heat and simmer, stirring occasionally, for about 1 hour, or until the liquid cooks down enough to just barely cover the beans. If the liquid cooks down too quickly—that is, before the beans are mushy and well flavored—add additional stock or water, a bit at a time.

Transfer the beans to a food processor fitted with the metal blade. Process, using quick on-and-off turns, until they are a chunky paste. Scrape from the processor into a clean container (or pan) and season to taste with lime juice and salt.

Use as directed in a specific recipe, or store, tightly covered and refrigerated, for up to 1 week.

Brazos River Beans *and* Tomatoes

My friend Angela Murry comes from Seymour, Texas, where her family still lives. Seymour is a spit of a town between Wichita Falls and Lubbock, a friendly community of ranchers and farmers. Angela grew up big and strong on this family favorite, which she introduced to our Dallas backyard barbecues.

By the way, Seymour is smack in the middle of bountiful hunting country, so people from all over the world come to take advantage of the great availability of game.

3 cups cooked brown beans

2 cups peeled, seeded, and chopped tomatoes

1 cup chopped onions

2 tablespoons seeded and minced jalapeño chile

2 cups favorite barbecue sauce

2 tablespoons light brown sugar

1 tablespoon Worcestershire sauce

2 teaspoons chile powder

1 teaspoon prepared yellow mustard

Salt

Freshly ground pepper

Preheat the oven to 350°F.

Combine the beans, tomatoes, onions, and chile in a large bowl. Stir in the barbecue sauce, brown sugar, Worcestershire, chile powder, and mustard. Season to taste with salt and pepper.

Pour the mixture into a 2-quart casserole. Cover, place in the preheated oven, and bake for 45 minutes.

Uncover and bake for an additional 15 minutes. Serve hot from the oven.

SWEET CORN CREAM SUCCOTASH   SERVES 4 TO 6

This is a rich and delicious way to get your children to eat their veggies. Best made in summer when everything is at its prime, succotash is a wonderful side dish at a barbecue or picnic alongside a grilled steak or half a chicken.

3 tablespoons corn oil

3 cups fresh corn kernels (or thawed frozen)

2 shallots, chopped

2 garlic cloves, minced

1½ cups heavy cream

1 teaspoon ground coriander

Salt

Freshly ground black pepper

½ cup small-dice red onion

½ cup small-dice carrots

½ cup fresh English peas

½ cup small-dice red bell pepper

½ cup small-dice yellow bell pepper

2 teaspoons chopped fresh thyme

Heat 1 tablespoon of the corn oil in a medium saucepan over medium heat. Add 2 cups of the corn along with the shallots and garlic and cook, stirring occasionally, for 4 minutes. Stir in the heavy cream and coriander and bring to a boil. Lower the heat and cook at a bare simmer for 7 minutes, or until thickened.

Remove from the heat and pour into a blender. Holding the lid down with a folded kitchen towel to prevent a steam explosion, process to a smooth puree.

Scrape the corn cream into a clean saucepan and season to taste with salt and black pepper. Set aside and keep warm.

Heat the remaining 2 tablespoons corn oil in a large sauté pan over medium heat. Add the remaining 1 cup corn along with the onion, carrots, peas, red and yellow bell pepper, and thyme and cook, stirring frequently, for 4 minutes, or until the vegetables are just tender.

Stir in 1 cup of the reserved corn cream. Taste and, if necessary, add additional salt and black pepper. Bring to a simmer and simmer for 4 minutes.

Serve as is, or as directed in a specific recipe.

BOURBON-JALAPEÑO CREAMED CORN SERVES 4 TO 6

This rich and delicious dish is a far cry from canned creamed corn. It is, of course, best made with fresh corn, but in a pinch, thawed, frozen corn can be used. It is one of my most popular corn-based dishes and is particularly suited to holiday entertaining.

1 tablespoon olive oil

1 large shallot, minced

4 cups fresh corn kernels (or thawed frozen)

1 jalapeño chile, stemmed, seeded, and minced

2 tablespoons Jim Beam bourbon

1 cup heavy cream

Salt

Freshly cracked pepper

Fresh lime juice

Heat the oil in a large sauté pan over medium-high heat. Add the shallot and cook, stirring occasionally, for about 2 minutes, or just until the shallot has sweat its liquid.

Add the corn and chile and cook, stirring, for 4 minutes.

Carefully add the bourbon and, tipping the pan slightly, allow the alcohol to catch fire. Lift the pan from the heat and let the flame die down. Lower the heat and cook for 2 minutes, or until the liquid has reduced slightly.

Stir in the cream and season to taste with salt and pepper. Bring to a simmer and cook at a gentle simmer for 6 minutes, or until very thick.

Remove from the heat and add lime juice as desired. Taste and, if necessary, season with additional salt and pepper. Serve hot.

MEXICAN CORN GRATIN SERVES 4

This is a slightly different take on creamed corn, but a really terrific one. An amazing side dish, this can be served with grilled or roasted meats, or even as an accompaniment to everyday tacos, burritos, and fajitas.

Butter, for greasing the dish

2 cups cooked corn kernels

½ cup mayonnaise

1 tablespoon seeded and minced jalapeño chile

1 teaspoon Sriracha sauce

1 teaspoon Fearing's Barbecue
Spice Blend (page 39)

Fresh lime juice

Salt

2 tablespoons crumbled Cotija cheese

Preheat the oven to 350°F. Lightly butter a 1-quart casserole. Set aside.

Combine the corn with the mayonnaise, chile, Sriracha, spice blend, and lime juice and salt to taste in a medium bowl and stir to blend well.

Pour the corn mixture into the prepared casserole and sprinkle the cheese over the top. Place in the preheated oven and bake for about 15 minutes, or until the top is golden brown and bubbling.

Remove from the oven and serve hot.

CREAMY CORNBREAD PUDDING   SERVES 4 TO 6

All kinds of savory puddings are popular Texas side dishes. This one is a terrific make-ahead dish that works well with grilled or barbecued meat and poultry. I have to warn you, this is totally addictive. If I take one bite, I can't rest till I've eaten the whole dish. Put this together the day before and store, tightly covered and refrigerated, and then bake just before serving.

Butter, for greasing the dish

4 cups crumbled Iron-Skillet Cornbread (page 213)

1 tablespoon olive oil

2 cups fresh corn kernels (or thawed frozen)

1 shallot, minced

¼ cup minced scallions

1 tablespoon mashed Roasted Garlic (page 41)

1 teaspoon chopped fresh thyme

2 cups heavy cream

1 tablespoon pure maple syrup

1 teaspoon Tabasco Chipotle sauce

Salt

Freshly ground pepper

Preheat the oven to 375°F. Lightly coat the interior of a 2-quart baking dish with butter. Set aside.

Place the cornbread in a large bowl. Set aside.

Heat the oil in a medium frying pan over medium heat. Add the corn and sauté for 3 minutes. Remove from the heat and scrape the corn into the cornbread.

Add the shallot, scallions, roasted garlic, and thyme to the cornbread mix and stir to blend well. Stir in the cream, maple syrup, and Tabasco Chipotle and season to taste with salt and pepper. Scrape the cornbread mixture into the prepared baking dish.

Transfer to the preheated oven and bake the pudding for about 20 minutes, or until cooked through and golden brown and crusty on top.

Remove from the oven and serve hot.

Sweet Corn–Sage Pan Stuffing SERVES 4

When time doesn't allow for a full-blown stuffing for a bird, this is a quick and easy way to bring a tasty stuffing to the table. It is also a great side dish for game or game birds.

1 tablespoon olive oil

1 tablespoon minced shallot

1 tablespoon seeded and minced jalapeño chile

1¼ cups fresh corn kernels (or thawed frozen)

1 teaspoon chopped fresh sage

1 cup crumbled Iron-Skillet Cornbread (page 213) or your favorite cornbread

½ cup heavy cream

½ cup chicken stock or nonfat, low-sodium chicken broth

Salt

Freshly cracked pepper

Heat the oil in a medium sauté pan over medium-high heat. Add the shallot and chile and cook, stirring, for 1 minute. Stir in the corn and sage and continue to cook, stirring, for 2 minutes. Add the cornbread and stir to blend well. Add the cream and stock and continue to cook, stirring, for 2 minutes, or until the cream has reduced and begins to coat the corn. Season to taste with salt and cracked pepper and serve.

Jalapeño-Cornbread Stuffing MAKES ABOUT 2½ CUPS

This is my go-to stuffing for game birds. It carries a little bit of tradition with the cornbread and a little Texas style with the chile and garlic. It offers just enough zest to balance the delicacy of the birds. You can double or even triple the recipe to make a terrific party side dish.

2 cups crumbled Iron-Skillet Cornbread (page 213) or your favorite cornbread

1 teaspoon olive oil

2 tablespoons seeded and minced jalapeño chile

1 tablespoon minced shallot

½ cup heavy cream

½ cup chicken stock or nonfat, low-sodium chicken broth

1 tablespoon chopped Roasted Garlic (page 41)

1 teaspoon chopped fresh thyme

1 teaspoon pure maple syrup

Salt

Freshly ground pepper

Place the cornbread in a medium bowl. Set aside.

Heat the oil in a small frying pan over medium heat. Add the chile and shallot and sauté for 1 minute. Remove from the heat and scrape into the cornbread.

Add the cream, stock, garlic, thyme, and maple syrup and stir to thoroughly combine. Season to taste with salt and pepper.

Use as directed in a specific recipe, or use as a side dish. To use as a side dish, transfer to a small buttered casserole and bake in a preheated 350°F oven for about 20 minutes, or until cooked through and golden brown on top.

SMOKED VEGETABLE DRESSING SERVES 4

Rather than just sautéing the aromatic vegetables usually found in a stuffing, I smoke them to give a real campfire taste to the finished dish. This dressing is a terrific side dish for game and game birds.

2 onions, cut into medium dice

2 celery stalks, trimmed and cut into medium dice

2 carrots, trimmed and cut into medium dice

1 red bell pepper, stemmed, seeded, membranes removed, and cut into medium dice

1 tablespoon olive oil

1 tablespoon chopped fresh sage

2 teaspoons chopped fresh thyme

3 cups crumbled Iron-Skillet Cornbread (page 213) or your favorite cornbread

2 cups medium-dice white bread

3 to 4 cups rich chicken stock or nonfat, low-sodium chicken broth

Salt

Prepare a smoker to cold-smoke (see page 177).

Place the onions, celery, carrots, and bell pepper into the prepared smoker and cold-smoke for 20 minutes.

Remove the vegetables from the smoker and set aside.

Heat the oil in a large sauté pan over medium heat. Add the smoked vegetables and cook, stirring, for 4 minutes, or until the onions are translucent. Stir in the sage and thyme and cook for another minute.

Add the cornbread and white bread and stir to combine. Stirring constantly, slowly add the stock, adding just enough stock to make a moist but not wet dressing. Cook, stirring, just until the mixture is hot. Season to taste with salt.

Use as directed in a specific recipe or as you desire.

JALAPEÑO GRITS SERVES 4

Breakfast, lunch, or dinner, Texans love grits. This combination of flavors takes them from the breakfast table to a special dinner. We like them spicy, but you can use as little chile as suits your taste.

1 tablespoon olive oil

1 cup diced onions

1 tablespoon seeded and minced jalapeño chile

1 teaspoon minced garlic

1 teaspoon chopped fresh thyme

6 cups chicken stock or nonfat, low-sodium chicken broth

2 cups Homestead Gristmill, or other high-quality white grits (see sidebar, page 50)

1 tablespoon Tabasco sauce

1 teaspoon smoked paprika

Salt

Freshly ground pepper

Heat the oil in a large saucepan (remember, grits expand!) over medium-high heat. Add the onions and sauté for 3 minutes, or until translucent. Stir in the chile, garlic, and thyme and stir until well blended.

Add the stock and bring to a boil. Boil, stirring constantly, while slowly adding the grits. When all of the grits have been added, reduce the heat and cook, stirring frequently, at a gentle simmer for about 25 minutes, or until thick and soft.

Remove the grits from the heat and stir in the Tabasco and paprika. Season to taste with salt and pepper and serve immediately.

CRISPY SWEET ONION RINGS SERVES 4

These are so, so delicious you can feast on them, alone. However, good sense will have them served as a side dish or a component of a more complex main course. We love our Texas Shiner Bock beer, but any fine-quality dark lager will work.

Vegetable oil, for frying

2 Texas sweet onions (see sidebar below), peeled and cut crosswise into ½-inch-thick rings

1 cup tempura flour

1 cup cornmeal

1 bottle Shiner Bock beer

Salt

Heat the oil in a deep-fat fryer over high heat until it registers 350°F on a candy thermometer.

Pull the onion slices into rings and set aside.

Combine the tempura flour and cornmeal in a medium bowl. Whisk in the beer to just form a loose batter. If too thick, add cold water, a tablespoon at a time.

When the oil has reached the desired temperature, begin dipping the onion rings, one piece at a time, into the batter, allowing excess batter to drip off. Carefully drop the rings into the hot oil and fry for about 30 seconds, or until the bottoms have browned. Turn gently, so you don't break the crust, and fry for another 30 seconds, or until golden brown on all sides.

Using a slotted spoon, transfer the rings to a double layer of paper towels to drain. Continue making onion rings until you have fried and drained all the rings. Season with salt and serve immediately.

NOTE: Tempura flour is a blended flour, usually wheat flour mixed with some type of leavener, such as baking powder. It is available from Asian markets, specialty food stores, and well-stocked supermarkets.

Texas Sweet Onions

Texas sweet onions, the state's leading vegetable crop, have a long and fascinating history. The Bermuda onion was first introduced into South Texas in 1898 when a packet of seed was planted near the town of Cotulla. The resulting onions were shipped off to Wisconsin, where their sweetness was so eagerly endorsed that farmers quickly increased production. By 1946, more than ten thousand freight-car loads of sweet onions were shipping annually. Originally, the yellow and white Bermuda and the Crystal Wax onions were the predominant crops. As hybridization occurred, many other types were brought into the mix. The Texas-bred Granex is now a worldwide favorite, planted under many different names, including the well-known Georgia Vidalia. Most, if not all, of these sweet onions are grown from Texas transplants. A favorite Texas saying is "A Lone Star sweet onion is so sweet you can eat it like an apple."

CRISPY TOBACCO ONIONS   SERVES 4

I got this recipe from a customer more than twenty-five years ago when he wanted real thin and crisp onion rings. The name came about because once fried, the onions get all brown and crinkly and look just like loose tobacco.

Although I usually serve these sweet, spicy onions as part of a main dish, they could easily be used to add zest to a great roast beef sandwich, or as a garnish for plain grilled meat or seafood. Just take care that you don't burn the onions; you want them to be caramel-like and slightly sweet.

Vegetable oil, for frying

1 Spanish onion, peeled and cut
   crosswise into very thin rings

3 cups all-purpose flour

2 tablespoons Fearing's Barbecue
   Spice Flour Mixture (page 39)

Salt

Freshly ground pepper

Heat the oil in a deep-fat fryer over high heat until it registers 350°F on a candy thermometer.

Carefully pull the onion slices apart into rings and set aside.

Combine the all-purpose flour and spice flour mixture in a resealable plastic bag. Season to taste with salt and pepper.

Working with a few at a time, place the onion rings in the flour mixture in the bag and shake gently to coat. Remove from the bag and shake off excess flour.

When the oil has reached the desired temperature, gently place the floured rings into the hot oil, a few at a time. Don't crowd the fryer or the onion rings will stick together. Fry for about 3 minutes, or until golden brown.

Using a slotted spoon, lift the onions from the oil and transfer to a double layer of paper towels to drain. Serve warm.

"LOADED" MASHED POTATOES   SERVES 4

I like to think of these potatoes as twice-baked potatoes without the skin. There is nothing better than these rich, creamy potatoes served alongside a sizzling steak right off the grill. Only in Texas would we gild the lily with all of this richness. When you need just plain ole mashies, stop before adding the cheese and sour cream. They will still be pretty darned good.

6 large russet potatoes, peeled and cut into chunks

¼ cup melted unsalted butter

About 2 cups heavy cream, warmed

Salt

¼ cup grated white cheddar cheese

¼ cup sour cream

1 tablespoon snipped fresh chives

Freshly ground pepper

Put the potatoes in a large saucepan with cold water to cover by at least 2 inches and bring to a boil over high heat. Lower the heat and cook at a gentle simmer for about 25 minutes, or until very tender. Remove from the heat and drain well.

Transfer the well-drained potatoes to a large bowl and either mash by hand (if you don't mind a few lumps) or beat with a handheld electric mixer until smooth. If you are really looking for perfect mashed potatoes, push the drained potatoes through a ricer and then beat with a wooden spoon until smooth and silky.

While the potatoes are still hot, beat in the butter. When the butter has been incorporated, begin gradually beating in the cream. Go slowly, as you may not need all of the cream to achieve the perfect consistency; the potatoes should be thick and fluffy, not wet and runny. Season to taste with salt.

Stir the cheese and sour cream into the mashed potatoes and beat to blend well. Stir in the chives and season with additional salt and pepper. Serve hot.

Avocado Fries   SERVES 4

These unusual "fries" came about when I wanted to add French fries to a dish but didn't feel they were just the right flavor, and I wanted something a bit healthier. So divine inspiration hit, and we decided to try avocados with their healthy oil. You need avocados that are firm but ready to eat. They must be frozen before frying, or they will fall apart in the hot oil.

These "fries" are extra-delicious dipped in Queso Asadero (page 26).

- 4 ripe but firm avocados
- 4 cups packaged tempura batter, prepared according to manufacturer's directions (see **Note**)
- 4 cups fine bread crumbs
- **Vegetable oil, for frying**
- **Salt**

Line a baking sheet with parchment paper and set aside.

Using a sharp knife, cut each avocado lengthwise into 8 wedges of equal size. Carefully peel off and discard the skins and pits.

Mix the tempura batter in a medium bowl, and put the bread crumbs in a large shallow container.

Working with one piece at a time, dip each avocado wedge into the batter and then gently roll in the bread crumbs to evenly coat. As coated, place each wedge on the prepared baking sheet. When all of the wedges have been coated, transfer the baking sheet to the freezer until ready to fry.

When ready to serve, heat the oil in a deep-fat fryer over high heat until it registers 350°F on a candy thermometer.

Remove the coated avocado wedges from the freezer. Add the wedges to the hot oil, a few at a time, and fry for about 3 minutes, or until golden brown. Season with salt and serve immediately.

NOTE: Tempura batter mixes are available at Japanese markets, specialty food stores, and most supermarkets in dry form.

QUESO FRESCO-CORN WHIPPED POTATOES

SERVES 4 TO 6

These are really, really Texas-style mashed potatoes overflowing with four-star flavor. The smooth mashed potatoes—which, by the way, are delicious on their own—mixed with fresh corn, a hint of garlic, and slightly salty cheese, are terrific with almost any beef but match up with a big Texas steak or short ribs particularly well.

6 large russet potatoes, peeled and cut into chunks

¼ cup melted unsalted butter

About 2 cups heavy cream, warmed

Salt

1 tablespoon unsalted butter

2 garlic cloves, minced

1 shallot, minced

1¼ cups fresh corn kernels (or thawed frozen)

3 ounces queso fresco or Cotija cheese

Put the potatoes in a large saucepan with cold water to cover by about 2 inches and bring to a boil over high heat. Lower the heat and cook at a gentle simmer for about 25 minutes, or until very tender. Remove from the heat and drain well.

Transfer the potatoes to a large warm bowl and either mash by hand (if you like lumpy potatoes) or use a hand-held electric mixer and beat until smooth. If you are really "into" your mashed potatoes, you can push them through a ricer for a very smooth, even consistency.

Beat in the melted butter and then begin to gradually beat in the cream; you may not need all of the cream, so watch the consistency carefully. The potatoes should be thick and fluffy, not wet and runny. Season to taste with salt. Set aside and keep warm.

Melt the 1 tablespoon of butter in a medium frying pan over medium-high heat. Add the garlic and sauté for 1 minute. Add the shallot and continue to sauté for 1 minute. Stir in the corn and continue to sauté for 2 minutes more. Remove the pan from the heat and scrape the mixture into the warm mashed potatoes.

Fold in the cheese until well blended. Taste and, if necessary, season with additional salt. Serve hot.

SWEET POTATO RAJAS SERVES 4 TO 6

In traditional Mexican cooking, *rajas* are roasted poblano chile strips cooked with onion and served over white rice. They are also used as an accompaniment to grilled meats, or mixed with potatoes or tomatoes as a side dish. This is just a slight variation on the classic, and a Texas favorite it is.

1 pound sweet potatoes, peeled and cut into thick wedges

3 tablespoons melted unsalted butter

Salt

2 medium roasted poblano chiles, stemmed, peeled, seeded, and cut lengthwise into ¼-inch strips

1 small onion, cut crosswise into ¼-inch-thick slices, then separated into rings

¼ loosely packed cup fresh cilantro leaves

Preheat the oven to 375°F. Generously butter a 10-inch pie plate.

Arrange the sweet potatoes in an even layer in the prepared dish. Using a pastry brush and 1½ tablespoons of the melted butter, lightly coat the potatoes. Season with salt.

Transfer the dish to the preheated oven and bake the potatoes for about 30 minutes, or until tender and just beginning to brown.

Lower the oven temperature to 350°F.

Combine the chiles with the onion rings in a medium bowl. Add the remaining 1½ tablespoons melted butter and toss to coat. Scatter the chiles and onions over the top of the hot sweet potatoes.

Return the potatoes to the oven and bake for about 30 minutes, or until the onions are cooked through and beginning to brown.

Remove from the oven and fold in the cilantro. Serve hot.

SWEET POTATO SPOONBREAD   MAKES 12 SPOONBREADS

I think that I've been eating some version of spoonbread my whole life. It is a Southern favorite, and there is even an annual Spoonbread Festival held in Berea, Kentucky, my home state. The history of spoonbread is a little vague, but it is thought that its pudding-like texture has evolved from a very basic cornmeal mixture introduced to white settlers by Native Americans. The usual is a simple mix of cornmeal and eggs, but here we add a little heart of Texas with the sweet potato and chile.

2 cups whole milk

1 tablespoon seeded and minced jalapeño chile

1 cup yellow cornmeal

1 cup sweet potato puree

½ cup grated jalapeño Jack cheese

8 tablespoons (1 stick) unsalted
    butter, at room temperature

Salt

4 large eggs, separated

Preheat the oven to 350°F. Generously coat the cups of a 12-cup muffin pan with butter or nonstick vegetable spray. Set aside.

Combine the milk and the chile in a medium saucepan over medium heat and bring to a boil. Whisking constantly, immediately add the cornmeal in a slow, steady stream. Lower the heat and simmer, stirring constantly, for about 5 minutes, or until very thick.

Remove from the heat and fold in the sweet potato puree, cheese, and butter. Season to taste with salt and mix until well blended. Set aside to cool.

When cool, place the egg yolks in a small bowl and whisk to lighten. Stir the yolks into the cooled cornmeal mixture, taking care that they are completely incorporated into the batter.

Place the egg whites in a medium bowl and, using a handheld electric mixer, beat until stiff peaks form.

Fold the beaten egg whites into the cornmeal mixture just until barely blended.

Spoon the mixture into the prepared muffin pan. Transfer to the preheated oven and bake for about 15 minutes, or until a cake tester inserted into the center of the spoonbreads comes out clean.

Remove from the oven and serve piping hot.

TANGLE OF GREENS   SERVES 4

This is about as simple and delicious as it gets! Greens, greens, and more greens—the addition of arugula here brings a contemporary taste to an otherwise Texas standard. You could combine almost any green you like to the mix—collard, mustard, dandelion—you name it, you can cook it up!

1 tablespoon olive oil

¼ cup cooked, small-dice smoked bacon

1 tablespoon minced shallot

1 teaspoon minced garlic

2 packed cups spinach leaves

1 packed cup arugula leaves

Salt

Freshly ground pepper

Heat the oil in a large sauté pan over medium heat. Add the bacon, shallot, and garlic and sauté for 1 minute. Add the spinach and arugula leaves, season to taste with salt and pepper, and toss to coat with the seasoned oil. Cook, tossing frequently, for a couple of minutes, or just until the greens have barely wilted.

Remove from the heat and serve immediately.

GUN BARREL CITY COLLARD GREENS SERVES 4 TO 6

Although I don't think many greens are grown along the shores of Cedar Creek Lake, around which the town of Gun Barrel City has been established, I liked the name so much that I decided to honor the town with this classic Texas side dish. Although the name evokes the Wild West, Gun Barrel City is a young town with lots of friendly folks located only about 55 miles southeast of Dallas. You don't need a shotgun to settle there!

1 cup chopped smoked bacon

2 tablespoons minced garlic

1 cup diced onion

2 tablespoons seeded and minced jalapeño chile

¼ cup malt vinegar

¼ cup pure maple syrup

2 bunches collard greens, well washed, large stems removed, roughly chopped

2 cups ham or chicken stock or nonfat, low-sodium chicken broth

Tabasco sauce

Salt

Freshly ground pepper

Put the bacon in a Dutch oven over medium-high heat and fry, stirring frequently, for about 8 minutes, or until well browned. Add the garlic and cook for 1 minute. Stir in the onion and chile and cook, stirring occasionally, for 4 minutes, or until lightly browned.

Add the vinegar and, using a wooden spoon, scrape up the browned bits from the bottom of the pot. Cook for about 2 minutes, or until the liquid has reduced by half. Stir in the syrup and continue to cook for 1 minute.

Add the greens along with the stock and bring to a boil. Lower the heat and cook at a gentle simmer for about 1 hour, or until the greens are fork-tender; there should be very little liquid left in the pan. Season with Tabasco and salt and pepper to taste. Serve hot.

CRISPY TEXAS OKRA SERVES 4 TO 6

Could you combine any two more specific regional tastes than Southern okra and Texas barbecue? I can guarantee that even the most die-hard okra haters will ask for seconds when you serve these crispy, crunchy little guys.

½ cup cornmeal

½ cup tempura flour (see Note, page 201)

2 teaspoons Fearing's Barbecue Spice Blend (page 39)

½ cup buttermilk

Vegetable oil, for frying

2 pounds okra, stems removed and cut in half lengthwise

Combine the cornmeal, tempura flour, and spice mix in a medium bowl.

Place the buttermilk in a separate small bowl.

Heat the oil in a deep-fat fryer over medium-high heat until it registers 350°F on a candy thermometer.

Working with one piece at a time, dip the okra into the buttermilk and then into the cornmeal mixture to evenly coat.

When the oil has reached the desired temperature, carefully drop the okra into the hot oil and fry for about 3 minutes, or until golden brown.

Using a slotted spoon, transfer the fried okra to a double layer of paper towels to drain. Serve immediately.

Fried Green Tomatoes   SERVES 4

I believe that green tomatoes have been Texas-fried for generations, but when I tried to find their history, I couldn't find one link to Texas cooks. In fact, some say that the recipe comes from Jewish cookbooks of the late 1800s. But in my opinion, since tomatoes were first grown in home gardens, I bet that home cooks were cooking with green tomatoes every year that there was a bounty crop. Farmers' wives whom I know tell me that their mamas were making fried green tomatoes for breakfast, lunch, and dinner just as their grandmas had done before them. I guess it really doesn't matter where the recipe started; Texas cooks have certainly embraced it—me included. If you really want the best old-fashioned taste, smother them in cream gravy…uhm.

Vegetable oil, for frying

1 cup all-purpose flour

½ cup Fearing's Barbecue Spice Blend (page 39)

4 large eggs, at room temperature, beaten

2 tablespoons buttermilk

1½ cups bread crumbs

4 green tomatoes, cored and cut crosswise into ¼-inch-thick slices

Salt

Freshly ground pepper

Heat the oil in a deep-fat fryer over high heat until it registers 350°F on a candy thermometer.

While the oil is heating, place 3 shallow bowls in a line on the countertop. Combine the flour and spice in the first bowl. Whisk the eggs and buttermilk together in the second bowl. Put the bread crumbs in the third bowl.

Generously season both sides of the tomato slices with salt and pepper. Working with one slice at a time, coat the tomatoes in the flour mixture, shaking off excess. Dip the flour-coated slice into the eggs, and finally into the bread crumbs. Take care that all sides are well coated.

When the oil has reached the desired temperature, working with a few slices at a time, place the coated tomatoes in the hot oil and fry for about 3 minutes, or until crisp and golden.

Using a slotted spoon or spatula, lift the tomatoes from the oil and transfer to a double layer of paper towels to drain.

Serve warm.

All-Day Green Beans   SERVES 4 TO 6

Home cooks have been making all-day green beans for generations. This method of cooking has almost been lost, with chefs, particularly, who are cooking their veggies until crisp-tender. I love these almost mushy beans—my grandma cooked them this way, my mom cooked them this way, and I still do, at home and at the restaurant.

1 tablespoon vegetable oil

½ pound diced, smoked bacon

1 packed cup sliced onions

2 pounds green beans, trimmed

1 quart chicken stock

Salt

Freshly ground pepper

Heat the oil in a large sauté pan over medium heat. Add the bacon and cook, while stirring, for 3 minutes, or until the bacon starts to brown.

Add the onions and cook for 1 minute. Add the green beans and chicken stock and bring to a boil. Lower the heat to a simmer. Season with salt and pepper and cook for at least 1 hour, or all day until the dinner bell rings!

ROASTED ASPARAGUS *with* SMOKED TEXAS PECANS

SERVES 4

Although you don't think of asparagus when you think of Texas, I can tell you that terrific asparagus is grown in Central Texas, where the cooler climate makes it very happy. The simple garnish of cold-smoked pecans and shallots accents the acidity of the asparagus in a perfect way.

1 pound medium asparagus, trimmed of tough ends

2 tablespoons olive oil

1 teaspoon salt

1 teaspoon coarsely ground pepper

¼ cup cold-smoked pecan pieces (see sidebar, page 139)

2 tablespoons minced shallots

Preheat the oven to 350°F.

Combine the asparagus with the oil and season with the salt and pepper.

Lay the seasoned asparagus out on a baking pan large enough to hold it in a single layer. Transfer to the preheated oven and roast for 8 minutes.

Remove from the oven and sprinkle with the pecans and shallots. Serve immediately.

PAULA'S GOAT CHEESE CROQUETTES

MAKES 12 CROQUETTES

Paula Lambert, owner of the Mozzarella Company in Dallas, was a pioneer in artisanal cheese making in Texas. I was her first customer when I was at the Mansion on Turtle Creek in 1981, and I have been using her cheeses ever since. Paula's goat cheese is, to me, perfection. It's not too tart but has a subtle rich flavor that shines in these croquettes. They are a wonderful accent to all kinds of salads.

½ cup all-purpose flour

2 large eggs, beaten

½ cup bread crumbs

1 pound soft goat cheese, preferably from the Mozzarella Company

Vegetable oil, for frying

Salt

Place 3 shallow bowls in a line on the countertop. Place the flour in the first bowl, the eggs in the second, and the bread crumbs in the third.

Using a small ice cream scoop or melon baller, form 12 goat cheese balls.

Roll the cheese balls in the flour, shaking off any excess. Then roll each floured ball in the eggs, taking care that the entire surface is coated. If any surface is uncovered, the cheese will ooze out during frying, making the ball unusable. Finally, roll the balls in the bread crumbs, making sure that the entire surface is well covered.

Heat the oil in a deep-fat fryer over high heat until it registers 350°F on a candy thermometer.

When the oil has reached the desired temperature, gently ease the cheese balls into the hot oil, making sure not to crowd the pan. Fry for about 1 minute, or until golden brown.

Transfer to a double layer of paper towels to drain and season with salt. Serve immediately.

8

BREADS

and

ROLLS

BACON-JALAPEÑO BISCUITS   MAKES 8 BISCUITS

Southern-style biscuits with a Tex-Mex twist, these are one of my favorite breakfast or brunch breads. They also add a little heat to a ladies' salad lunch. Just remember, biscuits have to be hot from the oven or they just don't taste quite right.

2 cups sifted all-purpose flour

½ teaspoon baking soda

1 teaspoon salt

4 tablespoons (½ stick) unsalted butter, softened

¾ cup buttermilk

1 tablespoon seeded and minced jalapeño chile

¼ pound cooked hickory-smoked bacon, crumbled

Preheat the oven to 350°F.

Sift the flour, baking soda, and salt into a large bowl. Add the butter and, using a pastry cutter or a kitchen fork, cut the butter into the dry ingredients until the mixture resembles cornmeal.

Stir in enough buttermilk to make a soft dough. Don't worry if you use less or more than called for—the amount will depend on the humidity in your kitchen.

Fold in the chile and bacon just to blend. Do not overmix.

Lightly flour a clean, flat work surface and scrape the dough out onto it. Knead the dough lightly for about 3 turns. Pat the dough out to a thickness of about ½ inch and cut it into circles using a 2-inch round biscuit cutter.

Place the biscuits on a baking sheet, leaving a couple of inches between them. Transfer to the preheated oven and bake for about 10 minutes, or until golden brown.

Serve immediately—nobody likes a cold biscuit!

Iron-Skillet Cornbread

MAKES ONE 10-INCH ROUND CORNBREAD

I use organic stone-ground yellow cornmeal from Homestead Gristmill (see sidebar, page 50), as it makes a deeply flavored bread with a terrific texture. Finely ground meal just doesn't result in the same corn flavor and coarse texture that I prefer.

1 cup yellow cornmeal, coarsely ground if possible

1 cup all-purpose flour

¼ cup sugar

4 teaspoons baking powder

½ teaspoon salt

1 cup whole milk

2 extra-large eggs, lightly beaten, at room temperature

¼ cup melted unsalted butter or bacon grease, plus more for greasing the skillet

Preheat the oven to 425°F.

Lightly coat a 10-inch cast-iron skillet with butter or bacon grease. Place in the preheated oven.

Combine the cornmeal, flour, sugar, baking powder, and salt in a medium bowl. Stir in the milk along with the eggs and butter and mix with a few rapid strokes just to moisten the dry ingredients.

Remove the hot skillet from the oven and scrape the cornbread batter into it. Return the skillet to the oven and bake for about 25 minutes, or until the edges of the bread are light brown or a cake tester inserted into the center comes out clean.

Remove from the oven and, if using as bread, serve immediately. If using as a component of another recipe, such as for a stuffing, transfer it to a wire rack to cool before cutting or breaking apart.

JALAPEÑO-BACON CORNBREAD MUFFINS

MAKES 24 MUFFINS

These muffins make a great addition to the brunch table but also work just fine at dinner. If possible, use bacon fat, as the flavor just expands the muffins to an almost indefinable richness. Corny, spicy, cheesy, and bacony—what more could you want?

1½ cups melted unsalted butter, plus more for greasing the pans

2 garlic cloves, finely minced

2 shallots, minced

½ cup finely chopped onion

2 teaspoons seeded and minced jalapeño chile

3 cups fresh corn kernels (or thawed frozen)

¼ cup finely chopped scallions

6 extra-large eggs, lightly beaten

3 cups buttermilk

3 cups cornmeal

3 cups all-purpose flour

½ cup sugar

¼ cup pure chile powder

2 tablespoons baking powder

2 tablespoons salt

2 tablespoons freshly ground pepper

1½ teaspoons baking soda

3 cups grated cheddar cheese

½ cup crumbled crisp bacon

Preheat the oven to 350°F. Lightly coat the cups of two 12-cup muffin pans with butter. Set aside.

Heat the butter in a large frying pan over medium-high heat. Add the garlic, shallots, onion, and chile and cook, stirring frequently, for 5 minutes. Stir in the corn and scallions and cook, stirring, for another 2 minutes. Remove from the heat and set aside to cool.

In a large bowl, combine the eggs and buttermilk and whisk until very well blended. Stir in the cooled reserved corn-scallion mixture. Set aside.

In a large bowl, combine the cornmeal, flour, sugar, chile powder, baking powder, salt, pepper, and baking soda and stir to combine. Add the egg mixture to the cornmeal mixture. Do not overmix; you want to just barely combine the ingredients. Fold in the cheese and bacon.

Spoon the batter into the prepared muffin pans, filling them about three-quarters full.

Place in the preheated oven and bake for about 15 minutes, or until a cake tester inserted into the center comes out clean and the muffins are golden brown. Serve warm.

PARKER HOUSE ROLLS   MAKES 24 ROLLS

Is there anything in the world better than a basket of homemade Parker House Rolls? Home cooks have been making them since the 1880s, and they have remained an American favorite since that time. I love the buttery sweetness of the dough that is accented by the slightly crisp crust.

> 1½ cups whole milk
>
> 1 package instant active dry yeast
>
> 2 tablespoons sugar
>
> ½ cup lukewarm (115°F) water
>
> 1 tablespoon salt
>
> 8 tablespoons (1 stick) unsalted butter, melted
>
> About 6 cups all-purpose flour

Pour the milk into a small saucepan over medium heat. Heat just until bubbles begin to form around the edge of the pan. Remove from the heat and set aside to cool to lukewarm.

Combine the yeast with 1 tablespoon of the sugar in the bowl of a stand mixer fitted with the dough hook. Add the water and let stand for about 5 minutes, or until proofed and bubbly.

Add the cooled milk to the yeast mixture along with the remaining 1 tablespoon sugar and the salt. With the mixer on low speed, add ¼ cup of the melted butter. Increase the speed to medium, add 1½ cups of the flour, and beat for 3 minutes.

Reduce the mixer speed to low and begin adding the remaining flour, 1 cup at a time. Continue adding flour until a soft dough forms.

Lightly flour a clean, flat work surface. Scrape the dough onto the floured surface and, using your hands, knead the dough for about 10 minutes, or until it is smooth and elastic.

Generously butter the interior of a large bowl. Using your hands, lift the dough and place it in the buttered bowl, turning to coat all sides of the dough with the butter. Cover and set aside to rest in a warm spot for about 1 hour, or until doubled in volume.

Again, lightly flour a clean, flat work surface. Gently deflate the dough and turn it out onto the floured surface. Let rest for 5 minutes.

Using a rolling pin, roll the dough out to a thickness of ½ inch. Using a 3-inch round biscuit cutter, cut the dough into circles. Using the back of a kitchen knife, make a crease down the center of each circle. Using a pastry brush, lightly coat the tops with the remaining melted butter. Fold each circle in half, on the crease, and gently press the edges together. Place the folded rolls, 2 inches apart, on nonstick cookie sheets. You will probably need at least 2 large cookie sheets.

Lightly flour 2 clean large kitchen towels and place one, floured side down, over each cookie sheet. Set aside to rest in a warm spot for 35 minutes.

Preheat the oven to 425°F.

Uncover the rolls and transfer the cookie sheets to the preheated oven. Bake the rolls for about 15 minutes, or until golden brown.

Remove from the oven and serve warm.

Spicy Cheese Crackers

Easy to make and so much better than store-bought cheese crackers, I'll guarantee that these neat little crackers will become a cocktail favorite. To make a terrific snack for kids, just reduce or eliminate the cayenne and black peppers.

2 cups all-purpose flour

¼ cup yellow cornmeal

½ tablespoon coarse sea salt

½ tablespoon cayenne pepper

Scant 1 teaspoon coarsely ground black pepper

8 tablespoons (1 stick) unsalted butter, cut into cubes and frozen, plus more for greasing the cookie sheets

½ pound white cheddar cheese, grated

1 cup whole milk

Combine the flour, cornmeal, salt, cayenne, and black pepper in the bowl of a stand mixer fitted with the paddle attachment.

With the mixer on low speed, add the butter and beat to incorporate until it is in pea-size pieces.

With the mixer still on low speed, add the cheese and milk and beat just until a soft dough forms. Do not overmix.

Using a rubber spatula, scrape the dough onto a piece of waxed paper and carefully roll it into a 2-inch round log. Seal the ends and place in the freezer. Freeze for about 2 hours (or up to 1 month), or until solidly frozen.

When ready to bake, preheat the oven to 325°F. Lightly butter nonstick cookie sheets. Set aside.

Remove the dough from the freezer and allow it to thaw for about 10 minutes, or just until a knife easily cuts into it.

Using a sharp knife, cut the dough crosswise into ¼-inch-thick slices.

Transfer to the prepared cookie sheets and place in the preheated oven. Bake for about 7 minutes, or until golden brown.

Remove from the oven and transfer to wire racks to cool before serving.

GRANNY EVANS' SHINER BOCK BEER BREAD

MAKES ONE 9-INCH LOAF

This bread is surprisingly simple but full of flavor. The recipe has evolved from the pioneer days with the recent addition of cheese, so it varies a bit from the original, but not by much. This particular recipe comes from one of Fearing's pastry cooks and has been passed down through generations of the Evans family from Texas to Arkansas. This beer-flavored bread is now so associated with Texas and steaks that almost every home cook willing to try their hand at bread making has done so with this recipe. It is a slightly sweet brown bread that is great at both the dinner and the breakfast tables. It is extremely important that the beer be at room temperature or the dough won't rise.

2 tablespoons melted unsalted butter,
   plus more for greasing the pan

3 cups all-purpose flour

3 tablespoons sugar

1¼ teaspoons baking powder

¾ teaspoon salt, plus more for sprinkling

1 bottle **Shiner Bock** beer, at room temperature

½ cup grated sharp cheddar cheese

Preheat the oven to 350°F. Coat the interior of a 9 by 4-inch loaf pan with butter. Set aside.

Combine the flour, sugar, baking powder, and salt in a medium bowl and stir to blend. Stir in the beer and beat until completely combined.

Add the cheese and fold it into the dough.

Scrape the dough into the prepared loaf pan and generously sprinkle salt over the top.

Place in the preheated oven and bake for 1 hour, or until golden brown and risen.

Remove from the oven and, using a pastry brush, lightly coat the top with melted butter. Serve warm.

KOLACHES *with* JALAPEÑO VENISON SAUSAGE

Talk to any Texan about memories of home and I'll bet you'll get a kolache story. From their origins in the ovens of Czech immigrants in the late nineteenth century, kolaches have become the state pastry. Savory or sweet, they are, no doubt, everyone's favorite snack—even those without any Czech heritage. Kolache festivals abound, with the most exciting ones in Caldwell and West (the town), Texas.

1 cup lukewarm (115°F) whole milk

⅓ cup sugar

1 packet or 2¼ teaspoons instant active dry yeast

3½ cups all-purpose flour

1 large egg, at room temperature

⅔ cup melted unsalted butter

1 teaspoon salt

1 teaspoon olive oil

6 cooked Jalapeño Venison Sausage links (page 129) or your favorite sausage, cut into 4-inch pieces

Finding the Best Kolaches in Texas

Around Austin you will hear long-standing arguments about who makes the best kolaches in Texas. Some of the most well-known bakeries are the Czech Stop in West, Kolache Creations in Austin, Shipley's Do-Nuts in Houston, and the Kolache Factory in Katy. I'm told that the Czech Stop makes so many that they can't even count the number. Now, that's a lot of dough!

Combine ⅓ cup of the warm milk with 1 teaspoon of the sugar in a small bowl. Add the yeast and stir until it dissolves. Set aside for about 30 minutes, or until it begins to bubble.

Put the flour in a large bowl. Using your hands, form a depression in the center of the flour and add the remaining ⅔ cup milk and sugar along with the reserved yeast mixture, egg, ⅓ cup of the melted butter, and the salt. Using your hands, mix to combine, then continue to knead the mixture together for about 3 minutes, or until a dough forms. The dough should not be wet; add flour in small amounts if needed.

Scoop the dough from the bowl and form it into a ball. Rub the ball with the olive oil and put it in a clean bowl. Cover with plastic wrap and set aside in a warm area for 4 hours, or until doubled in volume.

Preheat the oven to 350°F. Line a baking sheet with parchment paper. Set aside.

Uncover the dough and, using your hands or a dough cutter, divide the dough into 6 equal pieces.

Lightly flour a clean, flat work surface and, working with one piece of dough at a time, roll each dough piece out into a 3-inch square about ½ inch thick.

When all the dough is shaped, place equal portions of sausage down the center. You can now either fold both sides of the dough up and over the filling, pushing the seam closed, and place the filled dough, seam side down, on the parchment paper–lined baking sheet, *or* you can pull each corner of the dough up to the center and pinch the center closed, leaving a bit of sausage peeking out of the four corners. For the latter, the kolaches are placed right side up on the baking sheet.

Using the remaining ⅓ cup melted butter and a pastry brush, lightly coat the top of each kolache with butter, reserving some of the butter to brush on once the kolaches are baked.

Transfer the kolaches to the preheated oven and bake for 20 to 25 minutes, or until golden brown.

Remove from the oven and lightly brush the tops with the reserved butter. Serve hot or warm.

NOTE: You can wrap the dough around a sausage, leaving the ends peeking out. Other savory fillings might be ham, breakfast or Italian sausage, cheeses, or precooked and seasoned vegetables. Fruits, jams, and sweetened curd cheeses like ricotta or farmer's cheese make excellent sweet fillings. If using a soft-textured filling, such as those suggested for sweets, make sure that the seams are tightly sealed or the filling will spill out during baking.

BLUEBERRY MUFFINS MAKES 12 MUFFINS

Can you imagine that not very far from downtown Dallas, you can pick your own blueberries? These muffins are a summertime favorite made with berries from the local crop, but they can also be made year-round using frozen berries. Just let the berries thaw and drain a bit before adding them to the batter.

½ cup melted unsalted butter, plus more for greasing the pan

1¼ cups bread flour

1¼ cups all-purpose flour

1¼ cups sugar

1 tablespoon baking powder

¼ teaspoon ground cinnamon

¼ teaspoon salt

2 large eggs, at room temperature

1 cup whole milk

½ cup vegetable oil

¼ teaspoon vanilla paste

1 cup fresh blueberries

Preheat the oven to 400°F. Generously butter a 12-cup muffin pan. Set aside.

Combine the bread and all-purpose flours with the sugar, baking powder, cinnamon, and salt in a medium bowl. Set aside.

In a separate bowl, combine the eggs, milk, oil, butter, and vanilla paste and whisk to combine thoroughly.

With a wooden spoon, slowly beat the egg mixture into the flour mixture, stirring until well combined. Fold in the blueberries.

Spoon an equal portion of the batter into each of the prepared muffin cups. Place in the preheated oven. Bake for about 20 minutes, or until a cake tester inserted into the center of each muffin comes out clean. Serve warm.

NAVAJO FRY BREAD   MAKES ABOUT 12 FRY BREADS

It is thought that the recipe for Navajo fry bread came about when the American government relocated Navajos from Arizona to New Mexico in the 1880s and provided those Native Americans with government-surplus lard, flour, sugar, and salt. From these not very pleasant beginnings, fry bread has become part of the culinary history of these native people and is eaten at tribal celebrations as well as at home. Throughout Texas and the Southwest, fry bread is often served as a wrap for taco-like fillings at picnics, fairs, and other gatherings.

3 cups all-purpose flour

1 tablespoon baking powder

½ teaspoon salt

1½ cups warm water

Vegetable oil, for frying

Combine the flour, baking powder, and salt in the bowl of a heavy-duty stand mixer fitted with the dough hook. With the mixer on low speed, slowly begin adding the water, mixing until a soft dough begins to form. Continue to mix until the dough pulls together completely. Do not overmix.

Transfer the dough to a clean bowl, cover with plastic wrap, and refrigerate for 1 hour.

When ready to fry, heat the oil in a frying pan over high heat until it registers 350°F on a candy thermometer.

While the oil is heating, lightly flour a clean, flat work surface. Remove the dough from the refrigerator and place it on the floured surface. Pat the dough down slightly and pull off golf ball–size pieces of dough.

One at a time, roll the balls out to a thickness of about ¼ inch. Cut a hole in the center to keep the dough from curling as it fries, and place in the hot oil. Fry, turning once, for about 3 minutes, or until golden brown and cooked through. Using tongs, transfer to a double layer of paper towels to drain. Continue frying until you have used all the dough.

Serve warm, whole or cut into triangles.

NOTE: Navajo Fry Bread can also be used as the wrap to make a Native American–style taco.

MASA *for* TAMALES MAKES ENOUGH DOUGH FOR 12 TAMALES

This is the standard for tamale dough in the restaurant. However, the Maseca brand masa has a simpler recipe on the package. I will warn you that it takes some practice to make perfect masa. It took me some time to learn, and, even now, I prefer to leave it to my skilled Mexican cooks.

5 cups Maseca corn flour

¼ cup sugar

1 tablespoon baking powder

1 tablespoon salt

2 teaspoons Fearing's Barbecue
   Spice Blend (page 39)

1 teaspoon ancho chile powder

1 teaspoon chipotle chile powder

1 tablespoon vegetable shortening

½ cup Texas-Style Barbecue Sauce (page 19)
   or barbecue sauce of your choice

2 cups cool water

Put the flour in a large bowl. Add the sugar, baking powder, salt, spice blend, and ancho and chipotle powders and stir to blend. Add the vegetable shortening along with the barbecue sauce and the cool water.

Using a wooden spoon, mix just until the dough comes together. Do not overmix or the dough will be tough.

Use as directed in any tamale recipe.

9

DESSERTS

Banana Pudding *with* Caramelized Apple Fritters MAKES 6 PUDDINGS

This is my pastry chef Jill Bates' take on the Southern classic banana dessert. Although quite different from my mom's, it is as rich and addictive as the original. The fritters take this simple pudding over the top, but if you're lacking time, just make the pudding. And on another day, make the fritters; they are delicious on their own.

1¼ cups heavy cream

1 vanilla bean, split in half lengthwise

15 large egg yolks, at room temperature

¾ cup sugar

2 ripe bananas, peeled and cut crosswise into thin slices

Caramelized Apple Fritters, for serving (recipe follows) (optional)

½ cup Caramel Sauce, for serving (recipe follows)

Combine the cream and vanilla bean in a medium saucepan over medium-low heat and bring to a gentle simmer.

Put the egg yolks and sugar in a heatproof bowl, preferably stainless steel, and whisk to blend.

Fill a medium saucepan with about ¼ inch of water. The saucepan should be large enough to hold the bowl without the bottom of the bowl touching the water. Place the saucepan over medium heat and then place the bowl on top of the saucepan. Whisking constantly, cook the egg yolk–sugar mixture for about 5 minutes, or until the mixture forms a ribbon when the whisk is lifted from the bowl. At this point, increase the heat under the cream and bring it to a boil.

Remove the vanilla bean from the cream and, whisking constantly, slowly pour the hot cream into the egg yolk–sugar mixture. Cook, whisking constantly, until the mixture is beginning to thicken.

Remove the bowl from the saucepan. Pour the pudding through a fine-mesh sieve into a clean container. Cover with plastic film pressed directly on the surface to prevent a skin from forming over the top. Transfer to the refrigerator to cool completely. Once cool, the pudding can be covered and refrigerated for up to 3 days.

When ready to serve, remove the pudding from the refrigerator and fold the bananas into it.

Spoon an equal portion of the pudding into each of six small bowls. Place 3 fritters next to the pudding. Lightly drizzle the fritters with the caramel sauce. Serve immediately.

CARAMELIZED APPLE FRITTERS

MAKES 18 FRITTERS

¾ cup sugar

2 Honeycrisp or any firm, slightly tart apple, peeled, cored, and cut into a small dice

1½ teaspoons ground cinnamon

1½ cups all-purpose flour

1 vanilla bean, split in half lengthwise

½ teaspoon finely grated lemon zest

2 large eggs, separated, at room temperature

½ cup whole milk

2 teaspoons melted unsalted butter

Vegetable oil, for frying

About 1 cup cinnamon-sugar

Put ½ cup of the sugar in a medium heavy-bottomed saucepan over medium heat. Cook, stirring, for about 3 minutes, or until the sugar has begun to caramelize.

Slowly stir in the apples along with ½ teaspoon of the cinnamon and cook, stirring, for about 3 minutes, or until all of the sugar has melted and the liquid is a dark brown but not burnt color. Remove from the heat and set aside to cool.

When cool, strain through a fine-mesh sieve, discarding the liquid and reserving the apples.

Combine the flour with the remaining ¼ cup sugar and 1 teaspoon cinnamon. Scrape the seeds from the vanilla bean into the flour mixture. Stir in the lemon zest. Set aside.

Combine the egg yolks with the milk and melted butter in a small bowl and whisk to combine.

(continued)

Whisking constantly, slowly add the egg yolk–sugar mixture to the flour mixture and whisk until no lumps appear.

Place the egg whites in a small bowl and, using a hand-held mixer, beat until stiff peaks form. Fold the egg whites into the batter, leaving some small lumps.

Fold the reserved, cooled apples into the batter.

Heat the oil in a deep-fat fryer over medium-high heat until it registers 350°F on a candy thermometer.

Using a ¾-ounce ladle or scoop, lower portions of the batter into the hot oil. Fry for about 2 minutes, or until golden brown and cooked through. Do not crowd the fryer.

Using a slotted spoon, transfer the cooked fritters to a double layer of paper towels to drain.

Pour the cinnamon-sugar into a resealable plastic bag and, while still hot, add the fritters to the bag and shake to lightly coat with the sugar. Serve warm.

CARAMEL SAUCE

MAKES ¾ CUP

¾ cup sugar

½ teaspoon fresh lemon juice

2 tablespoons cold water

½ cup heavy cream

2 tablespoons to ¼ cup whole milk

Combine the sugar with the lemon juice and cold water in a medium saucepan over medium-high heat. Cook, stirring, for about 2 minutes, or until the sugar has dissolved completely.

Without stirring, bring the mixture to a boil. Continue to boil, without stirring, for about 3 minutes, or until the mixture is golden brown in color. Watch carefully, as the sugar mix can burn very easily. If it begins to burn, lift the pan from the heat for a few seconds.

While the mixture is boiling, carefully add the cream in a slow, steady stream, whisking to blend; be careful, the mixture may splatter when the cream is added. When all of the cream has been added, remove the pan from the heat.

Whisk in the milk, 2 tablespoons at a time, adding just enough milk to make a thin sauce. The caramel will thicken as it cools. Set aside to cool.

Use the sauce immediately, or store, tightly covered and refrigerated, for up to 1 week. Bring to room temperature before using.

Mexican Rice Pudding *with* Cajeta (Arroz con Leche)   SERVES 4 TO 6

This is a very rich and Mexican creamy rice pudding with just a hint of cinnamon. What makes it sing of Mexico is the *cajeta* drizzle, which, by the way, is also terrific on ice cream. If you love all things "dulce de leche," you will love this cajeta, a classic Mexican milk candy.

1 cinnamon stick

1 vanilla bean, split lengthwise, seeds scraped

4 cups water

2 cups long-grain rice

2 cups heavy cream

One 14-ounce can sweetened condensed milk

½ cup golden raisins (optional)

Cajeta (recipe follows)

Combine the cinnamon stick and the vanilla pod and seeds with the water in a heavy-bottomed saucepan over high heat. Bring to a boil, then, stirring constantly, add the rice. Lower the heat and simmer for about 30 minutes, or until the water has been absorbed.

Add the cream, one cup at a time, stirring constantly, and continue to cook until all of the cream has been absorbed.

Stir in the sweetened condensed milk and cook, stirring, for about 10 minutes, or until the mixture is quite thick. Remove the vanilla pod and discard.

Remove from the heat and stir in the raisins, if using. Pour the pudding into a shallow dish and set aside to cool.

When ready to serve, spoon equal amounts of the rice pudding into each dessert bowl and generously drizzle the cajeta over the top. Serve immediately.

CAJETA

MAKES 2 QUARTS

2 quarts goat's milk (cow's milk may be substituted)

2 cups sugar

1 vanilla bean, split in half lengthwise

½ teaspoon baking soda dissolved in 1 tablespoon water

Combine the milk and sugar in a medium saucepan. Add the vanilla bean and place over medium heat. Cook, stirring constantly, for about 7 minutes, or until the sugar has dissolved and the mixture begins to simmer.

Remove from the heat and stir in the dissolved baking soda; be careful, as the sauce will bubble up. This will happen more rapidly when goat's milk is used.

Return the pan to medium heat and bring to a brisk simmer; do not boil. Simmer, stirring frequently, for about 1 hour, or until golden brown. Continue to cook for a few minutes until the mixture begins to thicken and turn a deeper brown.

Immediately remove from the heat and set aside to cool. When cool, the mixture should have a thick sauce-like consistency. If too thick, add water, a teaspoonful at a time, to thin. Remove and reserve the vanilla bean. Pour the cajeta through a fine-mesh sieve into a clean bowl. Using a small, sharp knife, scrape the seeds from the vanilla pod into the cajeta and stir to blend throughly. Discard the pod.

Use the cajeta immediately, or store, tightly covered and refrigerated, for up to 2 weeks. Warm before using.

BROWN SUGAR PEACHES
with PISTACHIO ICE CREAM SERVES 6

This is a great Texas summertime dessert when the peaches are perfectly ripe. The grill gives an interesting taste to the dish and caramelizes the sugar. Of course, you can use the peaches on almost any commercial ice cream, and without all of the extras, but it sure wouldn't be a Texas dessert.

6 tablespoons Sugar in the Raw

6 peaches, peeled, pitted, and
   cut in half lengthwise

4 tablespoons (½ stick) unsalted butter

⅓ cup plus 1 tablespoon packed light brown sugar

1 cup heavy cream, sweetened and whipped

Pistachio Ice Cream (recipe follows) or fine-
   quality, store-bought pistachio ice cream

Pistachio Granola (recipe follows)

Preheat and oil the grill.

Pour the Sugar in the Raw into a large shallow bowl. Dip the peaches, cut side down, into the sugar. Turn and coat the remaining sides in the sugar. Place the peaches on the hot grill, cut side down, and grill for 1 minute.

Remove the peaches from the grill and cut into medium dice.

Put the butter and light brown sugar in a large frying pan over medium heat. Add the diced peaches and cook, gently stirring occasionally, for about 3 minutes, or until very tender.

Using half of the peaches, spoon an equal portion into each of four ramekins or sundae glasses. Follow with an equal portion of the whipped cream, then the ice cream, and finally the granola. Repeat the layering. Serve immediately.

PISTACHIO ICE CREAM

MAKES 2 QUARTS

4 cups heavy cream

4 cups whole milk

3 cups toasted pistachios

10 large egg yolks, at room temperature

1 cup sugar

Combine the cream and milk in a large heavy-bottomed saucepan over medium-high heat. Add the pistachios and cook for about 8 minutes, or just until bubbles begin to form around the edges of the pan.

Remove from the heat and set aside for 1 to 2 hours to allow the pistachios to deeply flavor the liquid.

Return the pistachio mixture to medium-high heat and bring to a boil.

Combine the egg yolks and sugar in a medium bowl and whisk to blend well. Immediately, slowly pour about 1 cup of the hot liquid into the egg yolk–sugar mixture, stirring vigorously to temper.

Whisking constantly, pour the tempered egg mixture into the hot liquid in the saucepan. Cook, whisking constantly, for about 5 minutes, or until it begins to thicken.

Remove from the heat and strain through a fine-mesh sieve into a clean container. Cover and refrigerate for about 2 hours, or until well chilled. Discard the solids.

When well chilled, transfer to an ice cream maker and freeze according to the manufacturer's directions.

PISTACHIO GRANOLA

MAKES ABOUT 2 CUPS

6 tablespoons grapeseed oil

¼ cup honey

¼ cup pure maple syrup

¼ teaspoon vanilla paste

¾ cup old-fashioned oatmeal

¼ cup pumpkin seeds

¼ cup sunflower seeds

1 tablespoon oat bran

1 teaspoon coarsely chopped pistachios

½ teaspoon ground cinnamon

½ teaspoon ground ginger

Preheat the oven to 325°F. Line a rimmed baking sheet with a nonstick silicone mat or with aluminum foil. Set aside.

Combine the oil, honey, syrup, and vanilla paste in a small saucepan over medium heat. Cook, stirring, for about 3 minutes, or just until hot and blended. Remove from the heat and set aside.

Combine the oatmeal, pumpkin seeds, sunflower seeds, oat bran, pistachios, cinnamon, and ginger in a bowl. Pour the oil mixture over the top and stir to blend well.

Spread the mixture out on the prepared pan. Place in the preheated oven and bake for about 20 minutes, or until golden brown and slightly crisp.

Serve immediately or store, tightly covered, in a cool, dark spot, for up to 1 week.

CARAMELIZED APPLE BUCKLE   SERVES 4

I grew up eating buckles and cobblers and all kinds of cake-based fruit desserts, and I never exactly knew one from the other—they were all good in my book. However, traditionally a buckle is made with a bottom cake layer, a middle layer of fruit, and a topping of sweetened crumbs. But it can also be made with the fruit mixed into the cake and then topped with crumbs. This version does a little of both.

Rather than the usual topping of vanilla ice cream or whipped cream, I like to serve this with slightly sweetened crème fraîche. (Just whip a little brown sugar into a cup of crème fraîche.)

2 tablespoons melted unsalted butter

½ cup packed light brown sugar

2 Granny Smith apples, peeled, cored, and cut crosswise into thick slices

Pinch ground cinnamon

1 cup granulated sugar

¾ cup almond paste

8 tablespoons (1 stick) unsalted butter, at room temperature

½ cup vegetable shortening

3 large eggs, at room temperature

1 teaspoon pure vanilla extract

Pinch salt

1 cup bread flour

Crunch Topping (recipe follows)

Pour the melted butter into a medium sauté pan over medium heat. Add the brown sugar and cook, stirring, for a couple of minutes, or until bubbling. Add the apples and cook, stirring occasionally, for about 10 minutes, or until the apples are tender and nicely caramelized. Stir in the cinnamon, remove from the heat, and set aside.

Preheat the oven to 350°F. Generously butter the interior of four 6- to 8-ounce ramekins and set aside.

Combine the granulated sugar and almond paste in the bowl of a stand mixer fitted with the paddle attachment. Beat on low for 3 minutes, or until smooth.

Add the room-temperature butter and shortening, increase the speed to medium, and beat for about 5 minutes, or until light and fluffy.

With the mixer still running on medium speed, add the eggs, one at a time, beating well after each addition. Add the vanilla and salt and continue to beat to blend.

Decrease the speed to low and slowly add the flour, beating until completely incorporated.

Using about half of the batter, spoon an equal portion into the bottom of each buttered ramekin. Then spoon an equal portion of the apples over the batter. Spoon the remaining cake batter over the apples, distributing it equally among the ramekins, and top with an equal portion of the Crunch Topping.

Transfer to the preheated oven and bake for about 25 minutes, or until cooked through and golden brown.

Remove from the oven and serve warm with ice cream, whipped cream, or my preference, sweetened crème fraîche.

Crunch Topping

MAKES 1½ CUPS

½ cup all-purpose flour

⅓ cup quick-cooking oatmeal

⅓ cup packed light brown sugar

½ teaspoon ground cinnamon

¼ teaspoon salt

4 tablespoons (½ stick) cold unsalted
  butter, cut into small pieces

Combine the flour, oatmeal, sugar, cinnamon, and salt in a bowl and stir to blend well.

Using your fingertips, work the butter into the dry ingredients to make a crumbly mix.

Use as directed.

PEACH COBBLER
MAKES ONE 9-INCH SQUARE COBBLER

It's said that in June you can find the best and biggest peaches in Texas in Parker County, and, when you find them, nothing could be better than making this cobbler. It is summertime in a dish. You can also make this cobbler with other stone fruits or berries.

8 tablespoons (1 stick) cold unsalted butter, cut into small cubes, plus more for buttering the dish

3 cups sliced peeled peaches

1⅔ cups sugar

1 teaspoon peeled and minced fresh ginger

3 cups plus 1 tablespoon all-purpose flour

2 teaspoons baking powder

1 teaspoon baking soda

1 teaspoon salt

½ teaspoon ground cinnamon

1⅓ cups buttermilk

Preheat the oven to 350°F. Generously butter a 9-inch square baking dish. Set aside. Line a cookie sheet with parchment paper or a nonstick silicone baking mat. Set aside.

Combine the peaches with ⅔ cup of the sugar and the ginger in a medium saucepan. Add 1 tablespoon of the flour and place over medium-high heat. Bring to a boil, stirring frequently. Immediately remove from the heat and spoon into the prepared baking dish. Set aside.

Combine the remaining 3 cups flour and 1 cup sugar with the baking powder, baking soda, salt, and cinnamon in the bowl of a food processor fitted with the metal blade. Process to blend.

Add the butter and process, using quick on-and-off turns, until it resembles coarse meal. Add the buttermilk and process just until a sticky dough forms.

Lightly flour a clean, flat work surface. Scrape the dough onto the floured surface and dust the top of the dough completely.

Using a rolling pin, roll the dough to a thickness of ¼ inch. Using a small biscuit cutter, cut the dough into circles or any other shape you desire. Transfer the cutout dough to the prepared cookie sheet.

Place in the preheated oven and bake for about 7 minutes, or until the dough is partially cooked and beginning to color. Do not turn the oven off.

Remove from the oven and place the dough on top of the peaches.

Place in the preheated oven and bake for about 15 minutes, or until the fruit is bubbling and the pastry is golden brown and cooked through. Serve hot or warm.

BLUEBERRY CRISP *with*
PECAN STREUSEL TOPPING   SERVES 4

This is now a year-round dish, as you usually find pretty sweet and juicy blueberries no matter the month. Blueberry Crisp is one of my favorite desserts, which, to my mind, cannot be separated from the American classic "à la mode."

1 cup all-purpose flour

1¼ cups packed light brown sugar

1 cup chopped toasted pecans

1 teaspoon coarse sea salt

1 teaspoon ground cinnamon or whichever sweet spice (clove, nutmeg, allspice) you prefer

8 tablespoons (1 stick) unsalted butter, cut into pieces, at room temperature

4 cups fresh blueberries, rinsed and dried

½ cup granulated sugar

¼ cup cornstarch

1 tablespoon fresh lemon juice

Preheat the oven to 325°F.

Combine the flour with the brown sugar, pecans, salt, and cinnamon in a medium bowl.

Add the butter and, using your fingertips, knead it into the flour mixture until the mixture is crumbly and all of the butter has been incorporated. Set aside.

Place four 12-ounce ramekins on a rimmed baking sheet. You might line the pan with parchment paper or aluminum foil to catch any spills and ease cleanup.

Combine the blueberries with the sugar, cornstarch, and lemon juice in a medium bowl and toss to make sure that the blueberries are completely coated. Taste for sweetness. If the blueberries aren't sweet enough, add more sugar, a tablespoonful at a time, until you reach the desired degree of sweetness.

Place an equal portion of the blueberry mixture into each ramekin. Top with an equal portion of the streusel.

Place in the preheated oven and bake for about 35 minutes, or until the fruit is bubbling and the top is golden brown.

Remove from the oven and let rest for about 5 minutes before serving.

NOTE: This dessert may also be made in an 8-inch square baking pan. The baking time should be exactly the same.

CHOCOLATE SHINER BOCK CAKE

MAKES ONE 9-INCH SQUARE CAKE

Who would ever think of putting beer in a cake? In this recipe, the hoppy flavor of the beer along with the acidity of the chocolate makes a winning combination. For sure, try our favorite Texas beer, but also don't hesitate to alter the flavor with your own personal favorite brew.

The toffee sauce is not only great with this cake, it is also a terrific ice cream topping.

2¼ cups light brown sugar

20 tablespoons (2½ sticks) unsalted butter, at room temperature, plus more for greasing the pan

3 large eggs, at room temperature

1½ teaspoons pure vanilla paste

1¾ cups all-purpose flour, plus more for dusting the pan

¾ cup Dutch process cocoa powder

1¾ teaspoons baking powder

½ teaspoon baking soda

¼ teaspoon ground cinnamon

½ teaspoon salt

1½ cups Shiner Bock beer

Preheat the oven to 325°F. Generously coat the interior of a 9-inch square cake pan with butter, then dust with flour, or coat with nonstick vegetable spray. Set aside.

Combine the brown sugar and butter in the bowl of a stand mixer fitted with the paddle attachment. Beat on low speed to blend, then increase the speed to medium and beat until light and fluffy.

With the mixer still on low speed, add the eggs, one at a time, beating well after each addition and scraping down the sides of the bowl with a rubber spatula. Add the vanilla paste and beat to blend.

Combine the flour, cocoa, baking powder, baking soda, cinnamon, and salt in a medium bowl, whisking to blend completely.

With the mixer on low speed, add the flour mixture to the creamed mixture, alternating with the beer. Beat just until well blended.

Scrape the batter into the prepared pan and smooth the top with an offset spatula.

Place in the preheated oven and bake for about 30 minutes, or until a cake tester inserted into the center comes out clean.

Remove from the oven and transfer to a wire rack to cool slightly.

Cut into squares and serve warm with the toffee sauce spooned over the top.

SHINER TOFFEE SAUCE

MAKES ABOUT 6 CUPS

4¼ cups sugar

1½ cups cold water

1¾ cups heavy cream

1 bottle Shiner Bock beer

2 tablespoons salt

Combine 4 cups of the sugar with the cold water in a heavy-bottomed saucepan over medium heat. Cook, stirring occasionally, for about 10 minutes, or until the mixture has turned a golden-brown color and caramelized.

Stirring constantly, slowly add the heavy cream; take care, as it may bubble up. When all the cream has been added, stir in the remaining ¼ cup sugar along with the beer and salt. Cook at a gentle simmer for 5 minutes.

Remove from the heat and stir constantly until cool.

TEXAS SHEET CAKE

I don't really have any idea why this is called a Texas sheet cake, but every native Texan home cook that I have talked to says that their mothers made it and called it that. Some say that it was invented by Lady Bird Johnson while others say that it got its name 'cause it is as big as Texas. The cake is very easy to make, but just know that it is as sweet as a Texas debutante and just as rich.

CAKE

- 2 large eggs, at room temperature
- ½ cup buttermilk
- 2 teaspoons pure vanilla paste
- 1 teaspoon baking soda
- 2 cups sifted all-purpose flour
- 2 cups sugar
- Pinch salt
- 8 tablespoons (1 stick) unsalted butter, at room temperature
- ½ cup pure vegetable shortening
- ¼ cup Dutch process cocoa powder
- 1 cup tepid water

FROSTING

- 8 tablespoons (1 stick) unsalted butter, at room temperature
- ⅓ cup whole milk
- ¼ cup Dutch process cocoa powder
- 1 pound confectioners' sugar, sifted
- 2 teaspoons pure vanilla extract
- 2½ cups chopped toasted pecans

Preheat the oven to 400°F. Generously coat the interior of a 15½ by 10½-inch sheet pan with nonstick vegetable spray. Set aside.

Make the cake: Combine the eggs, buttermilk, vanilla paste, and baking soda in a bowl. Using a whisk, beat until very smooth. Set aside.

Sift the flour, sugar, and salt together into a large bowl. Set aside.

Combine the butter, shortening, and cocoa powder with the tepid water in a medium heavy-bottomed saucepan over medium heat and bring to a boil, stirring occasionally. Pour the hot mixture over the flour-sugar mixture and, using a wooden spoon, beat to blend. When blended, add the egg mixture and beat to thoroughly incorporate.

Pour the mixture into the prepared pan and smooth the top with an offset spatula.

Place in the preheated oven and bake for about 10 minutes, or until a cake tester inserted into the center comes out clean.

About 5 minutes before the cake is ready, prepare the frosting: Combine the butter, milk, and cocoa powder in a medium heavy-bottomed saucepan over medium heat. Bring to a boil, stirring constantly. Immediately remove from the heat.

Using a handheld electric mixer, beat in the confectioners' sugar and vanilla until very light and smooth. Stir in the pecans.

Remove the cake from the oven, transfer to a wire rack, and immediately pour the hot frosting over the cake. If necessary, use a spatula to spread it out to the edges.

Allow to set before cutting into squares.

TEXAS CHESS PIE   MAKES ONE 9-INCH PIE

This Texas classic can be traced far back in state culinary history. In fact, this pie has been around longer than Texas has been a state. It is about as simple a filling as a baker can pull together, and that is probably one of the reasons it has been a Southern dessert staple for generations. No one really knows where the name came from, but it is thought that the original recipe came over with early English settlers. It is often called vinegar pie because of the addition of vinegar to cut the sweetness of the basic ingredients. Once you taste it, you will know that there is good reason why this dessert has never disappeared from the recipe boxes of so many Texas families.

16 tablespoons (2 sticks) unsalted butter, softened

2 cups sugar

3 tablespoons all-purpose flour

2 tablespoons white cornmeal

4 large egg yolks

2 large eggs

1 tablespoon distilled white vinegar

6 tablespoons water

Finely grated zest of 1 lemon

One 9-inch unbaked pie shell (see Note)

Unsweetened whipped cream, plain
    Greek-style yogurt, crème fraîche,
    or sour cream, for garnish

Melt the butter in a small saucepan over low heat. Remove from the heat and set aside to cool.

Preheat the oven to 350°F.

Combine the sugar, flour, and cornmeal in a medium bowl.

Place the egg yolks and eggs in a separate medium bowl and, using a handheld electric mixer, beat until well blended. Add the vinegar along with the water. Beat until light and frothy. Add the cooled butter and continue to beat until completely incorporated.

Add the sugar mixture and beat to blend thoroughly. Stir in the lemon zest. Pour the mixture into the pie shell.

Place the pie in the preheated oven and bake for about 35 minutes, or until set in the center and the pastry is golden brown.

Remove from the oven and transfer to a wire rack to cool before cutting.

When ready to serve, cut into wedges and serve garnished with unsweetened whipped cream or a dollop of Greek-style yogurt, crème fraîche, or sour cream.

NOTE: You can make your own pastry using my recipe for pastry given with the State Fair Pecan Pie on page 238, or use a commercially prepared unbaked pie shell, usually found in the frozen-foods section of supermarkets.

STATE FAIR PECAN PIE

In 1996, I judged the Texas State Fair pie contest and this was the pie that won that year. Bobbie Lee, the baker, gave me her recipe on the condition that I would serve it at the restaurant every year during the Texas State Fair. I've kept my promise and then some because it is just too special to serve only once a year.

PIECRUST

2 cups all-purpose flour

1 tablespoon granulated sugar

1 teaspoon salt

12 tablespoons (1½ sticks) cold unsalted butter, cut into ½-inch pieces

¼ cup plus 1 tablespoon ice water

FILLING

12 tablespoons (1½ sticks) cold unsalted butter

1½ cups packed dark brown sugar

¾ cup granulated sugar

½ cup light corn syrup

3 tablespoons whole milk

2 tablespoons all-purpose flour

½ teaspoon salt

½ vanilla bean, split in half lengthwise

4 large eggs, at room temperature

1½ cups (5½ ounces) toasted pecan halves

Unsweetened whipped cream or vanilla ice cream, for serving

Make the piecrust: Combine the flour, granulated sugar, and salt in the bowl of a food processor fitted with the metal blade, and process to blend. Add the butter, a few pieces at a time, and process, using quick on-and-off turns, just until the mixture resembles small peas.

Add the ice water and process, using quick on-and-off turns, just until the pastry is evenly moistened and begins to come together.

Scrape the dough onto a clean work surface and, using your hands, knead it a couple of times or just until it comes together. Form the pastry into a flat disk.

Place the disk on a lightly floured, clean, flat work surface. Using a rolling pin, roll the pastry out into a 12-inch circle about ⅛ inch thick.

Lift the pastry into a 10-inch, deep-dish pie plate, leaving an even overhang all around. Trim the overhang to ½ inch. Fold the overhang under and crimp all around the edge, using either your fingertips or a kitchen fork. Randomly prick the bottom of the shell with a kitchen fork and transfer to the freezer. Freeze for 30 minutes.

Preheat the oven to 350°F. Remove the pie shell from the freezer. Line it with parchment paper and fill with pie weights or dried beans.

Place in the preheated oven and bake for about 25 minutes, or until very lightly browned around the edge.

Remove from the oven and remove the paper and weights. Return the shell to the oven and continue to bake for an additional 15 minutes, or until golden.

Remove the shell from the oven and set aside to cool. Do not turn the oven off.

While the shell is cooling, make the filling: Melt the butter in a medium saucepan over medium heat. Add the dark brown and granulated sugars along with the corn syrup, milk, flour, and salt and stir to blend.

Using a small, sharp knife, scrape the seeds from the vanilla bean into the butter mixture. Cook, stirring frequently, for about 4 minutes, or just until the mixture comes to a boil. Immediately remove from the heat and let rest for 5 minutes.

Place the eggs in a small bowl and, using a whisk, lightly beat to aerate slightly. Gradually whisk the eggs into the sugar mixture and beat until thoroughly blended.

Sprinkle the pecans evenly over the bottom of the pie shell. Pour the hot filling on top and spread out to an even layer.

Place in the preheated oven and bake for 45 minutes, or just until the center is barely set and the crust is golden brown.

Remove from the oven and transfer to a wire rack to cool completely before cutting.

When ready to serve, cut into wedges and garnish with whipped cream or vanilla ice cream.

PARKER COUNTY FRIED PEACH PIES

MAKES ABOUT 1 DOZEN PIES

These little pies are my all-time special dessert— a childhood favorite turned into a grown-up treat. They are just like turnovers except they are fried. They can also be baked if you like, but they just aren't the same. There is nothing better than eating a warm fried pie stuffed with ripe Texas peaches, but don't hesitate to make other fruit fillings, and when you don't have any sweet and ripe fresh fruit, a fine-quality jam will fit the bill nicely.

- 8 ripe unpeeled peaches, pitted and sliced
- 1 cup packed light brown sugar
- ½ teaspoon fresh lemon juice
- 1 teaspoon plus a pinch salt
- 2 cups all-purpose flour
- 1 tablespoon granulated sugar
- 12 tablespoons (1½ sticks) unsalted butter, cut into ½-inch dice
- ¼ cup plus 1 tablespoon ice water
- About 4 cups vegetable oil, for frying
- 1¼ cups confectioners' sugar
- 3 tablespoons whole milk

Combine the peaches with the brown sugar, lemon juice, and a pinch of salt in a large sauté pan over medium heat. Cook, stirring frequently, for about 6 minutes, or just until softened. Remove from the heat and set aside to cool.

Combine the flour with the granulated sugar and 1 teaspoon of salt in the bowl of a food processor fitted with the metal blade. Process to blend.

With the motor running, add the butter, a few pieces at a time, and process, using quick on-and-off turns, until all the butter has been incorporated and the mixture resembles small peas.

Again with the motor running, add the water to make a lightly moistened dough that just comes together.

Lightly flour a clean, flat work surface and scrape the dough out onto it. Using your hands, lightly knead two or three times to just bring the dough together. Then, using a rolling pin, roll the dough out to a thickness of about ¼ inch. Using a 3½-inch round cookie cutter, cut the dough out into circles.

Working with one piece at a time, place a tablespoon of the cooled peaches in the center of each circle. Fold the dough up and over the filling and, using a kitchen fork, crimp the edges closed. Continue making pies until all the filling has been used.

Heat the vegetable oil in a deep-fat fryer over high heat until it registers 350°F on a candy thermometer. Add the pies, a few at a time, and fry for about 4 minutes, or until golden brown and slightly crisp around the edges.

Remove from the heat and place on a double layer of paper towels to drain.

Place the confectioners' sugar in a small bowl. Slowly add the milk and whisk to blend. Add just enough milk to make a slightly thick mixture.

Using a teaspoon, drizzle a bit of the glaze over each pie. Serve warm.

SOURCES

Chiles, Spices, Seasonings, Mexican and Southwest Cooking Materials

Pendery's World of Chiles and Spices
1221 Manufacturing Street
Dallas, Texas 75207
email@penderys.com
1-800-533-1870

Artisanal Cheese

Veldhuizen Texas Farmstead Cheese
Raw milk cheeses
www.veldhuizencheese.com
254-968-3098

Mozzarella Company
Mozzarella, goat's milk, and cow's milk cheeses
2944 Elm Street
Dallas, Texas 75226
www.mozzco.com
1-800-798-2954
214-741-4072

Olive Oil

Texas Olive Ranch
www.texasoliveranch.com
855-TX-OLIVE

Natural Grains and Grits

Homestead Gristmill
800 Dry Creek Road
Waco, Texas 76705
www.homesteadgristmill.com
254-754-9665

Tortillas

Luna's Tortilla's, Inc.
2225 Connector Drive
Dallas, TX 75220
www.lunastortillas.com
214-747-2661

ACKNOWLEDGMENTS

Eric Dreyer—if it weren't for you, we would still be working toward finishing this book! Thank you for your dedication, knowledge, thoughtfulness, creativity, humor, drive, muscle, empathy, focus, determination, and coolness, and for being a good friend. Thank God that you know how to type!

Judie Choate—my dear friend through all these years: I couldn't have done this book without you! Thank you for all that you did beyond the call of book duty, and for first telling me I needed to write "The Texas Food Bible" and then making it happen. Can't wait until we do it again!

Jill Bates—your desserts are the best I've ever tasted! I couldn't have done this book without your "sweet" recipes.

Dave Carlin—we have shot many pictures together in the past, but nothing like we did for this book! Thank you for seeing the food with a camera and making the dishes come alive. I had the best creative time of my life!

Karen Murgolo—who would have thought a chef from Texas might have a chance of bringing a new book idea to New York City? Thank you for believing in me and my story and my love of food. You envisioned the book before anybody!

Grand Central Life & Style—thank you for giving me a chance to help people know the great food of Texas! It is a pleasure being associated with a publisher that loves to share food and stories through its books! Thank you specifically to Tareth Mitch, Pippa White, Claire Brown, Sonya Safro, and all who helped get this book to its readers.

Jason Snyder—thank you for evoking the feel of Texas through your design! The look of the book is what the state is all about!

The Tasters—Gaby and Dani—thank you for the long hours of cooking and adjusting the recipes. You are both a joy to be around, with such dedication to whatever you do!

The Fearing's Restaurant staff—thank you for the great experience I feel every day as I work with the most professional and caring team of my career. Every one of you is a Texas Star in your own right, and it is my pleasure to work beside each of you!

John Goff—thank you for giving me the opportunity to have the restaurant of my dreams. Without Fearing's, this book would have never been created—you are the greatest partner!

ABOUT THE AUTHOR

Long known as the father of Southwestern Cuisine, **Dean Fearing** has been recognized as a Pioneer of American Cuisine by the Culinary Institute of America. He was presented with the Silver Spoon for sterling performance by Food Arts and has won the James Beard Award for Best Chef in the Southwest. In 2007, after more than twenty years as the chef at the Mansion on Turtle Creek, he opened Fearing's at the Ritz-Carlton, Dallas, which has been named Restaurant of the Year and Table of the Year by *Esquire*, and No. 1 in Hotel Dining by *Zagat Survey*. It was nominated by the James Beard Foundation for Best New Restaurant and has received stellar reviews from the *New York Times*, *Newsweek*, *Food and Wine*, *Texas Monthly*, and others.

Judith Choate is a multiple James Beard award–winning cookbook writer and pioneer in the promotion of American food. Through her company, Custom Cuisine, Judith works as a consultant in product development for international companies, chefs, and restaurateurs as well as in marketing and culinary trend forecasting.

Native Texan **Eric Dreyer** always had a passion for food, and early on he followed this feeling to California where he explored the culinary world, honed his skills, and earned a nomination as a Rising Star Chef for The Ritz Carlton Company. In 2007, Dreyer returned to his Texas roots and joined the team at Fearing's Restaurant, where he serves as executive chef.

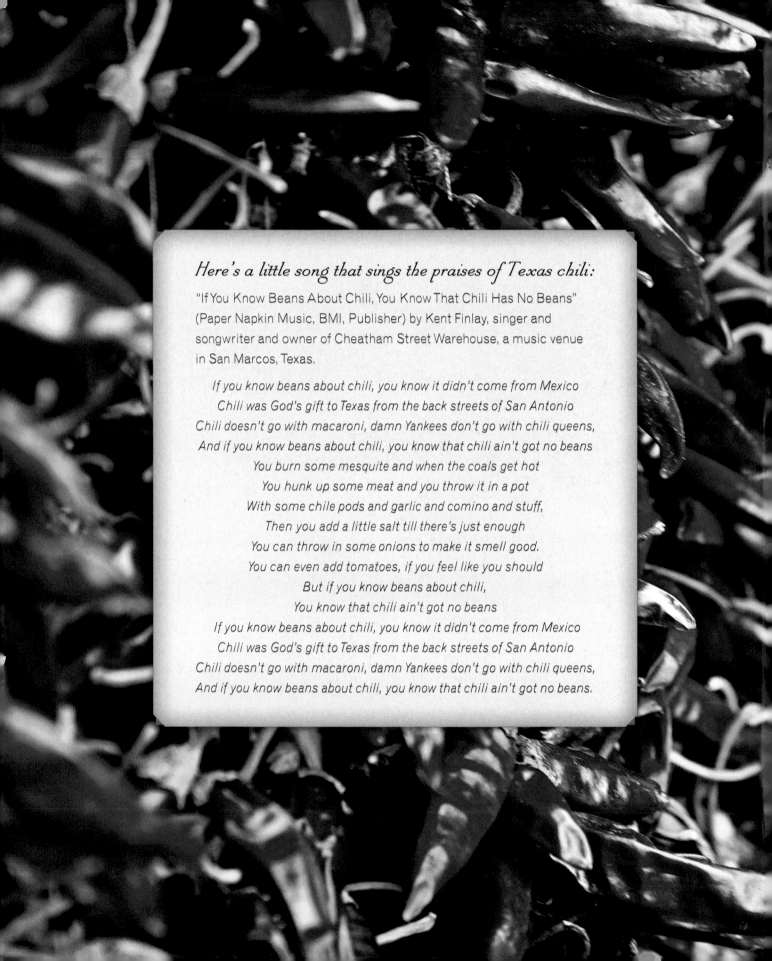

Here's a little song that sings the praises of Texas chili:

"If You Know Beans About Chili, You Know That Chili Has No Beans"
(Paper Napkin Music, BMI, Publisher) by Kent Finlay, singer and
songwriter and owner of Cheatham Street Warehouse, a music venue
in San Marcos, Texas.

If you know beans about chili, you know it didn't come from Mexico
Chili was God's gift to Texas from the back streets of San Antonio
Chili doesn't go with macaroni, damn Yankees don't go with chili queens,
And if you know beans about chili, you know that chili ain't got no beans
You burn some mesquite and when the coals get hot
You hunk up some meat and you throw it in a pot
With some chile pods and garlic and comino and stuff,
Then you add a little salt till there's just enough
You can throw in some onions to make it smell good.
You can even add tomatoes, if you feel like you should
But if you know beans about chili,
You know that chili ain't got no beans
If you know beans about chili, you know it didn't come from Mexico
Chili was God's gift to Texas from the back streets of San Antonio
Chili doesn't go with macaroni, damn Yankees don't go with chili queens,
And if you know beans about chili, you know that chili ain't got no beans.